CRITICAL MOVES

CRITICAL MOVES

Dance Studies in Theory and Politics

Randy Martin

Duke University Press   Durham & London 1998

© 1998 Duke University Press

All rights reserved

Printed in the United States of America on acid-free paper ∞

Typeset in Minion by Tseng Information Systems, Inc.

Library of Congress Cataloging-in-Publication Data appear
on the last printed page of this book.

Contents

Acknowledgments

This book was occasioned by my own involvement in a very special encounter of scholars with heterodox training and a shared commitment to dance, convened by Susan L. Foster at the University of California Humanities Research Institute (UCHRI) in the first half of 1993. My residency there allowed for intensive interaction with Professor Foster and Professors Mark Franko, Heidi Gilpin, Lena Hammergren, Sally Ness, Peggy Phelan, Nancy Ruyter, Marta Savigliano, and Linda Tomko, as well as frequent guests and other fellows at the institute, especially Jennifer Brody, who provided very helpful insights on what is now Chapter 2. Most of what was to become this book was initially composed in Irvine. Writing, so often crafted by hands playing solitaire, was given a thoroughly collective slant during our seminar, Choreographing History. So much of what moves through these pages can be traced to the participation of the colleagues named above. To the staff and then director of UCHRI, Mark Rose, I extend special thanks for their kind assistance.

The wisdom and support of Ken Wissoker and Richard Morrison, who have shepherded the project through Duke University Press, have been invaluable. The meticulous assistance and attention of the Press's editorial, production, and marketing staff, especially Jean Brady and Anna Haas, and the fine copyediting of Nancy Malone, earned my deep respect and appreciation. I was fortunate to have the opportunity to publish some of this material in venues that offered keen editorial guidance. Portions of what is now in Chapters 1, 2, and 3 have appeared in the journals *Social Text* (Winter 1993) — a journal for which I am a member of the editorial collective — the *Journal of Sport and Social Issues* (May 1997), edited by Toby Miller, and the collections *Choreographing History* (Bloomington: Indiana University Press, 1995) and *Corporealities: Dancing, Knowledge, Culture, and Power* (London: Routledge, 1995), both edited by Susan L. Foster.

I also express my gratitude to Sue Ellen Case, who offered helpful criticisms of an earlier draft of this book. Jane Desmond was incredibly generous in reading the work in its entirety, not once, but twice. Her comments energized me and opened fresh avenues of insight. Michael E. Brown and George Yúdice have been mainstays of intellectual support during the entire period in which this book was written. Pratt Institute has been a congenial place in which to pursue my scholarly and creative interests. Again, I offer my deepest appreciation and admiration to Susan L. Foster, whose enormous creative abilities made these musings on dance and politics possible.

My companion at so many stages of life and dance, Ginger Gillespie, keeps the words in perspective and the movement alive. She has lived this book in more ways than one. For those dancers and choreographers whose friendship I cherish and who have allowed me to see so much in dance, I hope that something of what I have learned from them is in evidence in the pages that follow. It is to them that I dedicate this work.

Introduction: Iterations of Dance and Politics

Critical moves. Steps we must take. Movement that informs critical consciousness. Dance lies at the point at which reflection and embodiment meet, at which doing and anticipation are intertwined. Dance is, therefore, the acute moment of its conditions, appearing as if with warning but no prior diagnosis. It has all the intensity of an emergency, yet one that is invariably survived. Dance occurs through forces applied to the body that yields to them, only to generate powers of their own. Dance makes for quick thinking, thinking on one's feet. Dance generates a sense of being in the midst of a crisis, a break, a rupture, even a loss and a prospect at the same time; thus while dancing may appear to be a series of stops and starts, for the dancer, next steps are already in motion, already passing from one (im)balance to the next.

The commonsense view of crisis is that it arrests movement. Therefore it seems that breaks are total, and ruptures irreparable, as if each moment involves a rethinking of what is to be done. When applied to political life, the idea of crisis suggests a series of unconnected moves, each of which is prompted by a thought and a decision, rather than something continuous in itself and capable of going beyond itself. Applied to dance, crisis is only a metaphor, since no one could deny that the special motion and momentum of dance is inherently progressive, hence creative. Yet we still think of what dancers do as if they are constantly in the crisis they appear to be in. What is important is to move beyond that metaphor to recover a sense of what motion, progressive movement, dance are, in fact, for the dancer.

Taking dance seriously in this way helps us to see beyond the despair of an arrested present to the opening that any present forges for enhancing social life, as activity done together. The sense that the present could be made other than what it is — namely, that movement is possible and unavoidable—is intuitive for those who dance or attend to it fully. But the social significance of this goes beyond what is formally recognized as dance to apply to life itself and therefore to politics—the uncertainties and motions of life in the contemporary world.

If one grants that along with dance, politics cannot have a solitary form or unitary object, if neither can be one thing or about one thing, it becomes possible to notice a proliferation of political activity throughout the social fabric and not simply confined to what are formally considered to be political institutions. Once politics is no longer reserved for events that constitute a sort of big bang that suddenly changes the world (if only one could find the fuse), then it can be recognized as far as the eye can see. Political activity, conceived beyond any given site or type, is viewed here as the contest over what difference difference can make (in the double sense of that which diverges from what is dominant in the present, and the expansive multiplicity of human expression that demands adjudication and decision). In this regard, politics is activity already in motion. It does not await ignition.

I am not very far into this volume and already dance is encumbered with political significance beyond a given tactical stance toward a particular issue, commitment, or moment. For me, this reference to the political is crucial for addressing a yet more general paradox that is clearly displayed in dance. Many observers of the current political scene have claimed that political action has shown itself to be futile, at least when judged by standards posed by past attempts to improve society. Others have suggested that existing politics, such as it is, requires an absolutely new set of historical and theoretical criteria for assessing the efficacy of any movement for social change.[1] Yet these contrary conceptions must reckon with what we now must see as a bountiful politicization of cultural practice, issues, categories of experience and identification, and economic formations across the social landscape. Minimally, one could ask, Why does the discussion of politics consistently refer to a scarcity (the lack of prospects) when lived politics takes place in the midst of such manifest abundance? Or, to put this question another way, How, then, in this ocean of the political, is it possible to feel adrift? The ability to register politics already in motion as what gives shape to the world, and not as some sickness that visits a passive body, requires special analytic focus.

I believe that the critique of politics in this regard can illuminate dance and that illumination can work back on our sense of what is to be done more generally in life. My purpose in this writing is initially to destabilize the conventional ways of thinking dance and politics so as to appreciate their interdependence more fully. The concrete studies of dance that make up this book vary from those on improvisationally based performance to large-scale concert production, to aerobic dance, to instruction in dance technique. This range of examples, while by no means exhaustive, is intended to refer to the contours of the entire field of dance so as to grasp what it means to study that field as a whole and, from this perspective, to theorize politics in the more amplified and abundant key that I suggest above. In this chapter I examine the theory of social movements to see where a critical understanding of dance might make a contribution to conceptions of politics, then I situate the particular studies that compose the body of the book with respect to the issues they raise for dance and politics. Finally, I address the question of my own participation as a dancer and writer in relation to those studies.

Politics concerns the forces that devise the social world. The collision and mutual displacement of forces — their motional flows — is what makes for difference, and difference can be summed up, organized, and contextualized in myriad ways that produce a given society and structure its divisions along lines of class, gender, sexuality, race, and much more. Theories of politics are full of ideas, but they have been least successful in articulating how the concrete labor of participation necessary to execute those ideas is gathered through the movement of bodies in social time and space. Politics goes nowhere without movement. It is not simply an idea, decision, or choice taken at a moment but also a transfigurative process that makes and occupies space. When politics is treated merely as an idea or ideology, it occurs in stillness, awaiting something that will bring people to action or mobilize them. But this presumed gap between a thinking mind and an acting body makes it impossible to understand how people move from a passive to an active state. The presumption of bodies already in motion, what dance takes as its normative condition, could bridge the various splits between mind and body, subject and object, and process and structure that have been so difficult for understandings of social life to negotiate.

This is not the first attempt made to bridge these various rifts. The very ability to notice the problem belies a long and fruitful history.[2] More modestly, I want to address a way of thinking that tempts us to judge politics in an abrupt and overly conclusive manner and, paradoxically, places theory outside the very practice it most wants to be part of. The corrective offered here takes the form of a certain approach to writing that is aimed at embodying the sense of being in the midst of what it looks at, hence, writing about dance that seeks to be captured by the movement of performance. For political theory in general (that would not necessarily take dance as its object of analysis), this writing elaborates the dynamics of mobilization that is already implicit in politics. In this respect, thinking about politics has scarcely grasped the language of mobilization. A critical reflection on dance can help promote fluency in the language of mobilization that political theory makes reference to but barely speaks.

By mobilization I want to stress not an alien power that is visited on the body, as something that is done to bodies behind their backs, so to speak, but what moving bodies accomplish through movement. Mobilization is situated through dancing so as to indicate the practical dynamic between production and product. Here, production is what dancing assembles as a capacity for movement, and the product is not the aesthetic effect of the dance but the materialized identity accomplished through the performativity of movement. Hence, through mobilization, bodies traverse a given terrain that by traversing, they constitute. Further, by constituting that immediate context for movement, bodies display as their identity the practical effects of dancing. Mobilization foregrounds this process of how bodies are made, how they are assembled, and how demands for space produce a space of identifiable demands through a practical activity. Mobilization incessantly mixes metaphors of time and space because it displays the means through which one is transformed into the other. If movement can be plotted on a grid of space and time, mobilization is what generates the grid.

Dance has much to offer this problem of theorizing participation and mobilization, for dance emerges through the mobilization of participation in relation to a choreographic idea. This, at least, is what I take to be a general idea about dance, irrespective of its cultural and historical particularity in terms of style, genre, social location, or relation to other aesthetic forms. Ideas about dance have at times spoken to what the politics of dance might be, but as the inspiration for thinking through politics in general, these dance thoughts have not assumed a place at the tables of political theory.

Although "performance" as such has made an appearance as an organizing figure or trope for thinking politics,[3] the more recent currency of the

term derives from an act of speech rather than a reflection on those particular practices that especially feature bodies in motion.[4] The spoken word is
also embodied, but the presumption of speech act theory that the utterance
accounts for the performance does little to clarify how the word is carried
to act, what I am calling the "mobilization of participation." Correlatively,
there seems no reason to assume that the process of identifying certain practices as political and focusing on them as objects of study will necessarily
generate the concepts that engender those practices with the fullest appreciation of their possibility and plentitude. The distinction between theory —
the effort to grasp something whole in order to reflect on it, as if from the
outside — and practice — the experiential engagement with something as if
from within the process of doing it — retains some utility only if reflection
and experience are not treated as separable acts but as two interconnected
moments of the same activity.

"Move," "movement," and "mobilization" are doing double duty here.
They are words that are being used to name a relation between dance and
politics. That relation, however, must itself be named lest dance appear with
a kind of false innocence to wipe away thorny intellectual problems or be
mistaken for those problems. Not only must dance be specified as a cultural
practice, but both its resources and its limitations as a reference for supple-
menting the vocabulary of political theory need to be acknowledged as well.
Exploring what dance practices and political theory offer each other in no
way collapses the two. What dance can bring to the scene of theoretical critique needs to be established; it cannot presume to *be* that scene.

Dance is best understood as a kind of embodied practice that makes
manifest how movement comes to be by momentarily concentrating and
elaborating in one place forces drawn from beyond a given performance
setting. The constituent features of any given dance work include technical
proclivities and aesthetic sensibilities that elaborate and depend on aspects
of physical culture and prevailing ideologies. While dance is neither language nor politics, it is clarified and qualified through these means. The
question, What is dance? is not usefully answered by description (as if the
categories used to inventory putative dance activities were somehow taken
to be empirical rather than conceptual). The efforts to identify dance as
purely different or clearly demarcated from any other cultural practice are
complicated by the fact that venues, promoters, and practitioners have
self-consciously mixed dance with other aesthetic forms, nothing novel in

itself but surely disruptive to any firmly established classificatory schemata. Equally unsatisfying is the elimination of the question altogether by saying that dance is whatever people call dancing, unless, when such statements are made, we ask, What is being called for?

Definitions of dance, given the field's cultural, historical, and technical diversity, if they are to remain open to these differences, cannot presume either transcendent or immanent criteria. Instead, a concept of dance needs to be formulated some steps removed from any concrete dance practice to avoid excluding particular expressions before adequate reflection on them is possible. It is insufficient, however, merely to state what dance is not. To delineate a field called "dance" requires a positive construction as well. In what follows, dance is treated as the reflexive mobilization of the body—that is, as a social process that foregrounds the very means through which bodies gather. Through dance, the means and ends of mobilization are joined together and made available to performers and their publics. Dance, so conceived, does not name a fixed expression but a problem, a predicament, that bodies find themselves in the midst of, whose momentary solutions we call dancing. Unlike most political practice, dance, when it is performed and watched, makes available, reflexively, the means through which mobilization is accomplished. In this regard, the relation of dance to political theory cannot usefully be taken as merely analogical or metaphorical.

Just as dance has no defining ideal form or aesthetic model, there can be no simple resemblance between dance and social movements. What is social in dance could never substitute or stand in for the politics of other situations. Dancing cannot, by itself, cause change in other social arenas, but clearly connections and mediations can establish a certain legacy for dance beyond the scene of its performance. Nevertheless, what is situated in the world, what people contest in myriad forms, can also be found in dance. More pointedly, dance displays, in the very ways that bodies are placed in motion, traces of the forces of contestation that can be found in society at large.

Theorizing Mobilization

The study of social change has had a long career in the humanities and social sciences, from certain perspectives, figuring as their central problematic.[5] In the chapters that follow, it will be possible to reflect on the question of mobilization from a variety of literatures and disciplinary orientations. For now, to frame some of the stakes of my argument, I want to focus on the concept as it has developed specifically and explicitly within the historically informed sociological literature on social change through social movements.

In increasing recognition that, to paraphrase Marx, people make history, but not under conditions of their own choosing, much writing has extended the emphasis on states, leaders, and formal institutions to common experiences, namely, those shared by people without recourse to offices of power. Social movements result from the organization of these quotidian sentiments which are directed toward transforming patterns of life, altering regulation and law, and generating and reallocating resources for collective benefit.

The growth in research on social movements over the past three decades in this country reflects both their historical elaboration as political formations and the rejection of notions going back to the nineteenth century of the crowd or the collective behavior of commoners as irrational and therefore incapable of generating any socially constructive activity. This earlier social psychological approach, exemplified in Gustave Le Bon's *The Crowd: A Study of the Popular Mind,* ascribed irrational behavior to those unruly assemblages of people protesting in the streets who lacked the dignity that property confers on speech through, say, ownership of the press.[6] Instead, the dynamics of social movements were modeled, just like the actions of formal institutions, on assumptions of economic rationality. In *The Logic of Collective Action,* Mancur Olson argues that participation in social movements is a function of a decision taken by an individual. This decision is based on a cost-benefit analysis of what might be gained by joining the movement in the light of external constraints, such as the power of authority that is being opposed, or other issues that demand protest and attention. The conception of affiliations made in a virtual marketplace of potential actions a person could undertake is effectively equivalent to the economist's understanding of how commodities are selected by consumers. What complicates the market analogy is what Olson calls the "free rider" problem, in which the successes of the social movement are institutionalized and enjoyed by people whether or not they personally participated in the movement. Because the benefits of a movement are translated into what are called "collective goods" in the form of entitlements, legal protections, tax abatements, and the like, they need not be purchased individually. If this is the case, then the gains that accrue to all who have an interest in social change can be compromised by calculating individuals who realize that they need not pay the costs of participation, especially in terms of personal risk of arrest, loss of income, or strain, to reap the benefits of societal progress.[7]

Inspired by the work of Olson and others, research on social movements began to contend with the gaps left by the earlier theory and, increasingly, to challenge many of its assumptions. The literature on the topic came to be known as resource mobilization theory because it focused on resources located in society rather than on the psychological disposition of participants or social actors. Resources included a variety of necessary inputs that could be obtained and used by participants, such as rights to petition, access to public space and media, finances, and tactics or repertoires of disobedience that were created and recognized in different historical moments. By the 1980s, the vast majority of work published on social movements in the most prominent scholarly journals in sociology and political science identified itself with resource mobilization theory.[8]

As the field expanded, emphasis on individual choices in the face of selective incentives shifted to group actors with varying measures of internal solidarity. Resources such as finances and access to the media were appreciated as not equally available to all, and a theory of the state inflected with marxist analysis complicated the meaning of institutionalizing movement success. From this last perspective, the state embodied class divisions in society more broadly, and thus social movements could contest the contours and material form of the state itself so that oppositional currents could not be assimilated to the formal apparatus of power without effecting it as well.[9] By the end of the eighties, aided particularly by the influence of feminist theory, issues of subjectivity and social psychology were reemphasized but now without the prior assumptions of an ideal, universal individual responding to external constraints with an objective calculus of rationality.[10]

Instead, the individual actor was relativized in response to collective identities and ideologies. If principal identification was made through collective identification or shared practice, such as the mother-daughter relation, rather than the lone male wage earner, then individual self-interest could no longer be assumed to possess a fixed content or predetermined effect.

Further, emphasis on immediate, face-to-face interaction could open up the questions of motivation and involvement thought key to understanding the subjective aspects of participation, which came to be called "micromobilization." The consequent reference to local or community-based struggle had the appeal of subverting the model of an individual, universal rational actor and of focusing on the content of what animated people's process of participation. In epistemological terms, the challenge lay in how to articulate the earlier model of rational choice derived from the natural sciences with the interpretive framework that concentrated on subjective meanings.

The willingness to cede this split between subject and object, structure and process, which characterized sociological theorizing in general during the past decade,[11] still left resource mobilization with an untenable gap between micro and macro levels of analysis and consequently between interests imputed to actors generated at the former level and an efficacy to action only discernible at the macro level of social structure, or over the long run. No matter how intimate with actors one became, their social activity was still largely cognitive, disembodied acts spurred on by locally generated common interests. However much the importance of subjectivity to account for mobilization was recognized, it remained an interest, an ideational form that could not account for what kept people in motion, for what maintained or mobilized participation. Even in its most sophisticated forms, resource mobilization theory could not account for what separated the inner life of participation from the outside effects of mobilization.[12]

Typically, then, where the concept of mobilization has appeared in research on social movements, it is already subject to the logic of efficiency in applying available means or resources to ends or interests. Despite recognizing that participants share certain beliefs, these inquiries have scarcely addressed the dynamics of how mobilization occurs. Consequently, the participation generated through the gathering of bodies is undervalued in a theory of politics whose putative means and ends are cognitive, an analytic maneuver that separates a moment of pure thought from its embodiment in and fluency as practice.[13]

Further, the question of how people become identified with a particular political movement is reduced to a matter of interest, a notion that assumes that it is possible to know what situation is best for people as if an outcome could be projected that would be free of the very contradictions that posed the problem of social change to begin with.[14] Interest as an idea remains tied to objectively discernible divisions between costs and benefits that can be derived from one's position in a given social structure. If interests can be given independent of the efforts to attain them, then analysis will face the disappointment of mobilizations that do not meet its expectations.

The fixing of identification in relation to political actions robs history of that which makes it dynamic and renders incomprehensible the present conjuncture as one where interests are discrete and difference is absolute. For if such were the case, we would not be in a conjuncture at all but in an eternal present of decision optimizing without an inkling of the setting in which all these independent, well-reasoned moves became efficient or co-herent. What is more grave, we would be confronted with the insufficiency of political mobilizations to meet the standards of interest, of participants doing what is best for themselves, that analysis itself places on what it scru-tinizes. This is not to suggest that there can be no evaluative criteria in as-sessing what generates or results from mobilization or that all mobilizations can be equally preferred. Rather, the responsibility of a self-critical analysis is first to allow what it looks at to be possible, then to notice what allows it to continue, and finally to evaluate what it facilitates and what it limits with respect to the larger project of social change in the service of which the analysis is presumably operating.

In other words, the very proliferation of politics that may turn out to be the present moment's greatest resource is minimized when the current situation is understood to be no more than a marketplace of ideas that has overwhelmed its demand. This disjuncture between political ideas and social mobilization, or agency and history, has contributed to a certain sense of stasis on the Left. Indeed, to speak of the Left, as if progressive politics were stable or singular, has already become controversial. Yet despite the problems that inhere in extrapolating from a bipolar model based on the architecture of power in the French Revolution, reports of a crisis in leftist politics have issued from many quarters of the globe. Even if the practical referents for leftist politics are not constant or the conditions of opposition between left and right universal, the model itself persists in many habits of imagining politics. By way of shorthand definition, the Left is taken to be those forces mobilizing against the fixity of what is dominant in the social order and on behalf of what is productive of society as a means for elaborating human association and not simply an expanding universe of exchange. The Right may couch its project as one of freedom, and at the most basic level its mobilizations are no less authentic than those which generate a left, an ambiguity that complicates analysis and makes it possible for the political orientation of persons and movements to change. But the Right's project frequently turns out to entail excluding many from the resources of society so that some can be free to expend those resources.

The literature on social movements reviewed above, with its conceptual divide between interest and action, raises a problem that can be framed more generally in terms of a conception of politics that separates agency and history, two moments of any political activity that are, in practice, irreducibly interconnected. When the split between agency and history becomes a perspective from which the political scene is judged, the movement is taken out of ideas. The ongoing motion of historical change can somehow be placed on hold or be seen as having come to an end. Although many on the Right and a few on the Left would subscribe to this latter position, it remains influential because it is one of the persistent points of reference around which debate is joined and in this way retains its influence.[15] If, for example, through pronouncement of the collapse of socialism the most comprehensive efforts to date to counter capitalism are seen as coming to naught, then the unambiguity of the past renders the present flatly negative, a blank slate without the means to write on it.[16] The irony here is that these self-limiting notions for social change had been the very ideas against which the Left had historically constituted itself. The Left had always taken as its brief the need to dissent from the claim that those in official positions of power had a hold on what could pass as social reality.

It does not seem useful to me at this point to attempt to refute particular pronouncements of crisis, collapse, or ends for progressive politics. For they exist in an arena that forecloses so much other terrain before it can even be imagined. I am more concerned to address an entire climate of thought that could seem appealing in its clarity and resolution to anyone considering the conditions for meaningful social change. No doubt that chilling intellectual climate is grounded in its own conditions: corporate hostility to the social base of labor; state defunding of social programs; moralizing hostility toward those most mistreated by the rush to cultural, political, and economic austerity; and a generalized violence that takes only selective notice of crime.

But even so short a list of obstacles to further mobilization grants all force to an external source of power, usually the state, or other formal and official institutions, without generating the means to recognize what those very forces seek to repress, coerce, and contain. One may be moved to wonder: if the newly established order is so successful, then why are the putative victors so manifestly unhappy, so wedded themselves to the mantra of collapse and crisis? Perhaps we need to learn to recognize more acutely what is making the triumphant so anxious, without at the same time denying that they make us anxious as well. We also need to ponder why, so soon after the trumpeting that history is over, the struggle to modernity seemingly complete and resolved, different noises, other rumblings, are again discernible. For such noises to be rendered coherent with respect to what is recognized as politically significant activity, the conception of social movements, and of agency and history more broadly, requires some adjustment.

For anyone involved in efforts to change the world, doubts about what will become of struggle or history are ever present not only because the future is uncertain but also because it is difficult to know, in the face of opposition, how to value one's own activity. It is unhelpful to rehearse yet another postmortem of the Left that rings of self-prophecy because idea and participation, theory and practice, and agency and history are divided from one another in a manner that arrests their development and stops critical movement in its tracks. Rather, I want to see if it is possible to imagine politics from within mobilization, instead of considering power as an external force that seeks to move people. Within this perspective, therefore, mobilization is a means rather than an end. This orientation shifts a key theoretical and political question from how to mobilize people to how to recognize what any given instance of mobilization could produce.

Within cultural studies, the intrinsic relation between everyday life and social change has frequently been studied under the purely oppositional rubric of resistance. Resistance is the consequence of refusing the logic, values, and sensibility of the prevailing order or, in Raymond Williams's term, the "dominant culture."[17] Cultures of resistance, or what were called "subcultures," turned notions of assimilation and co-optation in the perpetuation of extant power relations on their heads, by reproducing the pleasures of transgression rather than obedience to dominant societal norms.[18] These studies of resistance, particularly when applied to colonial and imperial subordination, continue to have political and conceptual value.[19] Yet to the extent that resistance assumes the perspective of that which blocks an offensive movement, it already cedes much to the forces of social control. Control rather than change becomes the principal problematic of society. Alternately, theory can seek to grasp the internal dynamics that generate social formations through the ongoing activity of people in motion. From this perspective, mobilization may turn out to provide a more constructive framework than resistance in which to value and evaluate social change. It is necessary to preserve a space where new formations germinate, to avoid assimilation and co-optation of the energies and demands that issue from social movements, to refuse to unsee what difference difference makes in the world. Yet, it must also be remembered that dominance too has much to lose and prepares itself incessantly to resist this possibility. Ultimately, the state takes on the responsibility to marshal forces that resist the societally creative energies of mobilization. In its myriad concrete forms, mobilization is activity that is already offensive.

Dance Studies

Dance has been written about in many ways and to many ends. Yet much writing in the twentieth century, following on the modernist conventions of an autonomous aesthetic domain distinct from other aspects of social life, has labored to affirm the distinctness of dance from other artistic and cultural forms. A series of critics sought to establish the artistic legitimacy of modern dance as a bodily practice without the associations with the sublime that the body, especially with reference to sexuality and popular culture, held. For dance writing of this sort, the separation of art and life could be considered strategic, if dance were to achieve recognition in a cultural environment increasingly being partitioned into high and low, avant-garde and kitsch. With respect to the prospects for the professionalization of dance, from the types of venues available for performances to touring opportunities and salaries for dancers, the stakes of these arguments were not incidental, for critics helped to institutionalize modern dance in the United States. Yet the successes in legitimating certain emergent dance forms (although certainly to the exclusion of many others) frequently came at the expense of bracketing off dance from social life. Particularly during the thirties when dance, like other arts, often regarded itself as a form of political practice as well, formalist criticism sought to insulate dance from political interpretations (not the least, from other critics).[20] Much contemporary dance criticism and scholarship is still inflected with the assumptions of this earlier formation, namely, that looking at dance politically might somehow interfere with its efficacy.

As is by now apparent, I would like to brush against the nap of these assumptions and explore not simply the politics of dance but also what dance has to offer politics. The question of what dance does for politics cannot be answered a priori; its effects need to be specified in any given instance. But, as the inspiration for a critical method, the study of dance can help one appreciate the context for "mobilization" and "agency" — two terms that register what is expansive and creative in the imagination of any political project. In my analysis of dance practices and choreographic works, I hope neither to omit the aesthetic vitality of dance from my writing nor to confuse life on the dance floor with that beyond it. Because politics appears, first, in the context of mobilizing forces within which dance and all other social practices are located and, second, as the particular bodily relations that contest a given space, the multiple effects that form a given instance of dance and politics can be understood as overdetermined.

The multiple forces that give rise to mobilization, easily taken for granted in the rush of political activity, are foregrounded in dance. An effective dance study, therefore, would expose both a political specificity and an entire political horizon. Such horizons, with their promise to enlarge the sense of what is possible, generally lost in daily experience to the enormous scale of society, are thereby condensed and made palpable. Hence mobilization in dance, because it is overdetermined, does not simply reflect the politics outside it but displays as well the activity of participation that is constitutive of the political as a field replete with myriad practices. Although the politics of dance cannot be directly translated or transcribed into other activities, it remains a source for generating concepts that are available to theoretical appropriation, as I sought to indicate in preceding discussion of mobilization.

Yet this sort of theoretical appropriation can always be tempted by the very idealization of dance as a kind of perfect world that would make dance

the solution in formal terms to absences in other domains of social practice. This idealization can occur when aesthetics and politics are treated
as the mirror of each other (notwithstanding their institutional separation)
rather than as the inextricably joined terms of an uneasy relation of form
and content, as true for the politics of form as for the forms of politics.
While aesthetics and politics can be conceptualized apart from each other,
any expression of one—whether in the concert hall or the statehouse—assumes an articulation of the other. All politics possess a form that cannot be
reduced to its ideational content any more than material art forms are free
of political significance, but both are in need of specification. Hence, dance
must be suffused with the politics of all the various domains of society to
the point that it cannot be free of any of them. Dance must also be subject to
the critiques that have been generated through the range of diverse political
practices that struggle with the multiple and uneven effects engendered by
the histories of exploitation, racism, sexism, homophobia, and xenophobia.

Dance, without losing its relation to the political and critical energies
that enter it from without, can also indicate how those energies are mobilized within the confines of a particular setting. If studies can be crafted
that present these dance insights cogently, the methodological platform for
all political imaginings (including how manifestly different politics could
circulate in the same sphere) might be enlarged and enabled. In the five
investigations that compose this book, I aim to identify and apply certain
methodological insights gleaned from dance studies to political theory.

Thus far, I have spoken of dance and political theory at a level of gener-
ality that has permitted some clarification of their meaning. I do not presume, however, that conceptions of dance or politics are immune to their
own sociohistorical context. While much strain from the global political
economy has been placed on the boundaries of nation-states and their internal ability to respond to those strains, they continue to operate as the most
powerful frame that shapes political activity. The setting of my own studies
within the contemporary United States is not meant to deny the global circuits of dance practice, to neglect the more inclusive frame of world society,
or to ignore mobilizations that transgress national borders. Like dance itself,
politics must be situated in order to take some responsibility for the scene
from whence I speak.

In Chapter 1, "Dancing the Dialectic of Agency and History," I explore the relation of agency and history through a double narration of a performance event, first from the perspective of my own participation in the performance and then from that of the vantage of the audience as simulated by a video-tape of that same concert. The narrative of performance and the reception that licenses it are used to disclose issues that arise in the attempt to conceptualize the relation of agency, or the execution of an idea, to history, or the mobilization of a critical presence. The performative idea, materialized in choreographic form, gathers a given public at a particular place and time. Although the choreography takes shape over weeks of rehearsal, it exists in anticipation of an audience that has not yet come to be. The audience is the occasion for the performance but is also transformed into a collective body, having been moved together by means of performance. No sooner does this public make itself audible by applauding the dancers off the stage than it disperses without leaving a trace of itself, other than the impression left from that time enacted together with the dancers.

The written review of the event that appears in the press and even the video of it are limited in their ability to capture by means of representation what made the dance performance possible. These limits to representation of an actualized occurrence are here marshaled as resources to grapple with the complexities of political mobilization, specifically, the problem of what to make of historical phenomena, which, like the audience, very often leave scarcely any traces of their passage. Further, the separation of agency and history, as two moments of historical process more broadly, offers a corrective to those radical notions of history that seek, almost tautologically, to locate evidence of common people's experience and, by so doing, to identify the true motor of history. While the absence of people who hold neither wealth nor office and their experience from historical records is not easy to recover, their presence is not as stable or efficacious with respect to what is termed "progress" as accounts of popular culture and history often claim it to be.

My own participation in the performance complicates the question of voice or agency in the discussion of historiography insofar as I am already initiated as a participant in an occurrence of which, after it has passed, I am also the observer. The frame of my own observation and the potential of the performance are both situated historically by examining the legacy of Judson Church, where the event took place, to reflect on that site as a kind of alternative public sphere.

Dance can have a transformative effect on a particular methodology that enhances the grasp of the issue of participation. The insights acquired through these means can also be applied to the reading of dance to see what image of politics such a reading yields. I term the methodological strategy for encumbering dance with politics "overreading," a procedure that appropriates the internal movement of dance—its own capacities of mobilization—to the conceptual ordering of social context. I have selected a very ambitious choreographic work by Bill T. Jones, *Last Supper at Uncle Tom's Cabin/The Promised Land* (1990), as the basis for my exemplification of overreading in the second chapter of the book, "Overreading *The Promised Land:* Toward a Narrative of Context in Dance."

This chapter is composed in the same manner as the choreographic structure of the dance piece itself. Both writing and dance are organized into a prologue, four sections, and an audience response. A choreographic prologue, consisting of the cast as slaves arriving on the shores of the stage, corresponds to an initial methodological reflection in the writing. The dance then tells a version of Harriet Beecher Stowe's *Uncle Tom's Cabin,* and the essay narrates the choreographic work so as to show how the dance complicates the very process of narrative as such. The dance was first performed at a time when the National Endowment for the Arts (NEA) had introduced antiobscenity pledges into choreography grants, and the second act of *Last Supper* comments on various meanings of authority, while the subsequent section of the writing explores the critical reception of Jones's work. This context for the reception of the dance is further elaborated in the next section of the chapter by tracing the attempts by conservative politics of the eighties to police the boundaries between so-called public morality and private behavior in an effort to politicize the former and depoliticize the latter. The concern to keep social and political ideas separate from matters of aesthetic form is confronted directly in an encounter of profane and sacred staged with Bill T. Jones and a local cleric in the third act.

The final act of the dance, called "The Promised Land," offers a certain utopian excess that has room for the ample diversity of bodies that fill the stage. So this chapter winds down with a reflection inspired by Jones's work of how the overwhelming sense of austerity that characterizes the present might be rebuked to reenvision certain utopian possibilities and concludes, where the audience would make itself heard, with a reflection on the politics of overreading. Throughout the essay, insights from the dance are enlisted to read the present conjuncture for theory and politics. What I claim the piece ultimately makes available is a vision of the social totality and, against an abiding rhetoric of scarcity, a sense of political possibility, termed the "utopia of the real." This expanded imaginary is produced by overreading but does not exhaust further interpretive action.

Part of what makes Jones's work so successful is that it permits politics of labor, race, gender, and sexuality to occupy the same space. Such a shared site of difference suggests a strong version of multiculturalism that genuinely thrives on the diversity it creates. Outside of dance, the scene of multiculturalism is the nation-state, where diversity becomes a political issue against the presumption of a unifying and self-contained national culture that, in practice, seems to be more and more exclusionary of global and domestic populations. While the existence of borders around a given territory grants a juridical definition to a nation-state (assuming that they are recognized by others), what it means to be one of that nation's citizens, to take one's identity from the national culture, does not follow simply or directly from the fact of those boundaries but must be constantly established or imagined. Yet the existence of ideological machinery, such as mass media or political parties, to imagine the nation as a singular community and not the population of strangers it turns out to be, in no way guarantees that those persons will experience themselves as one people. On the contrary, national cultures are both internally and externally selective of who is being ideally imagined to make up the nation. In practice, then, any nation-state contains a number of imaginings as to its identity, each of which may make reference to different principles for ordering society. The nation-state, which is the contemporary version of the body politic, is often discussed as not only wishfully unified but also oddly disembodied, with the act of imagining national unity merely a matter of mental reflection. Such a perspective can hardly account for the passions that enflame the nation.

In the third chapter, I want to employ dance to reflect on how national sensibilities are embodied. Rather than begin with the presumed affinity of citizen-body and nation-state, I examine hip hop culture in music and dance to evaluate what might be different about multicultural circuits of nationalist sentiment. Unlike the discussion of dance as a stage event in the previous two chapters, popular practices are sited but not so clearly bounded in a given space. Precisely what makes the forms popular is their circulation through the entire space of the nation (or globe). I treat multi-cultural bodies as composite, in the sense that their identification as physical presence comes about through mediated and direct participation in popular entertainments. Composite bodies are fundamentally diverse in that they are formed by different sorts of cultural processes, rather than simply disparate variants of the same means for imagining and sensing the affiliation of self to community.

In its mediated aspect, the composite body assumes national contours, and as such, the means through which this body gains its sensibility at the scale of the nation-state needs to be discussed. Perhaps the closest thing we have to an official and ongoing broadcast of national identity is the evening news. Although many stories are told there, among the most persistent are those of violent crime. Crime stories are significant not only because they aim to evince a desire for unifying order through application of coercive means but also because they tell their story in a way that fortifies a racial divide. That the crimes portrayed, such as homicide, misrepresent what is most commonly an intraracial phenomenon as interracial needs to be related to the imagining of a nation as more threatened and divided by crime than the criminality of an increasingly divided and exclusionary economy.

In Chapter 3, "The Composite Body of Dance: Re(w)rapping the Multi-cultural Nation," I juxtapose the racialized and criminalized embodiment of nation on the evening news to a form of popular culture that has been accused of being divisively nationalist. My aim is to read the nationalist currents of hip hop against the grain of these accusations to see how aspects of this music and dance form might embody a different principle of association on which not simply a nation but also a society could be founded. Composite bodies are constituted across sites of production and reception. To examine the linkages between those sites, I have selected two instances of hip hop culture. One is a music video of *Wicked* by rapper Ice Cube that directly responds to broadcast news events and conventions, specifically those of the urban rebellion of spring 1992. The other is a hip hop aerobics class in Orange County, California, a geopolitic initially designed to be free of multicultural difference. Together, they serve as incidents of performance and audience in a thoroughly *media*ted and unexpectedly differentiated national environment. The music video is analyzed through repeated viewings, and the aerobics class, once again through my own participation.

The ethnographic study of the hip hop aerobics class suggests that dance techniques can orient bodies quite differently to their own (national) desires. That otherwise nonblack bodies would be propelling themselves across a racial divide by means of dance technique introduces the possibility that technique does more than tool the body to what is dominant in the social order. Bodies can also be trained—or learn—in a manner that is inconsistent with dominance as such, which assumes investment in the logic and sensibility of exclusion and subordination. The key to subverting dominance lies in the antinomies of the participation necessary to be mastered by technique. At the most basic level, the dance class is impossible without participation, and so too with society. The problem for any society structured in domination is how participation can be managed and appropriated in a way that allows the fact, if not the particular formation, of those structures to persist, for it is never clear how much change a given social order can tolerate and still remain true to itself. In the last instance, the state bears responsibility to maintain physical mastery over its subjects. For this, armed forces are kept. But the state's monopoly over these legitimate means of coercion generally remains a latent threat to the potential of an unruly citizen body. In daily life other techniques take up this charge, and whether explicitly or not, techniques such as those found in a dance class are called on to align bodies with state authority.

At the most general level, techniques bring together the practical accomplishment of a given activity with the means to regulate what is considered appropriate to that activity. As such, the fundamental contradiction of all technique is that the very training which allows those who participate to be mastered by discipline also allows them to achieve mastery over technique itself. For mastering a technique develops the fluency in practice that loosens the fixed hold on the body initially commanded by that very technique. Surely this contradiction does not necessarily translate into a politics that challenges state authority, particularly if the pleasures of accomplishing a given bodily practice are identified with the law of technique—the juridical structuring of opportunity—that assigns credit to the existing state order for what the citizenry accomplishes by dint of its own collective labors. It could be said that by virtue of the law of technique, the United States can be called a free country in that the technical means through which people get things done are seen as guaranteed and released rather than constrained and coerced through the state. Paradoxically, then, although coercive forces are more extensively deployed on behalf of the state throughout social spheres than is typically thought, bodies are also less subordinated than they would appear to be through standard means of political reckoning. The dance class foregrounds this paradox, which is also that of state authority wherever it is instantiated.

The teaching of dance technique is a privileged site for examining how mastery of the body that is otherwise latent in society becomes manifest. In Chapter 4, "Between Technique and the State: The Univers(ity) in Dance," I draw on my experiences in a college modern dance technique class to examine the tension between the manner in which a given technique takes hold of the body and what competencies those trained bodies bring to the subversion of authority that is driven by technical mastery. The institutional setting of the university is here taken as a weak link in the state armory that exposes in detail the machinations of authority that seek to embody the coercive principle of the state in everyday life, particularly in a site thought privileged and therefore exempt from being subjected to such forces. As governmental resources at all levels are shifted from constructive social programs aimed at a modicum of inclusion in civil life, to exclusionary instruments of coercion such as prisons and police, this line of analysis may assume increasing relevance.

In addition, modern dance technique is often cited as a distinctly (North) American form and as such is loaded with certain national aspirations, which have been explicitly stated by dance pioneers such as Martha Graham. It has also been said that modern dance techniques have been posed as universal forms that fuse the impartially scientific with the transcendentally aesthetic so as to ground a well-rounded citizen-body as a naturally occurring condition. In the university technique class, what appears at first sight as the mimicry of this singular national body reveals, through the influence of other techniques, a multiplicity of demands that the dancer learns to negotiate and, within limits, to surpass the strictures of technique to display the intrinsic diversity that composes each citizen-body. That these dance students are women and the techniques themselves multiculturally inflected further complicates the claims to a universality made by nationalizing corporeality and ideology.

The university produces not only trained bodies but trained minds as well. Dance studies materializes where these two trainings intersect. The flourishing of investigations that take the body as their object of analysis might logically cede a central place to the theory and practice of dance. But this has rarely been the case. Dance scholarship has only recently begun to incorporate into its own methods of reflection the interdisciplinary theoretical language of cultural studies that has attended to the radical moment of what bodies and minds produce. Writing about dance is now encouraged in this development across disciplinary boundaries by parallel occurrences in the field of dance performance. This phenomenon of cultural production overspilling its boundaries is consonant with my understanding of cultural studies. What I consider in the concluding chapter is a more formal undertaking of certain issues I have raised in this introduction, namely, what a critically informed approach to dance can bring to the emerging field of cultural studies that has itself been closely allied to forms of knowledge generated in the multicultural context beyond (but also through) the academy. Here I imagine the conceptual conditions and potential alliances for a dance studies that could participate more fully in the development of contemporary cultural theory by foregrounding what dance can offer to the understanding of politics.

Hence, in Chapter 5, "For Dance Studies," I return to the problematic of mobilization and attempt to articulate the institutional and epistemological emergence of dance studies. Although the roots of university dance programs can be traced to certain feminist impulses in liberal arts education of the 1930s, departments proliferated with the Great Society expansion of the 1960s. Along with the institutionalization of the arts generally that gave rise to the NEA, the formalization of dance study emerged alongside a number of other social movements engaging gender, sexuality, race, and environment that privileged the bodily. As an object of writing, dance has enjoyed attention for centuries. But as a field of study, it did not begin to generate epistemological foundations until the 1980s. Dance studies, however, emerges with the benefit of specifying an already existing theoretical interest in the body, one that is also grounded as a practice and not merely as an object of analysis. As a cultural practice, dance has the potential to offer certain moves out of the entrapping splits between structure and agency, context and text, that have ensnared the humanities and social sciences even as they have come together in cultural studies. The mutual implication of choreographic structuration and of dance process, in which choreography already begins within dance technique and the means to dance already incorporate choreographic invention, suggests insights into what has plagued the theory of mobilization, the unworkable divide between agency and history. These nascent ambitions provide powerful interdisciplinary foundations for the participation of dance studies with other efforts to transform the techniques of self-understanding.

Toward a Realignment of Participation

Judson Church, Bill T. Jones, university dance, MTV, and hip hop aerobics: What do these instances of dance have to do with one another, what dance topography do they imagine, and how do they map a political landscape? On the surface, these examples share no conventional aesthetic or stylistic unity or common technical foundation, nor do they issue from any single cultural location. On the contrary, the aesthetic and cultural diffusion that these examples display stands as a certain kind of evidence for the diversity of contemporary dance practice. Yet, on closer inspection all manner of mutual influence and relation are discernible. A hip hop mover need not study release technique, as did those in the Judson concert, to understand a downward use of his or her body's weight that is in counterpoint to the gravitational uplift of ballet (and certainly many ballet classes have incorporated similar kinesthetic insights). Both Bill T. Jones and the dancers in the university class are drawn to the rhythms of popular movement forms. An affinity for the dance identities of others is an undercurrent that connects these four examples and suggests that the standard taxonomies for sorting out different dance forms may overstate the discreteness implied by such dualistic categorizations as modern-postmodern, concert-popular, black-white, gay-straight dance. On the strength of these connections, it is possible to imagine the vitality and range of dance.

As points on a map of the dance field, these four instances suggest that no single point exists that all dancing must pass through, no privileged form of dance with which all others must be compared. The manifest distance at which these examples are located culturally and aesthetically suggests that any topography of dance must appreciate the relation between dancing as the reflexive mobilization of the body and physical culture more broadly.

Dance is a specification of bodies in a given historical conjuncture, and its coherence must be understood not simply in terms of resemblance among different expressions of dance but also with respect to the resonance between dance and the entire social kinesthetic. Because dance concentrates the social forces that make bodies what they are, it can be drawn on to rethink conventional views of politics as well.

As occasions for writerly reflection, each dance example poses different conceptual problems and offers certain resources in relation to the question of mobilization that I have sketched in this chapter. Judson reveals the fragile link between agency and history that social movement theory assumes to be initially unconnected. Jones's *Last Supper at Uncle Tom's Cabin/The Promised Land* suggests a way of thinking politics in terms of abundance rather than scarcity. Hip hop moves offer a way of imagining the underlying linkages among the manifestly diverse communities that compose the nation. University dance technique exposes how coercion and consent are actively negotiated outside the formal apparatus of the state. Dance studies as a recent entrant into the field of interdisciplinary ways of knowing not only galvanizes and disseminates the growing interest in dance but can also offer a fresh theoretical vocabulary that may help move certain clots and blockages in our entire epistemological enterprise. If politics is already in motion, dance studies suggests that so too is the practice of thought.

Ultimately, however, Judson, Bill T. Jones, university dance, and hip hop are but moments in the larger movement of my own dance life. Taken together, they help imagine the current dance terrain; their selection was not preordained but the consequence of my own participation in what led to these essays, an issue that deserves comment. While dance is being foregrounded here analytically, this strategy cannot be detached fully from the place of dance in my own biographical background. Ontogenetically speaking, dance appeared late in my body, relative to the recommended life course of a dancer. After some initial encounter with modern dance classes in 1975 as a college freshman at the University of California, San Diego, my training began in earnest when I transferred to Berkeley a year and a half later. There, I auditioned for a daily class as a way, I told myself, to satisfy my appetite for physical activity. At the end of the audition, there were piles of dancers in different corners of the studio. The perceived lack of men compensated for my own technical deficiencies as a dancer, and at the last moment, I was moved from the "out" pile to the "in" pile. This affirmative action, contrary to claims of reverse discrimination, is altogether too common and continues in all manner of special attentions from teachers and choreographers long after the initial access to dance is granted. Here it occurred in the face of lack with respect to normative expectations of what would make classes, and subsequently the ascendant movement of women in the modern dance world, more "balanced." Beyond the phallocentrism that dance, like other practices, is also susceptible to is perhaps a hint that the presence of male bodies can be taken as the site of technical insufficiency, rather than prowess, as assumed by the ideology of a male-centered world.

I entered dance by means of a certain access to unearned gender privilege, by which I mean attributions of a value in identity made without reference to the labor performed to generate them. While there are many domains in which this privilege is invoked, it was particularly apparent to me in dance. My prior history of masculinization, including the requisite exposure to sports (albeit the less gender-divided tennis and swimming, with their own associations of privilege), accustomed me to movement but not to the flexibility associated with a technique that was developed from the strengths of a particular woman, in this case, Martha Graham. The relative inflexibility in my pelvic architecture, clearly not shared by all male dancers, nonetheless came to figure for me a definite lack that could be attributed to gender. In this regard, the effacement of my particular male history became part of my training not only at Berkeley but also when I danced during graduate school (in sociology) at Madison, Wisconsin, and subsequently when I moved to New York to study professionally in 1980.

Without pretending to have freed myself through dance from the webs of unearned privilege, my desire to move was animated by appropriating what could be found in the bodies of others. This explicit dependence on and crediting of others at least introduced a measure of interference with the strictures of dominance that called me out and through the pleasures of dancing offered immediate gains by means of a deliberate realignment of bodily identity. It is a great leap to take, but I would hope that the pedagogy of realignment to move through others and against the inflexibility in oneself that dance offers might apply elsewhere as well. I venture this hope at a time when it is claimed that those who benefit from privilege have no interest in breaking their own affiliations with the dominant order and are thereby rendered indifferent to the violence that order does to themselves and others. The very appeal of the dominant order that is typically taken as operating behind people's backs might be subverted by a movement that is more fully sentient of a realignment of forces that is altogether more appealing than the power relations with which we currently contend.

With the prospect of that movement in mind, I return to the particular studies that follow and want to implicate my dancing self in them. In both the dance performance at Judson Church and the university dance technique class, I was the only male dancer. With respect to the choreographer and dancers in the Judson project, I was among friends. Not only were the gendered relations more fully negotiable than in other settings, but the movement vocabulary was also generated largely through improvisation and without the formalized gender roles of, for example, partnering and lifting that characterize certain dance divisions of labor.[21] When I began that project, I had no notion of writing about it and reserved for myself no special authority of the observing gaze that is conventional to the male posture in ethnography and art. The same cannot be said for the dance technique class. There, my presence could not be fully separated from that of the other males in the studio, the teachers, and accompanists, who gazed on the bodies of women. Although for the other students I had no formal authority, my writing of them after class, while dependent on them during it, traded on the split between the private role of the participant and public pronouncements of the observer that has been taken to task in feminist critiques of ethnography.[22]

The affinity of whiteness for black culture that informs the discussion of hip hop clearly pertains to my own attraction to the work of Bill T. Jones as well. It is the concern to grasp the political implications of that affinity, and the questions of racial classification more broadly, rather than any special claim to expertise regarding African American cultural practices, that underwrites my efforts at understanding these two particular instances. Obviously the categories race and gender are not identical (nor are they exhaustive of either hip hop or Jones's choreography), but as historical constructs they share features of the process of unearned privilege I have described that makes it possible to live through others without acknowledging and constructively incorporating the debt that is incurred. Today, racialized divisions within society attack the very viability of racial difference. It is with no small degree of urgency that attempts must be made to realign the terms of identification across the violating chasm of race.

The problem of speaking for the other, especially from these positions of dominance from which I hail, cannot be underestimated. The ability to appropriate what others produce by means of cultural identity is predicated on a larger cultural economy of unequal exchange and cannot be remedied simply by locating oneself. Even to be self-reflexive about the ability to speak to others can be problematic when that particular voice of self only amplifies a privileged position that we may need less, not more of, at this particular moment. Yet if my experience of dance practice continues to assert itself in these writings, it is precisely in the manner invoked in Chapter 1 — namely, as a disruptive other to the fixating powers of representation.

I cannot dance to write, but reinvoking dancing can help to mobilize a realignment of the complex economy of identification and difference that is never far removed from the economy of things. Drawn to these divergent affiliations, I can be moved to support powers other than those of dominance. The endeavor to learn about my own desire for the disruptive presence of difference may be of some assistance to counter what is dominant in the lives of myself and others. The prospect of such desirable and self-effacing affiliations with others is fundamental to the call for a more generalized climate of participation — what for me makes socialism and democracy of a piece — that animates the present writing. Once we accept that we are already in motion, already at work in an ongoing process of realignment, the resistance — in the name of dominance — to those differences which make for abundance in and of society may lose more and more of its luster to these superior mobilizing forces.

There are no wings in Judson Church. Stained glass. A marble altar. A gilded organ. These and not the conventional tokens of theater architecture are the markers of a space transformed. In an evening of works shared by two choreographers, dancers in the last piece of the concert await their moment of display in a gallery immediately above the audience. In anticipation of their own performance, they witness now in others what others will soon see of them. They join in the audience response to this just completed spectacle that they are now called on to provide. Dancers descend from this elevated perspective on a narrow staircase and walk along the audience's flank, brushing against the perimeter of that congregated body as if to measure its density. They enter the darkened space that holds a diffuse focus. The markings of "church" at Judson — quite eccentric, no doubt, to the experience of a good part of the crowd — is enough of a departure from the familiar to grant the performers the distance that will privilege their activity as spectacle, despite their entrance on the scene through means of such casual contact. What has accumulated over three months of rehearsals at sites with little resemblance to this one will now dissolve in fourteen minutes of performance.[1]

The transcription from disparate spaces of rehearsal to this one of performance has occurred only once in a run-through of the piece an hour before the concert. This concert is one of a series of single-evening showcases on Monday evenings, when many other theaters are dark, and it is offered without charge to the public. Freed from competing demands of time and purse, a space that appears as if it were just outside the market for spectacle is filled to capacity. There is a certain drama to what will pass through the opening of an opening night performance that must be regathered for subsequent shows. In this case, the expectation of a future must itself be deferred. Without the presumption that this moment would be repeated on the eve of some further performances, four of us assume places in the darkness that we take as the illusory origins of something that culminates but did not actually start here.

I sit farthest downstage watching, along with the audience behind me, the minimal beginnings of a recurrent gestural phrase, suggestive of but without specific signification. Kim, who sits perched on the edge of the marble altar, appears silently absorbed in these handmade gestures. I share in the audience's gaze on these initially tiny movements, but with a decidedly more instrumental interest. One of those movements brings me to join in their general articulation and, by so doing, to depart from that gaze whose name is audience which had effectively formatted the performance space and as such facilitated the performance.

There is now music to provide an aural frame of reference for the four of us and to allow the visual dependencies among us to abate. The escalating movement, punctuated like so many questions still listening for response, brings me from the floor to my feet. Randa intervenes on my behalf as I begin to fall back again toward the floor. She takes over the weight that had been me freestanding. She flips it, shifts it again, and departs. Corporal interdependency continues in a duet with Greta composed of a series of embraces that slip away as we grasp for them. Well inside of the piece by now, the movement that has brought me here is all linked through permutations and disruptions of that initial gestural phrase. The physical contact of two yields to the unison of four in the first frontal encounter of performers to audience. There are no lights angled at the stage at Judson Church that normally would blind performers to those who gaze on them, generating the visual asymmetry on which spectacle depends. On the contrary, the general illumination does little to discriminate between the two parties, and in the moments of movement that open outward, it is possible, albeit only fleetingly, to regard them as they do us.

Soon this mutuality of regard will become more explicit. The unspeakable state of my body as an object of the gaze is broken when I address the audience with a line that I had previously spoken only in rehearsal, without the audience being there: "I suppose you were hoping to get some sort of meaning out of that? Well did you?" These words carried my gaze back to the gazers and inquired as to what their sight had seen. But my momentary fixity could bring me only to gaze without being able to sustain such a visual stance. In movement, the boundary between the volume of the performance space and that of the audience could be effaced. Motion, collected in me as a medium of exchange between the history of rehearsals and the aggregated body of the public, operated across the spaces divided by staging and seating. In sight, I could not match the mass of audience with its detail. Framed in the aggregate, faces lost their claims to portraiture. There was the brown beard against blue plaid sitting in front and, several rows back, the curve of glasses matched in a facial furrow. Such sightings had to be quickly relinquished to preserve my own visuality as something available to the audience and to lend my corporeality to those three to whom I owed an imminent allegiance.

Racing through the performance space in a collision course with audience and lofting myself into verticality, I am caught by three standing in for many more beyond them. In the seamless circulation of weight that is dancing, what was caught is now deposited for the transit of others. These exchanges continue, enlisting dancers to effect the equivalent of localized polar shifts. Whole bodies are remapped along altered axes of arrival and departure. Soft folds for sudden landings are created where there were flat surfaces associated with the boundaries of self-containment. The boundaries have been redrawn so persistently as to inflict a partial meltdown of that familiar da Vinci figure in its orb. For inside that sphere is no longer a renaissance of singularity exposing its genius. The canvas has been torn, and like figures momentarily released from the stillness of representation, we pour through the openings. There is now little movement that proceeds unmediated through the body of others. Space has become dense and bodies permeable to the point of narrowing the differences between them. It is possible to extend in a direction where no one yet stands and find support by the time of arrival.

Such explicit collectivity, dependent as it is on proximity, yields to an expanding distance among the four of us. The suggestion is made through movements echoed peripherally among us of that prior community of proximity, now continuing without touch, implicating not only ourselves in a shared project but also those others on whose gaze we have come to depend for our continued activity. But the piece ends. All of the motion in the space collects the place we each occupy as we regard those who gaze on us. Only their applause will break that tenuous obligation, and with it, our mutual unities disperse.

The genealogy of audience, as that other unity, is much more difficult to trace than is that of the performers. Like the latter, it is occasioned by and enables the performance, but unlike the dancers, whose specific unity as a company has a prior history, the audience in attendance is constituted only by that particular instance of the dance. Despite the indications that it exists for a specialized purpose, the chapel at Judson Church imposes fewer architectural and theatrical qualifications than many performance spaces do on the process of audience self-constitution. Without a functioning proscenium, the audience itself serves as a physical boundary of the performing space. The illumination of that space, which signals the opening of the dance piece for the audience, finds those in attendance scanning what lies before them — in actuality, looking for the dance. Given the absence of illuminated pools that are typically created in other stages by the canopy of focusable lighting instruments, or other visual aids, such as a curtain (both of which Judson lacks), and the minimal movements that begin this particular piece, it is not unlikely for an active participant of the audience to locate the figure upstage who makes the initial gestures after the dance has already begun. For audience members, then, it is the work of their own gaze that sets the piece in motion. Given too that the space is as wide as it is deep, the distance between dancers with which the piece begins imposes a certain sense that the origin of the dance may be lost. This loss is introduced by the work of the audience itself and takes the form of a suspicion that there may be more activity on the periphery of one's gaze than at its focal point. Watching the piece entails looking for something to look at. The candidates in this visual field are not limited to the dancers. The carved details and inscriptions of the church may provide as likely a momentary resting place for the gaze as would the attire or attributes of others in the audience. The public is arrayed in a U shape around the performing space and is therefore difficult to avoid catching sight of. This particular seating arrangement resists the disappearance of the collective self in the act of viewing others that is said to be the stock-in-trade of the proscenium stage.

The shifting character of the gaze is also activated by the specific inscription of the choreography in this space. Yet the promise of the choreography — to deliver the space whole to an intended viewer — is violated through the very activity of viewing. This occurs not simply because each participant in this process sees it from a different perspective but additionally because the different perspectives are generated by an indeterminate but distinct process of audition, a tryout, so to speak, for the senses. What audience members share is not what they have seen, as if the dance produced a common set of images exposed to a population with diverse propensities toward their reception (the model of mass media), but rather a common predicament of looking for the dance as they view it. This predicament is not inconsistent with the idea of this piece of choreography, as evidenced in the constant shifting of who moves through space and who moves in place in the opening sections of the work, or who moves and who observes or speaks in the latter part of the dance. There are, no doubt, moments of common focus for the audience that the choreographer has designed into the piece, and these make the reflexivity of viewing more immediate. When the muteness of the dancers is broken by the initial verbal address made to the audience, their common attendance to what they have heard breaks their own silence. The creakings of chairs and clearings of throats, the prior noises of the listeners, which usually go unrecognized as solitary acts of self-acknowledgment, are now expressed as a corroborative laughter. The laughter in this case was not a common roar that might have come from the spongy mass of a homogenous body in attendance. It was instead punctuated through the house, accumulating its aural presence in response to the question I had asked them, without waiting for a reply, as to whether they had gotten any "meaning" out of the dance. Part of what the audience was trying out for was the assertion of its capacity for evaluation. The audience was listening to itself.

The other opportunity for audition comes when the public brings the piece to a close. Applause emerges at the audience's moment of fullest self-recognition. It is certainly occasioned by the dancers' activity, but it is a response to a question that the audience must by this point have posed to itself: Was that the dance? By initiating this common reflective activity on what has just transpired, the audience imposes a direct physical imperative on the dancers, an authority that until now was reserved for the choreographer. For, when the audience decides that the dance is complete, it gets them to bow and then quite literally applauds the dancers out of the performing space. What the choreographer began — getting dancers to move with something in mind — the audience here continues. But as soon as they have succeeded in assuming their choreographic role, they disband themselves, leaving behind the very authority that their work had assigned to them.

One of this night's audience members was a critic for the *New York Times* who did invoke that lost authority. Several paragraphs appeared in the Home section of the paper a few days later. That a review appeared at all could not have been expected, especially for a concert of experimental dance that ran for only a single evening. But that it did appear meant that the dance could have an efficacy beyond the concert hall, at least in the minds of those who had not been at the event. Conventionally speaking, the review entered the dance into history by translating it into the representation of a past occurrence that could be interpreted by others. Yet both as a document of the event in which the artistic object was presented and as an instrument for understanding what made the event possible, the review in this rather truncated form is a weak device for historical representation. The review, the most common form of dance writing, is weak as much for how it attempts to describe the object of that performed event as for what it leaves out.

Dancing among the Arts

Clearly this problem of representing the artistic object impinges on any writing about art or, for that matter, other historical events whose deeds are invariably more than words. There is always something left out of the attempt to represent in words work executed in a nonverbal medium. Although all art exists within history, it does so, "as it were, twice": first, as an object that gains the status of a discrete and originary appearance, namely, as a creative event; and second, through the history of that object's reception, which while subject to different conventions of interpretation typically treats the object as an authentic instance of its past context rather than as a reflection on how representation of the object bears what, from the perspective of the present, is called history. Reference to the art object can thereby serve to elide the critic's own separation of past and present by means of the critical writing itself. This written representation of the object can then take the place of the object itself as an authentic, albeit mediating, authority. But dance presents special problems of how to move between representation and object, not the least because as a performance, it is an object that dissolves into the temporal medium in which it occurs. In the same event, the performance incorporates the historical appearance of a choreographic idea and the history of reception for a given instance of dancing. The fact that the

performance occurs is already represented as history rather than as a problem presented by the historian of how to write about events that leave no
traces in the form of archival evidence or material remains.

It might be possible to imagine a sort of technological solution to the
problem posed by the review, insofar as it serves as a document that writes
the object into history. If writing itself is not an adequate device to document performance event-as-object, is there another technique that resolves
some of the issues posed for representing dance? For example, better documentation of the dance might have been provided by either of two video
cameras that recorded the performance at Judson Church that evening, insofar as they supply an index of the self-dissolution of the dance object during the course of the performance. But this assumes that it is the passage of
time per se that constitutes the object of dance, an idea that may turn out to
yield as little insight into dance as it does into history, not the least because
time would have to be conceived of as an objective measure of some linear
movement of the universe that is abstracted from human experience, rather
than being produced through the process of living history.

Instead of taking a notion of objectified time as the medium within which
dancing occurs, dance may help elaborate an understanding of how a sense
of time and space is generated through social life. Dancing features as its
artistic object the motional dynamics of gathering together physical presence (mobilization), the incessant change of bodies moving in space. This
process of mobilizing bodies in space can be simulated in video only by subjecting various shots to an editing process that results in a visual perspective
distinct from any single view by an eye in the audience, of the actual dance
in performance. Indeed, the more the video pursues the kinesthetic content
of dancing through its own visual form, the more it disrupts the appearance
of continuity in the standard documentary shot that purportedly places the
camera in the seat of the audience. Whereas audio recording might replicate
at least the signifiers of a musical performance, video relies on a displacement of an activity that occurs within a three-dimensional space into some
virtual equivalent. Videography reinscribes dancing in another medium
that, although not a mere reflection of performance, can, by its assimilation
of the active looking that editing shots from different angles allows, introduce an awareness of how history is written.

When the video gaze assumes the perspective of audience, it imagines a generalized viewer that is consolidated under its watchful eye as a unity-in-the-name-of-collectivity (it speaks as audience and as event). In this way it does not depart from the claims to authority that make possible any form of representation. Yet, as an artifact of the performance, video may readily conceal the asynchrony and heterogeneity of audience activity. Hence, even the more self-conscious forms of documentation (when dance videography is that) focus on reconstructing an event-as-object rather than on recapturing something of the social processes — namely, the very participation of performers and audience — that made that event possible.

Dance performance highlights this participation precisely because of its resistance to representation. Yet this resistance can be apprehended only in the course of representation itself — for dance is associated with a variety of representational forms.[2] Properly theorized, however, the limits to representation that dance poses become a resource for writing about all activities that share with performance the passage through the present and, as such, can deepen our grasp of what constitutes history. But any gains realized from dance analysis must specify dance adequately. Without moving too quickly to a set of essentially defining positive traits that make dance seem wholly exceptional from every other practice, it is useful to clarify what dance is by differentiating it relative to representation. In the 1950s and 1960s, semiotics gained currency as a transdisciplinary framework that allowed all forms of cultural representation, irrespective of their particular material form, to be understood as a kind of language, with corresponding regularities of form, structure, and function. By joining in this intellectual movement, a semiotics of dance could indicate what dance shared with other cultural practices and provide a systematic way of speaking and writing about dance. Yet, at the most basic level of its construction, the operation of the sign, dance is unlike language, in which at least a relation of the material image (or signifier and associated concept, or signified) is identifiable if not immutable. At the "zero degree" of dance movement, meaning is indeterminate because movement in practice lacks the discrete equivalents of sound images that words provide. In this respect, it departs from music, which, as Jacques Attali notes in a similar mode of inquiry, can be said to possess a determinate signifier, without an equivalent signified. As he puts it, "the 'meaning' of the musical message is expressed in a global fashion, in its operationality, and not in the juxtaposed signification of each sound element."[3] Despite stylistic consistencies within dance forms, the association between particular movements and concepts has not been culturally established by any equivalent of a "community of speakers" that would systematically equate a lexicon of dance movement with a more generalized circulation of gestures.

All this raises the question of what would constitute a unit of meaning in dance. While in his semiology in *Course in General Linguistics* Saussure is careful to avoid attributing a signifier with a determinate content, what makes one signifier distinct from another is a function of a process of recognition through difference.[4] Yet where dance idioms such as ballet carry this kind of logophilic similarity, the meaning is still said to lie in the dancing as a whole, which constitutes the "speech act," not in each gestural movement as if it were a detachable utterance. Even this connection belies a certain cultural and historical specificity as evidenced by recent developments in concert dance (such as contact improvisation), in which the continuity of movement or motion usurps sequences of gestures as the object of the dance.[5]

Although dancing relies on any number of structural devices as part of the choreographic craft, even such experienced dance-goers as professional critics do not evidence anything as efficacious as demonstrable codes of interpretation that mark what of the choreography is translated into words, though clearly there are continuities in the critic's own philosophical disposition toward dance (a question that will be taken up in the next chapter). Nor has a secondary literature emerged that has articulated a grammar of dance criticism specific to its object or a more general meditation on this predicament for the representation of dance in writing. The other side of the resistance of the dance object to representation, therefore, has been the challenge (that only recently has begun to be addressed) to generate a theoretical language of its own or a sustained dialogue with theory from other sources.[6] Suffice it to say that the belated entry of dance writing into the domain of theoretical reflection is here taken as a resource rather than a deficiency. For what appears at first glance to be merely muteness, fragility, or silence can be marshaled self-critically to speak of that difficult conjuncture between the irreducibly concrete and its vanishing point that constantly moves in dance.

The distance between representation and object has engaged the intellectual energies of those writing on dance as a kind of bricolage where the concrete dance event appears to occasion writerly structure or the conceptual framework of representation. Following Claude Lévi-Strauss, this process of event-into-structure does not display its relation between theory and technique but produces an impression of the totality of relations within a culture.[7] In other fields of inquiry, the question of how to represent the object of analysis has been addressed by a theoretical language that simulates the complexity of what is being discussed, so that the form of writing approximates the form of what it represents. If this idea is applied to the case of dance performance, the audience, when taken as an object of representation, is best understood as a means of participation. Participation, in my usage, assumes the internal perspective of the performance event. As event, audience-as-participation cannot see or observe itself from without but is labor that, through its association and expenditure, enables the event to occur. The audience is not only part of the event's reason for being but also its means of becoming, what momentarily embodies the communicative idea of the performance. The traces of participation, the work an audience does to create a sense of the object as it is presented to them, are nowhere to be found in the standard means of representation and documentation. These traces are absent from the ways in which history is conventionally conceived.

Reception of dance, quite evident in the kinds of dancing referred to at the opening of this chapter but also characteristic of Western concert dance more broadly, is realized only in and through the execution of a particular performance event. This particularization is precisely the uneasy conjuncture of creation and execution, of a birth that is a death, a consequence of this operation that is known beforehand. The dancers constitute themselves in anticipation of performance. This anticipation bears the anxiety of uncertainty, of something that can be completed only through its communication. The performance is the execution of an idea by dancers whose work proceeds in expectation of an audience that is itself constituted only through performance. The audience has no identity as audience prior to and apart from the performative agency that has occasioned it. As such, the audience is intrinsically "unstable," both in terms of its own presence and in its ability to occasion and then disrupt the very anxiety of performance.[8] The uncertainty, the indeterminacy of performance, is momentarily actualized by the audience and therefore itself disrupted. At the same time, it is the work that the audience does, the participation that it lends to performance to make the latter possible, that is irrecuperable to representation. It is, like the dance activity itself, an untranslatable object. But unlike dancing, toward which writing may express a certain overconfidence in its ability to "capture and chronicle" the event,[9] representation rarely makes an effort to recognize the fundamental participation audience offers to enable performance. Participation springs from this disruptive potential, an indeterminacy of representation internal to the performance.

Put more strongly, the preceding analysis of dance shows that representation generates a misrecognition of what, by virtue of its very relation to performance activity, cannot be represented or is lost to it. If writing and documentation can refer to performance but cannot recuperate the traces of participation found in performance, minimally they can recognize the disruptive effects of the work of participation lost to representation. This is the problem that was hinted at in the writing that opened this chapter, writing that, in effect, stood in for the activities of performance and audience. My double account of the dance was meant to indicate a disruption of narrative forms, one that in this case depended on a kinesthetic memory of my part in the dance and the other on a video of that performance with visual and aural traces of audience in it, which I viewed six months later. A limitation of my writing, beyond altering typographical format, is that, as writing, the two narratives appeared as a sequence of discrete events, whereas during the performance event, the work of dancers and audience was simultaneous. What a fuller elaboration of these narratives would want to show was that the performance event could be grasped only as a process of exchange through the mutual interruption and displacement of narratives. A single privileged narrative perspective, whether that of the dancers, the audience, the choreographer, or the critic, is not adequate analytically to the complexity of the event.

Performing the People

The conceptual challenges posed by dance based on the particularization of the performer-audience relation suggest a shift in analytic perspective from something I have called "representation" to participation. This reorientation has an import beyond dance writing, one that can contribute to recent debates over the constitution and representation of historical agency. Nietzsche anticipated these debates in his discussions of the ways in which the very representation of history can interfere with living history. He characterized an abusive presence of the past as either "monumental" or "antiquarian," the former referring to the problem of exclusion and the latter referring to immutability.[10] The monument alludes to those vanished moments of eternal greatness that eliminate from consideration much of what transpired in the past and all of what goes on in the present as capable of providing value in human affairs. Similarly, the antiquary preserves in relics and mementos an unmediated survival of past times as compensation and grounding for a present that bears no ethical substance. Although each approach styles itself differently, as lofty and as humble, both views of the past allow it to be treated as a negative reference for the present, undermining the recognition of the means through which social change is generated — that is, of historical agency.

Here I want to argue that what at first glance may look like a misconception of history turns out to be something more complex. Conventionally speaking, what is taken to be the past in actuality appears as an idea or force within the present, and yet, paradoxically, past and present are conceived of as absolutely disjoined from each other. Nietzsche's critique is, after all, occasioned by a concern with what the present has become to those who live it. He is attempting to articulate the experience of modernity as an awareness of the interminable loss of the present that is possible only when what is felt as "just now" (modernus) becomes a central cultural referent.[11] It is the culture of an incessantly passing "now" that allows the past to figure as compensation for the imminent death of what is. Hence the temptation to reify the past — to displace a subjectivity onto the pure exteriority of things (monument or relics) — to stabilize an ungovernably vanishing present. Nietzsche was committed to confronting the present more directly without the mystification of what was confusing about modern life, which he saw as being swept aside in the exclusive focus of so many other intellectuals on reason as a force of progress.

Like Nietzsche's work, and seminal as well to the contemporary discussions of history that I will focus on, is the work of Karl Marx, who also opens the horizon for a self-critical awareness of history as crucial to the agency of social change. The historical conditions under which the production of a present could simultaneously appear as its loss were central concerns to Marx in volume 1 of *Capital*. His analysis of the movement of concrete (the efforts of living people expended in production) to abstract (the now dead consequence of that expenditure referenced in the whole universe of exchangeable objects) labor can also be read as an account of how labor is temporally set in motion. In the most fundamental sense, it is his work that provides the theoretical context for the points I would like to make about agency and history with reference to dance.

As an account of how labor is set in motion, the labor theory of value is also consistent with Marx's own historical writings. It is in *The Eighteenth Brumaire of Louis Bonaparte,* the most well known of these writings, that Marx makes the claim that people "make their own history, but they do not make it just as they please."[12] Taking their cue from this claim, a group of British historians associated with the Communist Party committed themselves to locate the popular forces absented from monumental histories. Contrary to the antiquarian view, the people were, in the accounts of these British historians, invested with a generative capacity for social change that treats the past as always in motion. The "people's historians," as they were called, sought to include the everyday life experience and activities of those who had been excluded from the historical record and to render contingent the very authority of those who wield official power so often thought to be fixed in the present. Among the group's efforts could be counted such seminal works as Eric Hobsbawm's studies of popular resistance, George Rudé's reversal of the historic antipathy toward the crowd, and Raphael Samuel's development of oral history.[13] Edward Palmer Thompson's *The Making of the English Working Class*[14] is perhaps the most influential in the efforts to treat the relation between historiography and history as a political project that takes as its object "the social constructions of the relation between past and present which intervene in daily life."[15]

But the move toward the people was not without its own problems. Thompson especially expressed great skepticism toward those very conceptual frameworks that sought to problematize the relation of representation to its object. In *The Poverty of Theory,* Thompson was concerned that the politics of history writing would be lost by the attempt to theorize it.[16] He focused on the work of Louis Althusser, specifically, Althusser's critique of historicism, or the linear unfolding of history in a uniform temporal field.[17] Consequently, the historian's identification and location of "the people" in history was tantamount to an assurance that history was being made to their benefit, a position that risked an essentializing reduction of the subject of history to the object of historical analysis. In the words of Bill Schwarz, " 'History' is at once both the practice (in the sense of people making history) and the theory of the popular."[18] Hence the radical historians traded a fully interventionist intellectual practice for the risks of essentialism and historicism that Nietzsche was alert to in calling for a "critical history."

Yet, Thompson's polemic with Althusser, in which the latter is accused of blinkering historical consciousness by overly abstract language and refusing to recognize the progressive movement of history, constitutes an impasse for thinking the relation of history and historiography only if we accept the theoretical claims that Thompson makes for his own work. If, instead, historiography and history can never be fused as something on the order of the representation of a historical idea with the living voice of those who make it, then the work of Thompson and his colleagues may rest on more complex theoretical premises than they have been willing to consider. This is the argument made by Michael E. Brown in his appreciative reading of Thompson's work against the grain of its own claims. According to Brown, Thompson's historiographical practice assumes a theory of representation that, with great conceptual complexity, "makes too much of too little" and, as such,

> is constructive, an aspect of a project in which past and present must be shown as of the same order of human reality if the future is to be conceived as capable of "production" through the actions of people. It attempts to *display* the fact that any account of class interactions and political life is "complete" only when it takes account of the possibility of underground activity, inchoate resistance, and the whole panoply of minor events and unregistered acts that must be a feature of any event or outcome if history is to have occurred and to have been part of our own history—if history is to be conceivable as human action such that we too could have acted.[19]

The status of "unregistered acts" is not that they can now be registered but that they offer a perspective on "human action" that effaces the demobilizing divide of past and present. Brown posits history as a feature of all social life and therefore rejects the historicizing separation of a past time of significance from a present that cannot recognize history in itself. The force of the popular consists in an ongoing ability to occasion itself without ever being fixed in the manner of a pure presence like that of the monument or relic that, paradoxically, in its immutability, renders ahistorical the very conception of history. Rather, inclusion of the popular prohibits any simple monumentalization that would make of the hitherto excluded merely the same as what they had been opposed to, as yet another monument to add to the registry, or a kind of rectification of the injustice of historical accounts through addition. The twin problems of essentialism and historicism are thereby averted insofar as the people never becomes a substance with a voice whose very expression is of the order of a forward movement in time (as in the expression "progressive forces"). Against the conventional view that time constitutes the most fundamental historical agency that generates change, it is instead the production of difference through human activity that makes sense of time. Time as it relates to history is not the abstraction that makes human life concrete but an effect of the various densities, aggregations, and mobilizations of human activity.

Brown emphasizes the centrality of difference—here as internal to a historical moment rather than being what separates one moment from another—to the constitution of history and of time per se. His own work notwithstanding, the historiography of the Communist Party (CP) in the United States has only recently begun to apply some of the principles developed by historians of the British CP and to move away from an almost exclusive focus on the leadership, shifts in the party line, and the relation with Moscow, toward the practices of the rank and file in relation to other social movements.[20] Brown's discussion of these issues once again merits citation:

> The contradictory and history-constituting character of the relationship between formal and informal aspects of organization, and its implications for the critical project, can be appreciated in its application to the sociology of organizations or ensembles. The main point is that such unifying formations cannot be understood as merely resolving momentary differences of interest or perception, but must be seen as increasingly complex sites of certain unresolvable tensions responsible for whatever appears to be their identity (of form or project) and course of self-transformation in regard to their historical and historicizing situation. The alternative, characteristic of orthodoxy, is to see human ensembles mechanistically and as passing through rather than constituting historical time.[21]

As was the case with the French historians of the *Annales* school and Fernand Braudel, Brown seeks an articulation of history and sociology, but it is one informed by the theoretical considerations of representation and agency that characterize the so-called new cultural history.[22] Hence the formal and informal aspects of social organization (the structured arrangements of human interactions), like the relation between what is representable and what is "unregistered" in history, encounter each other as an "unresolvable tension" that constitutes historical time. Here, time is the self-production of "ensembles," not a medium through which people can pass. If the ensemble that makes time pass is not of a single piece but an entity internally divided against itself, then perhaps we must reconsider the unity of its object, historical agency.

In sociology, the development that could be said to parallel that of the people's historians was the study of social movements and collective behavior. Alain Touraine, a sociologist of social movements, has found it useful to speak of "historicity," the collective work done by social actors that produces ensembles or, as he puts it, "the production of historical situations by actors."[23] This perspective suggests an internal divide of the sort that Brown speaks of between the actor or agency and history. It distinguishes two moments of any ensemble: the production of voice, idea, or agency and the movement or the capacity to gather that generates historical time, or history. The radical project of relating representation (whether it be called historiographic, sociographic, or choreographic) to its object assures the ongoing productivity of politics without assuming that the political tendency of a mobilization can be reduced to its identifying source. While any representational act constitutes an object for analysis, it also makes reference to a larger practical field out of which that object is constituted. Representation does not exhaust what it purports to cover, nor does the construction of an object subsume other dimensions of activity that remain unnamed. People make history, but the history they make cannot be evaluated simply by noting the presence of the people. This is the perspective I hope to encourage by privileging that ensemble identified as dance performance, in which the relation of formal and informal, represented and unregistered, is materialized in the tension between performers and audience that enables performance to produce itself as historicity.

This analytic attitude toward history simulates a relation of performance and audience in which performance pertains to the execution of an idea implicit in the notion of "agency," and audience suggests a mobilized critical presence intended by radical notions of "history." This distinction between agency and history points to a conception of history in which historical project, seen as the formation of an identity, and historical possibility, taken to be the capacity for continued mobilization, are dialectically joined. Agency and history, thus conceived, focus on the moment of reception in relation to the object. The full appreciation of the place of reception, of the unstable audience, has the potential to expand an understanding of the political beyond its conventional register in representation, which grants agency an impossible autonomy as an idea disembodied from its material expression and takes participation for granted. As a consequence, quotidian and "great" events are disjoined from each other within any given historical moment, in a manner that minimizes those forces of participation that grant all ideas their reception. Hence, this is not a problem of scale—of micro versus macro levels of social activity—as it has been posed in the sociological literature.[24] There, much gets made of the difference between face-to-face encounters among small groups and impersonal processes that operate through large numbers of people. It strikes me that in practice as well as in theory, the question of what social dynamics can be attributed to the difference between small and large, micro and macro, local and global, is not simple to resolve, nor, ultimately, are the distinctions themselves easy to maintain. The most intimate interactions are subject to constraints of the global economy or widely circulating formations of pleasure that result from the commingling of the world's peoples. Concomitantly, the exquisite range of diversity from which we draw our differences refers each putatively local instance of human expression to the whole societal field in which it is located. As reviewed in the last chapter, the sociological literature on social movements has the greatest affinity to the work of the people's historians and shares many of the latter's conceptual challenges. Participation must be considered irrespective of the scale of collective action.

In sum, joining the politics of history and of performance rests on a specialized application of dance analysis. Dance does display a particular agency, but its place in politics generally cannot be privileged with respect to other practices. It is offered here as a site of analysis whose resistances to representation offer special resources. Briefly stated, dance can be more particularized than performance idioms such as music and theater, whose scores and scripts exist both within and beyond the moment of performance. Dance treats the mobilization of bodies more reflexively than quotidian bodily acts. The efforts to represent dance index their limitations and exclusions more pointedly than other instances of cultural production and reception. The point is not, therefore, what other political activities dance resembles or is representative of but how dance analysis develops concepts that can be applied to other spheres of practice. Rather than proposing dance in any form as a model for political activity or prescribing models for political dance, both of which assume a priori responses to what can be only conjuncturally based questions, the specificity of the relations of performance and audience in dance can provide methodological insights for recognizing politics where it would otherwise be invisible. Two avenues of expansion deserve mention: first, the study of what gives rise to politics but leaves no traces, and second, the identification of the politics of those situations frequently thought to be politically irrelevant. In the context of this analysis, dance should be considered as an analytic frame, not as a particular activity that should be extended or emulated in other social arenas.

Fuller recognition of the moment of reception in dance performance not only brings the issue of participation in historical processes to the fore but also can be applied beyond the narrow confines of a venue such as Judson to reconceptualize the place of audience in a culture of mass communication. Since the 1980s, media theorists have critiqued the view in which culture is mistaken for a market transaction that proscribes the public as passive consumers of images who lack the capacity for critical presence suggested by the term "participation." In this market view, the image on the screen is only a decision taken that requires no further effort and disappears somewhere in the demand of the audience.[25] Even in more complex conceptions of media consumption, it is often assumed that representation is the sole optic through which to view the prospects for mobilized publics or the making of history. Conversely, where readers are said to perform, embody, or enact what they receive, the question can at least be raised as to whether reading itself remains an appropriate term from which to generalize processes of cultural production and reception. The performer-audience relation seems closer than that of text and reader to approximating the object of history. As something that passes without a trace, like dance, the historical object lacks the stability of a text. Likewise, the conditions of history's production imply more participation than does the activity of interpretation or reading. This is not to suggest that dances cannot be read (a strategy for which will be pursued in the next chapter) but that reading must recognize the limits of its own approach to the object of analysis. Methodologically speaking, reading requires a corrective, which the performer-audience relations in dance provide, that recognizes the place of participation if there is to be historical agency.[26]

The sense in which that participation can be recuperated beyond those settings rests with the possibility of theorizing it as more than simply attendance at an event (even one as manifestly unique as the Judson performance), that is, as struggles over the context and configuration of an alternative public sphere. Without developing these oppositional spaces, the work an audience does in performance may not have a political efficacy beyond merely asserting a capacity as a public to mobilize productive energies. When questions arise as to whether the desire exists for more expansive and ambitious political mobilizations, appreciating the more fundamental social capacity to participate in and as audience serves as a not politically insignificant resource for politics.

More concretely, performance, like any other means of gathering a collectivity, cannot exist outside the social regulation of public space that directly or indirectly invokes the state. The history of contemporary political performance, from the Soviet director Vsevolod Emilevich Meyerhold to the Living Theater of the 1960s, is the history of boundaries for participation established as a particular conjuncture of civil society and the state.[27] The point, however, is that if performance is an agency that occasions participation, it also limits the scope if not the persistence of participation. The agency of performance is distinct from the one that transforms state or civil society as such, but in either case, such an agency elicits a desire for further participation.

In this regard, critical writing that takes its inspiration from dance identifies politics where there was thought to be none. This is not to say that we should expect to hear more from the audience at Judson that night; clearly, that would take some other event, tied to a sustained mobilization. But if critical analysis is to understand what keeps any audience coming back for more, if it is to grasp what sustains any mobilization irrespective of its duration, it had better attend closely to the dynamics of performance.

Difference hitherto relegated to some exotic other elsewhere now lies within the account of the object as destabilized and destabilizing. Context here is not what lies beyond the object but what it cannot grasp and in failing to do so what appears as a momentary assertion. The other, grounded in practical terms as the mobilized presence of the unstable audience, provides momentary context to the agency of the object itself, now the writing of spatial inscriptions or dancing.

Such a conception of critical writing could be applied to any number of situations from television watchers to soldiers in battle, from movements of capital to those against it. But to develop its terms of analysis, it should logically begin with the highly particularized relations of dance where the participation of audience refuses to be subsumed by the representation of performance. With these issues in mind, I will return to the particular performance at Judson Church that initiated these reflections and then offer some indication of how it might be placed in its social and historical context.

Judson in History

All the dance performances in which I have participated labored under the sign of repetition. The anxiety over whether the dance is possible and the affirmation that the dance is for others, both of which suffuse opening night, are tempered by assurances that the anxiety will return the next evening and that even when the run of performances expires, there is always the prospect of a revival. This urge to repeat that which is lost, the desire for more performances as a movement into the future, is, no doubt, what renders dance an instance of history. Yet this disposition depends on a situation that is exactly its opposite, namely, that the actual condition of appearance for any ensemble is that of a unique instance of mobilization that cannot be repeated. Dance as history can easily be misrecognized exclusively in terms of that which recurs, whether as choreography or the engagement that contracts the dancers to the performance space for a fixed number of shows. The piece of choreography performed once that November evening of 1991 (and not since) may well have aspired to recurrence. But it took the contractual situation of nonrepeatability as its performative disposition, foregrounding analytically the irrecuperable presence that gives rise to history.

Identifying that which cannot be repeated is not the same as asserting some pristine origin for the appearance of an ensemble. At the Judson performance, the performers emerge through the audience in several respects. Given the architecture of the church, with its gallery above the audience overlooking the performance space that is used as an area for warming up, our dancing is preceded by watching others. We enter the place where our dance is to be by passing through the audience. I sit as an extension of the audience, looking, like many of its members, at a dancer upstage and begin my own performance as a differentiation from within that audience gaze. While I am a representative of the agency that this public has gathered to see, its gathering is what offers my agency the place and perspective from which it can begin.

Once I have taken my initial movements, the piece is no longer simply there for me to see. Music intervenes where what had connected us was only looking. Some concert dances are set to music. Some scores are metered to measure dancing. Although the score was composed especially for this dance, it offered a field, a medium internal to the performance, in which the choreography could occur, rather than an index for the passage of movement. The music was a mediation of the performance activity that soon usurped that of the gaze. Yet this power of the gaze (an extension of the audience through the performers) that is interrupted by the music reemerges with a certain mutuality in the course of the performance. The dancers address the public verbally and motionally, to see what has occasioned them. The gaze stands in for a kind of first contact between dancers and audience that the dancers took as their own condition of possibility. Thus, the physical contact among the dancers, through the vehicle of bodies that by touching give rise to further movement, develops in the choreography as a subsequent form of mediation. But, like the gaze, once this touch is established, it can become virtualized in the sense that the dancers remain in touch kinesthetically even when not in contact. This play between actual and virtual touch could be taken as precisely what gets particularized in the space occupied by performers and audience. That the mutuality of the gaze establishes the terms of performance and subsequently becomes a mutuality of touch suggests what is specifiable about the object of dance. For while being seen by others brings the performers in touch with one another, that ability to touch is ultimately left with the audience, who by touching themselves in applause mobilize the dancers to yield their agency to the audience and in so doing bring what had opened that night to a close.

For the audience, history is initiated in the self-constituting boundary that fills as its members gather to mark where the space of performance begins. Here, too, the architecture of Judson is more sympathetic to presenting the problem than designing its solution. While the audience takes its place in chairs arranged before it arrives, it is asked by the producer of the series to stack the chairs in racks before leaving, making it complicit in erasing the boundary it had formed. Since some in the audience, like myself in the performance, sit on the floor, it is a boundary defined more by living tissue than a given activity. This labor of collecting itself, distributing its mass, and marking its boundaries is formalized only when the lights go out and on again to illuminate the gaze that seeks its object in performance. When the audience finds what it seeks, it incorporates the loss of that initial pleasure that comes from the indeterminacy of looking, so that it can now follow the dance. Such active engagement in the face of indeterminacy generates for the audience what could be understood as the idea of the choreography, the dependence of reflexivity on others. Such dependence is now the predicament that the audience finds itself in as it seeks through its gaze what will allow it to perform its object. In this reversal, which is but a moment of the performance event, there is evidence that history as the gathering, critical public reproduces and mobilizes agency.

The glimmers of agency in audience are also given voice, one gathered from the intermittent throat clearing (to open what had been closed by sight?) and the cascading titters that are more explicitly understood as responses to the situation. This voice does not state what the audience has always been but is educed through audition, as the audience listens to itself. These articulations of agency in the body of history are as unstable as the audience itself. Ultimately, the gain of agency is the loss of history, for when the audience gets the idea of the piece (the moment of reception), it is moved only to disperse. That what began as a spatial boundary has now become temporalized as the audience departs tempts the reading of the capacity for history as something past, a sacrifice to agency without monument or relic. This is the loss from which "orthodoxy" in historiography takes its cue. The audience at Judson may have many words for what it saw but is likely to register far fewer for what it did to allow that history made in the past to have been present.

In the case of the audience at Judson Church, its inability to speak of its self-constituting activity comes at the expense of its continued mobilization in the larger public arena, and as such, the powers it appropriated during the performance are expended without recognition of their politics by audience, critics, or others. Such politics would be interesting to pursue in the recent conjuncture of anxieties over dance (and other artistic) output that substitute the work of audience with a negative idealization of the public's capacity for critical reception. Instability of presence has been translated as a kind of moral fragility in need of the protections of censorship in the minds of those willing to talk about contemporary art but unwilling to see it. The invisibility of audience's participation is misrecognized as an absence, a void into which is projected a fatuous intimacy. The materialization of publicness that performance enables is rendered in terms of an idealized Victorian privacy. Hence in the recent attacks on performance, public demands for resources are elided with a language of protective (but highly selective) private rights that seek to exclude difference as what is constitutive of the public. Reception gets conceived as a matter of simple transference of the idea of the art object to its audience, rather than a transformative social activity that brings context into performance. In this regard, such terms as "shock," "indecency," and "immorality" must be reconsidered as both problems and capacities of reception rather than properties of the object.

The Judson series was sponsored by another organization called Movement Research that had National Endowment for the Arts funds revoked for its putative foul play (it had published materials on AIDS and sexuality in a journal it produced that were considered inappropriate to art by the funding agency). It is not surprising that a critically inclined arts organization would turn to Judson Church, which has long figured as an oppositional public sphere that has included involvement with labor and antiwar movements.[28]

Historically, the cultural programming at Judson gave focus to the democratic project implicit in the production and collective appropriation of activity; but it gave equal focus to the context of mediations that inevitably compromised that project and opened the possibility of nondemocratic alternatives in art. No artistic movement controls the context that conditions its production, nor can it be assumed to provide a basis for mobilization beyond its particular audience. The democratic project could be sustained only if the critique of representation in regard to dance were to be incorporated into performance itself and if the agency of performance were to be expansively extended to include its public, a public that could then be identified with respect to other sites and activities—namely, the labor that generates any social value, including the sociality and critical capacity of audience.

In this chapter I have tracked dance activity at Judson Church from the vantage point of a participant and from the perspective of one searching for its traces of participation, its democracy. While these two takes on Judson are different in their ways and objects of writing and even in their historical moment, they share the problem of how to recognize the unrepresentable traces of participation that connect the labor of writing about something with what is being written about. No doubt these differences in perspective are, by now, familiar to those strategizing how to write self-critical history. Yet, whether a historical account offers itself as written from a perspective inside or outside an event, the issue of how to speak of the necessarily unspeakable labor of history remains. Similarly, the problems raised for writing participation in history by the dance review and for the people's historians in search of their object indicate that the distinction between a history written "from above" and one written "from below" is also analytically insufficient to grasp the internal relations that animate dance performances or history more broadly.

If the approaches to writing that inform the dance review are indifferent to the question of participation, those of the people's historians risk resolving the same question prematurely by collapsing the moment of historical idea or voice with the critical public or presence necessary to mobilize agency. The view from on high may refuse to recognize the participation generated by the people in history, but the attempt of historical writing to *be* the people's voice is also unsatisfying in its fixity of what, in practice, is always in motion. Ultimately, a revision in historical writing requires more than a shift from one perspective to another—that is, an appreciation of what is unsubstitutable among each of them with respect to the other as they are brought into mutual tension. To the extent that writing can allow the same object or event to admit the "*irreducible* plurality" of perspective, it will avoid the temptation to overstate its powers of representation in a manner that negates participation.[29] My concern here has been to expose these issues rather than offering any final resolution of them. In this chapter, therefore, the analysis of Judson has been in the service of encouraging a certain approach to writing dance and history together, and I assume a particular politics, the contours of which I want to indicate here and then pursue in the chapters that follow.

In these more general terms, the analytic gains of critical analysis that incorporates the methodological insights offered by dance, aimed at the relation of agency and history, reveal the bad faith of the colonizing discourse of narrow market rationalities and supposedly noneconomic irrationalities (of race, gender, sexuality). To deny what audience produces in performance is to disavow its capacity to produce its own associations, in favor of an imperative to manage its desires with respect to a world of products run wild. The protection offered trades the unruly orders of difference that constitute society for a representation of harmony that serves as a nefarious performative fiction. But the wonder of fiction is the desire it sustains for another tale to be told. The magic of dance is to deposit this desire with the audience.

If writings on dance acknowledged their own resistance to theory and attempted to theorize that resistance, they would provide precisely the context of self-denial that has been so fruitfully engaged by contemporary critical theories of representation: the denial of history always ends by being and revealing history. Such writing would allow dancing to appear as an agency that familiarizes the strangeness of the commodified world, making that world yet more acceptable as an object of critique by being, as it were, the butt of jokes. Here a critical dance analysis would make its intervention. The analytic frame that a reflection on performance provides for theorizing history in terms of agency depends both on the distancing of the familiar that makes the problem of representation unavoidable and on the recovery of that unruly familiar otherness for a world that, from the heights of its imperial achievements, will always insist that the incessant disruptiveness of history is merely momentary and exotic.

2 *Overreading* The Promised Land: *Toward a Narrative of Context in Dance*

Play Bill

Dance has trouble staying still, and yet, one convention in writing about dance is to put it in its place. From this perspective, which I term "underreading," dance, as a purely aesthetic activity, is partitioned from its social and political context, generating in turn a stable and self-containing divide between what is inside dance and what is external to it. In the preceding two chapters, however, I have argued that dance foregrounds the mobilization of participation that is essential to grasp the dynamics of history, but difficult to notice through the standard means of reckoning with political activity, making dance a key analytic resource to develop a critical understanding of society. Here, I would like to use this notion of mobilization to examine the political significance of a single choreographic work but also to use the internal movement of that work to expand an appreciation of political possibilities in society as a whole.

The analytic procedure for enlisting a recognition of the movement in dance to evaluate the political horizons for mobilization in society is what I term "overreading." This approach entails employing dance to read the contours of context as well as reading through and past the dance to overcome what I perceive to be a certain scarcity in the means to imagine the prospects for fundamental social change. Underreading, to the extent that it promotes the isolation of what is, in practice, mutually interdependent, is also a purveyor of scarcity. Whereas overreading treats the internal movement of dance as an organizing principle in the conceptual ordering of context, when the politics of a dance are approached from an underreading, they are addressed as ever widening horizons to a work whose putatively stable interior renders it static with respect to that context.

The dance performance selected for overreading is the *Last Supper at*

Uncle Tom's Cabin/The Promised Land (November 9, 1990) at the Brooklyn Academy of Music (BAM) by the Bill T. Jones/Arnie Zane Dance Company, with Jones as artistic director.[1] This evening-length work draws on a range of historical narratives, from slavery to civil rights, Reconstruction to revolution, and through its danced relations, it sets in motion fundamental connections between race, gender, labor, and sexual preference to stage the historical context for the meeting of these political mobilizations. To heighten what can be learned from this dance, I will use its choreographic structure to inspire the rhetorical structure of the present writing. Before explicating that particular connection, however, I would like to reflect on how dance more generally presents the opportunity to create overreading.

Imagine two instances of Western concert dance. In one, a woman from some mysterious, exotic place appears in a man's domain. Her dancing provides his desire. She is pure movement. He, absolute boundary. He pursues her but cannot have her. He must acknowledge complete difference, the loss that returns him to his place. She perishes. In a second instance, bodies roll endlessly over one another. They rise and fall. Lift and are lifted. Moving forms dissolve into one another. Anatomies appear reconfigured from their pedestrian functionalities as movement is initiated from unexpected sources—the tops of feet, a shoulder, an inner thigh.

Perhaps these two instances could be named. One could be called *La Sylphide*, and the other, Channel Z. Further, to organize what the names differentiate, the former could be identified as dance narrative, and the latter, nonnarrative dance. This would not be the first time that such a distinction was made. But it is one that carries its share of problems. There is apparently a story to be told in the instance of Romantic ballet. It would seem more difficult to plot what happens between the beginning and end of the improvisational performance of the New York–based group of the 1980s Channel Z. But what are the implications of this distinction? Does it suggest that some forms of dance are intelligible and others are not, as Curt Sachs would claim?[2] Or does this imply that dance is fundamentally unmediated by intelligibility, as John Martin would insist?[3] In both cases we have a prestructuralist fallacy which assumes that some putatively universal cognitive process, or mind, is but a mirror for a nature that always offers itself to nature in the same way. Yet as Lévi-Strauss and others have made plain, culturally specifiable forms of the labor of signification operate in a domain of representation that, as is evident in their very global diversity, cannot be reduced to the world itself.[4] The notion that cultural practices such as dance could be wholly free or independent of cognitive processes is here replaced with the imperative to identify how those processes might operate.

What would happen, however, if we reversed the names and the descriptions? If recent improvisational dance was legible only against the background of what, with respect to Western performance narrative, Catherine Clement has called the "undoing of women"[5] and hence depended on a story of the ethereal female Sylph that gets told in reverse, then certainly the ballet story could be going through someone's mind during the Channel Z performance. Further, if one were willing to watch and take note, Romantic ballet rests on the kind of defamiliarization of moving bodies from their quotidian habits, associated with the dance form known as "contact improvisation" that Channel Z practices. At this point any facile opposition between what is within narrative and what is not would be troubled, not the least because it would no longer be clear what is inside and what outside the dance.

The very association of dance with narrative — or its absence — is an assertion not simply about how dances are made but also about how they are seen, for narrative assumes the passage, through a given medium, from inscription to reception, that is, from writing to reading. The bodily inscription of choreography no doubt complicates how this communicative passage might take place, particularly given that the body is always a referent within a dance and a reference to what is outside dancing. Even a dance composed of just a body moving is other than a quotidian body, while it cannot escape identification with any body that works for a living. Similarly, every story told within a dance is legible only in relation to the panoply of tales outside it, and as such, the relation of narrative and nonnarrative aspects are features of both the dance and its context. It is this doubling of the body as referring to itself and something else, operating across dance and its exterior, that makes for the complexity of dancing's relation to referentiality.

The slippage between narrative and nonnarrative through which dance is inscribed is also suggestive of a certain ambivalence for reading performance that is well appreciated by narrative theorists. As an activity, reading approaches a field of meaning that already exists prior to any given encounter with it, but reading itself is generated only in the course of acting on that field, in a manner that, in Roland Barthes's phrase, renders the reader "a producer of the text."[6] Because the reader brings a certain capacity for making sense out of the text to bear on it, the precise interpretive outcome cannot be predicted by the fact of the text, but more profoundly, this very multiplicity of outcomes is what grants each text its specificity. The text is in this sense fundamentally plural. For Barthes, the text has an openness that is a consequence of this encounter between reading and writing which problematizes narrative. Insisting on the plural text, he says: "This necessary assertion is difficult, however, as nothing exists outside the text, there is never a *whole* of the text (which would by reversion form an internal order, a reconciliation of complementary parts, under the paternal eye of the representative Model): the text must simultaneously be distinguished from its exterior and from its totality. All of which comes down to saying that for the plural text, there cannot be a narrative structure."[7]

Against the misconception attributed to Barthes and others that the world is only text, the claim that nothing is outside the text insists that the relation between a text and its world can be produced only through reading, which generates the differentiation of exterior and totality. The stable, a priori boundary that would allow what is within the text (its "internal order") to mirror or model the world as its representation (its "narrative structure") is here radically effaced. Hence, the productive practice that yields the plural text also brings what is outside it and what it is part of into view. Whereas Barthes reads the plural of the text to grasp its "infinite paradigm of difference," in overreading one aspires to sustain this complexity but reverse its emphasis so as to focus the labor of textual production on the identification of context and social totality. The paradox of overreading is that it cannot directly grasp what it seeks to understand. Rather, it must begin with reading to establish corollaries for the apprehension of historical and societal context, which, Fredric Jameson notes, while not itself narratively constituted, "is inaccessible to us except in textual form."[8]

Here, text and context are both distinguished by their disparate relation to narrative processes (constituted by versus merely accessible through) and are also joined in narrative. What is nonnarrative within the text is the very referentiality of what lies outside it. The efforts to textualize this reference constitute writing and generate the deep affinities between fiction, in the broadest sense of textualizing, and history, as the societally significant, temporally structured effects of human agency, that in turn make context accessible to reading. Paul Ricoeur calls this structural coreference of fiction and history, narrative and temporality, "interweaving."[9] The text, therefore, does not reflect context as if it were a passive surface acted on by forces of the real but provides a means to imagine societal order through the fragmentary social referents gathered in the text's own materiality. If fiction corresponds to the cultural process by which structures are provided to render meanings legible, and history pertains to the societal forces that move those very processes, then dance may turn out to be a privileged site to attend to their interweaving. For whatever significance dance carries is achieved through self-mobilization, which in turn generates whatever there is to be read of a dance. Recall that it was precisely this mediation of meaning and movement that apparently slipped between (but, more consequential, was what mobilized the interweaving of) my own accounts of the Romantic ballet and improvisational performance mentioned above.

Yet dance criticism, as it is traditionally practiced, has not assumed the complexity or ambivalence for reading suggested by narrative theory. For example, Edwin Denby (whose dance criticism for the *New York Herald Tribune* dates from the 1930s), counsels that "his most interesting task is to describe the nature of the dancing," while, as performance, its "particular essence . . . has no specific terminology to describe it by."[10] But because this tension between what can and cannot be narrated in dance goes unrecognized by the critic, the labor of reading that allows the critical text to reflect on its own conditions of production also goes unnoticed. The emphasis on a purely descriptive language that cannot account for either its own terminology or the narrative frame within which it operates generates a confusion between the critic's representation of the dance and a document of the dance event, what Michel Foucault called "history, in its traditional form."[11] In reading the dance, the standard critical procedure requires a certain fidelity to the object, trading on what is "elusive" about it for a certain confidence about evaluative judgment. In Denby's words, "An intelligent reader expects the critic—in his role of school teacher—to distinguish between good and bad."[12] The price of this normative critical confidence is to isolate what is internal to dance from its own exterior, thereby purchasing an underreading of dance with respect to its context.

The detachment of text from context, which has tempted dance and other

criticisms, parallels positions in political analysis that place themselves outside the very social situation of which they are part, thus pronouncing an
overly confident negative judgment of past or present political possibilities.
Like the simplifying normative evaluation of the critic toward dance (that is,
"good" or "bad"), political analysis that overspecifies its historical object is
dimmed by an inadequate theory of context. As Marx noted for the study of
political economy, the forcible separation of what had been joined together
produces a crisis for analysis. This crisis has yielded a rhetoric of collapse,
the adoption of which ultimately tempts a narration of the end of political
possibilities altogether. Here dance and politics share a relationship that is
more than analogical. In the manner of the interweaving of history and fiction of which Ricoeur spoke, Western concert dance has, in the past decade,
been subjected to an economic metaphor of boom and bust, and the circumstances under which a political Left could operate have been identified
as a narrative that has come to an end.

There is, no doubt, a common context that has affected the way in which
both dance and politics get (under)read, what I would term the assertion
of a rightist idea in the reception of culture. The deepest assumption of this
idea rests on conflating the real and its representations with a condition of
absolute scarcity. This conceptual regime of scarcity limits, on the one hand,
how economic growth and social development are to be coordinated and,
on the other, the tolerance of critical self-reflection, or theory, in public discussion. Symptomatic of this acceptance of scarcity for society and its theorization is the presumed autonomy of the object from its context and hence
an autonomy of objects from one another, so that each object must assume
the burdens of maintaining its own conditions of production, again, an orientation to analysis encouraged by underreading. The greatest risk that the
circulation of this idea of scarcity poses is its assimilation by the Left as its
own condition of self-understanding and, at the same time, the misappre-
hension of this idea as a critical trope for the activity of dancing as such.
Hence it is the shared problem of an insufficiently critical self-limitation, of
underreading, that urges an alliance between dance and politics in a common analytic strategy, overreading. The impulse for overreading emerges
from a conjuncture whose historical originality may be difficult to define,
given the way that historical ends and autonomous aesthetics have been
twinned in Western thought.[13] But much of current political rhetoric bears,

implicitly or explicitly, a conjunctural language whose criteria are generally expressed in the periodizing terms of the sixties as a high-water mark of leftist thinking and social possibility and the eighties as the moment of rupture and collapse. Without replicating the problem of origins, one must question and contest the implications of this periodizing gesture for dance and politics. Only by so doing can one counter the narrative of self-limiting scarcity that is said to be constraining art and social life.

The aspiration of overreading, a particular effacement of the stability between interiority and exteriority, is to mobilize the text in the service of context. In this regard the strength of the very ambivalence manifest in dance toward narrative can serve as a resource to develop both dance and political analysis. The internal movement of dance narrative, what moves the plot, so to speak, rests on the mobilization of what is nonnarrative in dance. What mobilizes a particular dance already draws the context for dancing onto the stage. As experienced critics such as Denby have noted, this mobilization is elusive or difficult to see partly because what any reader of dance notices are the effects of the mobilization, the describable dance, rather than what Denby calls the "particular essence" of a performance. This latter should not be taken as what is unchanging in performance but, more usefully, as the forces marshaled to accomplish the dancing. When we place the reading of dance in the service of politics, what is nonnarrative in dance—its conditions of mobilization—is precisely what may be difficult to see in the social context, namely, the horizon of possibilities for politics. The twist here, as Jameson observed, is that this horizon can be read only as a narrative or "prior (re)textualization." This displacement from what is nonnarrative in dance to the narrative of historical context is one feature of overreading that assumes a commitment to read through and past the dance to the point where it meets its own exterior. A second feature could, in the spirit of Althusser, be called temporal condensation, that is, the articulation of the differential temporal dimensions of nonreducible but interconnected social structures, from aesthetics to politics, into a "time of times."[14] The apparent temporal unity of dance—namely, that any given performance transpires over a given period of time—in practice rests on a compositional assemblage of divergent rhythmic structures. This is the case not only with respect to movement phrases with differentiated meters and sources but more profoundly in regards to the very relation between what dancing bodies accumulate to produce their motional effects and what they reference in the world. In dance, the divide between the nonnarrative forces that generate dancing and the narrative consequences of that dancing's effects is dramatic. Hence, the question of what would both mediate and sustain such radically disparate elements — some principle of totality displayed within the work — is produced by overreading without exhausting what a given dance offers to reception.

The exploration, occasioned by overreading, of how dance and politics are joined takes as axiomatic that no simple relation of reflection or expression exists that would unite the two terms and therefore no archetype or model for political dance exists. For the politics in dancing, like anything else, will always need to be specified. Whereas much dance that adheres to its own formal vocabulary might resist such analytic specification, Jones's *Last Supper at Uncle Tom's Cabin/The Promised Land* (hereafter *Last Supper*) pushes the ambition for dancing by loading it with politics. It is this encumbrance with the political that renders *Last Supper* so appropriate for overreading. Beyond being a work of tremendous scale and scope which critically reflects on the history and present condition of racism, sexism, homophobia, and exploitation, the form that politics takes in this piece is particularly germane to the issues that overreading seeks to address. Let me mention four.

First, *Last Supper* is a form of narrative dance in that it not only makes reference to events but also orders them, starting with slavery and emancipation and proceeding with civil rights and liberation. But African American history is not its only narrative register, nor is what flows within the dancing solely narrative. The work is also replete with dance events whose referentiality is, by contrast, far from explicit, and it is full of dancing that maintains its distance from narrative convention. By neither avoiding narrative nor subsuming choreography to narrative, *Last Supper* explicitly complicates narrative's relation to nonnarrative on which overreading's production of context rests.

Second, *Last Supper* provides for this labor of overreading by commenting on its own situation of reception and production, particularly against dance critics' temptations to contain the politics of a given dance and specifically against right-wing assaults on the political resonance of art that culminated in federally administered self-censorship pledges in the year that Jones mounted his piece. By the challenges it makes to those strictures, the dance constitutes an offensive against its own immediate context of possibility, therefore enlarging its admitted dependence on its own context.

Third, the interweaving of historical and fictional narratives from the Civil War era (Lincoln's second inaugural address and Harriet Beecher Stowe's novel) and the civil rights era (Martin Luther King's "I have a dream" speech and Amiri Baraka's *Dutchman*) rehearses narrative displacement for the audience. The effacement of the putative boundary between life and art is both represented in these narrative shifts internal to the piece and accomplished referentially by the way contemporary context is drawn into the dance. This opening of the work to its own exterior undermines any simple process of mimesis that had been attributed to art. Instead, a coupling is promoted between the aesthetic values of the cultural sphere and the institutional effects of the social. It is these two spheres that have been taken by conservative critics to be separate and inviolable when they propose the resegregation of private and public life by the standardization of the former under the authority of the latter.

Finally, if *Last Supper* imagines a resistance to this mythic resegregation of the private and public, aesthetic and political, it also mobilizes through the dancing of its "promised land" an imaginary terrain in which a social-aesthetic totality is momentarily displayed, one that I term the "utopia of the real." It is on this terrain that overreading seeks a nonreductive joining of politics that have been separated by assuming a context of scarcity that dims the horizon of historical possibility. Expanding the horizon of political possibility entails reading past the conceptual divide of so-called old and new social movements (whose putative process of disarticulation spans from the sixties to the eighties). Hopefully, a Left that had been tempted to narrate its own ends and deny its history can take a dance such as *Last Supper* as a means of imagining a certain temporal condensation that would recast its own political self-concept. At this level of abstraction, dance, by means of theory, is joined with politics.

If theory is to realize the potential for self-understanding that dance offers, overreading must survive beyond its significant debt to this particular choreographic work. Yet precisely because Jones's *Last Supper* so strongly takes on context as its own content, it holds out the promise to apply this analytic method to other instances of dance and theoretical form alike. For now, this partnership will serve as the central conceit of the present essay.

The four issues — or, more useful, analytic levels — for overreading just addressed name a certain relation between what structures the dance and what can animate theory. Like a sign, I will take the arbitrary (but significant) division of the dance into four sections and associate these with the rhetorical structure of this essay. But unlike the presumably stable opposition between the material image of the signifier and the intangible signified, here I seek to cross that divide to insist on the materiality of both elements of signification, which I prefer to name "narrative" and "nonnarrative."

In what follows, I first offer an account of the dance; then, a précis of the immediate context for its reception in terms of the conjuncture between the trajectory of Jones's own career and the tendencies in dance criticism; then, a reflection on the institutional effects between the art and social world that focuses on the National Endowment for the Arts and postmodernism; and finally, an analytic ordering of the social context inspired by overreading *Last Supper*. This quaternary structure of the essay in turn receives its inspiration from *Last Supper*'s first act based on retelling Stowe's *Uncle Tom's Cabin;* a second act that plays with the issues of authority and its resistance raised by the tale; an encounter of sacred and profane (or aesthetic and social) forces staged between Bill T. Jones and a local cleric; and a finale, titled "The Promised Land," the danced excess of which belies the scarcities that art and politics were presumed to be suffering from. Indeed, it is that very recognition of excess that moves theory in the direction of overreading, replacing the stable objects of its gaze with a resistant yet irresistible mobilization.

Dancing Particular Tales

Last Supper begins in the midst of the Civil War. The somber tones of Abraham Lincoln's second inaugural address precede the visibility of any dance movement: "One eighth of the whole population were colored slaves, not distributed generally over the Union, but localized in the Southern part of it. These slaves constituted a peculiar and powerful interest." Lincoln goes on to say something omitted in the libretto but enacted through the performance as a danced tension between containment and expansion. "All knew that this interest was, somehow, the cause of the war. To strengthen, perpetuate, and extend this interest was the object for which the insurgents would rend the Union, even by war; while the government claimed no right to do more than restrict the territorial enlargement of it." [15]

The stage is bathed in a deep blue light that casts the figures on it in the negative. What emerges from the darkness of this overdetermined past of revolution and apocalypse are dancers in V formation, simulating the prow of a slaver. The darkness of their own history forcibly severed from its root, they stamp out a march in place. They bear long oars that evoke their own movement toward another's promise of their emancipation. Given that they remain within the "territorial" confines of the performing arena (in this case, the Brooklyn Academy of Music) freedom and the peculiarity of the "powerful interest" will have to be sought and found somewhere within this circumscribed space.

R. Justice Allen, an actor I had initially misrecognized as Jones himself, appears in front of a painted flat of Uncle Tom's cabin, which has the look of an enlarged, movable theater for marionettes or, more to the point, a minstrel show, complete with curtain and racialized faces that conceal the race of their bearer.[16] Here the set serves as a narrative frame for the dancing, connecting Jones's choreography with Stowe's story. By reducing the actual area of performance, the set keys the eye to foreground movement in that concentrated space as something virtuosic, against the larger field of scenic space that remains open around the edges of the BAM opera house stage, and it also constructs a kind of human picture book at moments in the choreography when movement is arrested in illustrative friezes. That virtuosity would require such scenic support already indicates a certain distance this piece takes from other strains of dance narration, whose stories are told through the dance virtues of its star-protagonists, and implicates social conventions of scenic perception in what is generally taken to be an intrinsic property of the body. At the same time, this alternation of the synchronic (frieze) and the diachronic (movement) within the same frame could itself be a metonym for the dilemma of historical representation more broadly. The dilemma itself is, as it were, overrepresented in the very historical content of what is being framed, the textualizing of a foundation for the antinomies of blackness.

If my misrecognition of Allen for Jones was attributable to more than my own (in)discrimination or absence of vision, it could be explained by the position Allen assumes as one who interrupts the historical authorial representation of black by white. Here this interruption is choreographic, but the choreography assumes the dimensions of narration, a relation characterized as a symbolic encounter of choreographer and author. Allen as choreographer and also as narrator introduces the audience to that author, Sage Cowles, the actress who plays Harriet Beecher Stowe. Given that Stowe, the author, appears only in the "Concluding Remarks" of her novel to give account of its message, her presence here is something of a reversal. Her appearance signals both a backward glance through her text, for the epic is greatly compressed here, and an indication that the dance which follows comes after the text. She begins to spin her yarn, but Allen, the choreographic narrator, starts to yawn.

His success in quieting the author, textualizing her so that he can resume narration, begins the dancing in earnest. If virtuosity foregrounds the dancing, it also privileges Tom in the narrative. As is here retold, his virtue rests on his standing as a "spiritual leader" who is a "man of principle," the principle in question being slavery, which, in upholding his end of the Hegelian bargain, forbids him from betraying his master, even as such others as Eliza escape to "freedom." In Tom's interest we are asked, "What is there for those who are left behind? Freedom." Because slavery is a system of exchange, Tom circulates among many masters, who, despite their varied dispositions, do not alter his status, until he becomes the property of Simon Legree. This last whips him to death for refusing to whip or betray others.

Except for Tom, all the other dancers are masked, leaving their gender, among other identities, concealed but making possible a reassignment of identity on the basis of race. The masks are worn in reverse, on the backs of the dancers' heads. This permits a disorientation of the dancers' bodies onto which are grafted the multiple dance forms from jigs to ballet to gravity-friendly floor movement.[17] The parade of styles grafted onto a body as so many mastered techniques marks an accomplishment in dance (talent) homologous to the appropriation of a body whose relation of production gets stamped with a falsely singular identity (African), that is, both are, in a certain respect, naturalized. The emergence of modern dance out of the conjuncture between the naturalizing narratives of talent and race as bodily ascriptions/inscriptions is established early enough in *Last Supper* to become an object of the work's own critical activity.[18]

In his re-presentation of certain sequences, Jones permits the audience to reflect on what catches their eye. For example, in a dance-as-video sequence, Tom is resurrected and the whipping scene is played in reverse, with Legree now pealing the blows off of Tom's body, then in forward motion again, Legree being ultimately forced to confront an endless stream of slaves whose very return demands further repression. Denied the value in exchange, it is now Legree's mastery that is effaced. It is in this opening scene, with its masked faces, confused genders, citations of multiple dance traditions, and videolike replay, that narrative conventions are most intact and their presumed linear temporality most directly confronted. As Stowe's tale ends, it seems to spawn others less coherent, that together form a narrative of narratives, or epic.

One direction of this epic is to pursue the trajectory of slavery into the present, a move already anticipated in recent historiography and struggles against racism.[19] In subsequent sections, the dance eschews chronology for an abstraction of what might be the persistent presence of the historical, the traces of an authority that will not relinquish its command over the body. With "The Dogs," a men's septet that references and genders the relation of slave catcher and prey, we are treated to the full fleshiness of uncovered flanks with boots and a gas-mask-like facial garb that is suggestive perhaps more of a boar's than a dog's snout. This stomping surfeit of the masculine moves only to the verbal command of two upstage figures. With martial precision these loyal pets are taken through a rigorous but unattached semiosis of gesture until they get their final marching orders and depart the stage. The more they display their affinity for discipline, the more the frailties of sustaining this vision of masculinism are revealed. For it is precisely the exuberant pursuit of command that maintains the flaccidity of the men's buttocks, hinting perhaps that in strength there is weakness, or in dance terms, in movement there is release.

The relation of authority and subjection is further complicated in the next scene, "Eliza on the Ice." Four women pass the mask of a black female face, first among themselves and then to Sage Cowles, who, still attired as Harriet Beecher Stowe, now assumes the voice of yet another personage, Sojourner Truth. This ventriloquy mirrors that of the suffragette Frances D. Gage to Sojourner herself in recounting the famous speech at the Akron Convention of May 28–29, 1851. Gage was entreated by "timorous and trembling ones" not to let Truth speak due to the presumed havoc it would bring in the representation of the suffrage movement. "Every newspaper in the land will have our cause mixed up with abolition and niggers, and we shall be utterly denounced." [20] The speech that so effectively "mixed up" race and gender was here being used to accompany a series of solos that pass the word, initially among women and then across gender. For the first, Cowles incants, "Ain't I a Woman?" while Andrea Woods, a woman whose physiognomy conjures up that of Sojourner Truth's, braids balletic and black vernacular dance movement in a manner evocative of the scene at the cabin. But that legacy seems quickly foreclosed as "the dogs," newly trained from the prior scene, cross the stage and take her with them, thus delivering the soloist who follows.

Next, Cowles pursues Heidi Latsky with a wireless microphone. Latsky recites a text of her own about trust, abuse, and betrayal, allowing the sharp gestures of Cowles's probing pursuit to evince stinging words that then send her spiraling down and across the floor, apparently set in motion by what she says. "I believed my father. My father told me to turn the other cheek." The microphone effects the prealienation of voice so that when it finally finds Latsky's lips, she is given the word, a moment that also arrests her movement and then, in a condition of autonarration, enables it. For the solo by Betsy McCracken that follows, that phallic little stub that gave the word is now displaced by an oar from the opening of the piece. Affixed to the dancer's white unitard is a slender chain suggestive of an improbable bondage. The men, constantly intervening as they did from the gallery and pulpit where Truth herself spoke, are momentarily kept in check with the oar. But the leggy men return with their snout masks and jackboots to insinuate a partnership into the final solo that effects the dancer's own motive force as the men pass her among themselves. They appear to serve as her agency, a collective exterior, until the other women enter to save her, not escaping but dancing away the uninvited partners. Then Stowe returns, twisting Sojourner's "truth" through reversed recitations such as, "?from come Christ did Where. woman a wasn't Christ because men as rights much as have can't women says he, there black in man little that . . . woman a I Ain't." These reversals shatter any simple reflection of identity (Sojourner as truly woman), leaving gender overdetermined by race, precisely the persistence of bondage in the pursuit of desire.

The women who have soloed whip their own bodies in a figuration of the curvaceous that has been ascribed to the feminine. As they exit, Gregg Hubbard rises from upstage and, as he does, begins to emulate their movement, while pulling a tube of material down over his buttocks to a point midway down his thigh where it creates that illusion of leg associated with the broadcasting of female sexuality. Shod in high heels, he hops and caresses his breasts and crotch, then follows the path and motion through Sojourner's now deontologized question regarding womanhood. He reverses the orders that had made the men move as men while upholding the "truth" of that final reversed line, "woman a I Ain't." This concludes the first act.

The opening of the second act, "The Prayer," finds Bill T. Jones in a black suit and white shirt, standing a dozen feet away from his seventy-five-year-old mother, Estella Jones, herself a preacher and gospel singer. She speaks while he remains in silence. "I have a chance to sing for you again tonight, and y'all better sit quiet and listen." In her melodious prayer, she thanks Jesus and asks that the dancers be given strength. Of the tenth of her twelve children, born into their family of migrant farmworkers and now HIV positive, she asks, "Look down on my son, Lord, I feel that he needs you." She generates a gospel medley, beginning with "Wade in the Water," and Jones, at first impassive, is moved. His hand covers his mouth. The inertial residues of the pedestrian appeared contained in one hand that remains in his pocket until this too is freed to the service of Jones's kineticization of his mother's words; treating her phrases as if he were an oscilloscope, he dances in the same plane as she until coming to rest at her side, monitoring her, as it were. Yet in Jones's body, we clearly have an instance of multiple waves that can be set in motion in different directions simultaneously. In a later interview, Jones remarked on the transgressive significance of his mother's agreement to allow him to dance to her prayer. This acceptance was also "a kind of sacrilege" because such dancing would not be allowed in their church.[21]

When his mother departs, her evocation of Jesus is transmitted upstage to a frieze of the Last Supper, complete with its long table. A small reproduction of da Vinci's painting, Jones once recounted, had hung in his mother's living room. She apparently did not recognize it as a (great or famous) work of art but rather as a representation of faith.[22] Allen (in a further suggestion of his placement as Jones's double) faces the (dinner) company, and to the recorded sound of a basketball dribble, shoots an imaginary ball through the frieze image's metaphysical hoop—but the score of a ball softly bouncing off into the distance indicates that he missed. Perhaps he, like Estella Jones, faithfully took a shot in the dark and mistook a representation of art for something else. He then joins what he has just faced. The frieze itself breaks up into activities that explore the opposition and effacement of sport and dance, game and play, present and absent authority, suggested by that prior face-off. Dancing is used to block shots or is interrupted with chair games. It accompanies itself as an activity, then is juxtaposed to a dialogue of Lamentations (3:1–29) spoken between Allen and Andre Smith, who had played Tom. The decomposition and recomposition of a work of art whose form and content are considered canonical render problematic the generally implicit authority that frames both art and history.

The cast returns to their march formation of the first act and narrates participation in their own civil war as they sing against the "masters" in a version of the "Battle Hymn of the Republic," "We mean to show Jeff Davis that the Africans can fight." Now on American soil, the dancers-as-emancipat(ed/ing)-slaves have gained in agency and illumination since that first voyage across the Middle Passage referenced in the dimly lit opening of the dance. They reach a line of chairs downstage that they proceed to reorganize into that familiar musical game, but this time a surplus of places over persons exists. As they scramble and sit, there is an evocation of the earlier question of "those who are left behind," now not only in life but in death as well. The motifs of gaming slide between more martial authorizations as they move to commands that they parody in the strictness of their execution. They take further what "The Dogs" had only intimated, that the disciplining of the body never seems to exhaust what either discipline or a body can do and that any attempt to manifest the law as action exposes it as a dead letter. In the spaces created between the commands, necessary if they are to maintain their discrete instrumentality, dancers find time to slip into embrace. The embrace is here figured as a moment of volition rather than intrinsically volitional, an instant of freed will that opens up against the impossibility of an authority that could ever fully exhaust what it seeks to command.

In this section, the simpler instructions—numerical, monosyllabic—that had elicited their direct and indirect responses find their way to that most contemporary form of call and response. The company settles back into their "supper" while R. Justice Allen offers an autohistorical rap called

"Somethin ta Think About": "Young, gifted, and black was my identity, but I was blind, no I couldn't see, from Vietnam came dope in body bags, I started hangin' and bangin' and got hooked on skag. . . . I lost regard for life through my forgotten tears, picked up a gun, stick 'em up cost me fifteen years, hard time is whatyacallit, a ward of the state in a legal slave system full of death and hate." Once in jail he is now "rocking 'round the world with Bill T. Jones." Such forms of lateral mobility are rarely mentioned in dance, and the movement from street to stage is scarcely done in a way in which art does not suffer for its implication in mimesis. BAM is indeed amid the streets where rap is commonly heard. But that proximity is drawn on in a different manner in the section that follows.

At BAM and all other locations where the piece is performed, a local cleric is invited onstage to recite the story of Job, a biblical test case for faith of a wealthy and "blameless" man. For this performance, the cleric is Michael Perry, who happened to share my workplace, Pratt Institute, some minutes' walk from BAM. Satan ("a Hebrew word meaning 'adversary' or 'accuser' not the devil of New Testament thought"), when asked by God what he thinks of His exemplary follower, suggests that Job's adherence is based on material interest.[23] Rising to the challenge, God permits Satan to strip Job of wealth and inflicts "loathsome sores" on him. Job's suffering is the body on which his faith is tested, but it is a dialogic examination in which Job can challenge the principles of the test and in the strength of his intercession achieve the restoration of wealth and faith, body and soul.

This scene opens to the lush strains of "Round Midnight," played live by a saxophone-only sextet led by Julius Hemphill, who has also provided the musical score for the entire evening. That a piece so devoted to the elaboration of difference would find its musical accompaniment in a unity of instrumentation works to suggest the very conditions on which difference rests. That from these horns comes not only the functional differentiation associated with a jazz "combo" but also a musical combination of styles — in this case, from blues to free jazz — is certainly consonant with what Jones's own company can produce in movement equally framed by the incorporation of improvisation. In this instance, however, it is Jones's own dancing that is featured.

He is initially flanked by Arthur Aviles and Sean Curran, who effect hieroglyphic shapes and then rip Jones's shirt with a knife as the biblical commandment is handed down. Jones takes on his punishment in dance, but he does so in a way that appears to divide his body against itself. With bare back to the audience, his feet weave rapidly in finely articulated loco-motion. They seem almost weakened and intoxicated by the strength of his back arched in the contortion of pain but displaying in its stolidity the capacities to bear the weight of his sentence. Fluidity below, elegant carving above, he embodies the dualism of the fable while mobilizing the evidence of faithful suffering to the ends of kinetic "sacrilege." Having used dance once again to transgress the space of the sacred in the act of displaying it, Jones then steps outside dance altogether to engage in a sort of occupational discussion, allowing his dancing to serve as the referent for a foray back into the sacred. His self-emancipation from adherence to the principle that had just governed him draws the problematic of slavery into yet another setting.

After dancing, Jones sits down with the Father at the table of the last sup-per and engages the priest in a reflection on evil and anger. The good Father answers in the negative when queried as to the evilness of homosexuality, a response suddenly secularized in light of Perry's own referentiality in this context where one's presence is meant to represent another. But he could be speaking equally about the demands of representation when in analogy between dancing and preaching he says, "We are all inadequate . . . there is no way that either you or I in either of our forms can catch the fullness." This most explicit articulation of the relation between the theological and the secular, a historical materialism, as Cornel West would argue, that is particularly constitutive of the African American experience,[24] is twinned throughout the piece. The former is joined with the latter precisely in the desire (what Perry calls faith) that in Lacanian formulation emerges in the difference between the demands of authority (the impossible fullness) and the drive that makes activity itself possible.

For the final act, the cast is enlarged by the addition of forty-five dancers, drawn from whatever community the piece is performed in (fifteen cities in the United States alone).[25] This mass, not commonly associated with North American modern dance since the large group works of the thirties, dis-places the intimacy of a group of dancers who in the last two hours have begun to impart a certain familiarity. The larger group undermines the feel-ing of scarcity wrought by AIDS, defunding, and ideological attack that had descended on the dance world by the mid-1980s and instantly assumes the role of a raucous cheering public brought directly onstage in an effacement of the conventions of dance-viewing etiquette. They also, in effect, occupy the space outside the frame of the initial set for "Uncle Tom's Cabin," constituting a sort of human landscape for that promised land into which those first dehumanized characterizations had sought to escape. This public, however, is available for a display of mobilization in a manner unavailable to the paying audience. They are less a chorus offering commentary than a body that collects the desire for dancing. They are mobilized as witness, as movable props (as an antidote to the harried spearholder), and ultimately as that very excess of movement from which dance itself springs.

As props, they hold large, flat, painted masks which resemble African deities and which cover the dancers' heads and chests. For Jones, the masks as tokens of memory mark a problem of historical narrative. "I read Uncle Tom's Cabin in the same way that I collect black memorabilia—it's a testament to where we have been. The question is, were we ever there, or is that where Stowe, a well meaning white liberal Christian woman, said we were? When you look at it as a contemporary person, white or black, the memorabilia shouts, 'This is a lie,' The question remains, what is the truth." [26] As prop, therefore, the expanded cast takes on this task of forcing contemporaries to look at the memorabilia and see, as Eco said of signification more generally, the lie of representation within it. [27] Even after they shed these masks, the corps effected gestures that resembled the African icons—as if to make of themselves a fetish. This links them to the physical memorabilia and allows them to serve as an object lesson, albeit initially at their own (dancing) expense. This initial choreographic device of masking relies on hierarchy of dancers and corps (hence retaining the frame-implicated set of the first act—now as a virtual space—that had marked virtuosity in these dancers). Yet by the end of the piece, as will shortly become evident, the division of dancers will yield to shared conditions for the recognition of their difference.

This final act, like those that precede it, begins with an alluded opposition of sacred and profane, but here the positions are situated within the black community and the words are those of Martin Luther King and Amiri Baraka. Baraka's words retain their original form. King's final words of his "I have a dream" speech (delivered at the March on Washington demonstration of August 28, 1963) are reordered in a manner suggestive of their own historical profanation to proclaim "last at free are we." This often-repeated phrase sends the public back into King's text kinesthetically rather than verbally. It is interesting to trace the shift in King's speech from its moment of rapture to that of critique, where the urgency of mobilization is the order of the day: "This is no time to engage in the luxury of cooling off or to take the tranquilizing drug of gradualism." A few lines later in the speech, King prophesies: "Nineteen sixty-three is not an end, but a beginning. And those who hope that the Negro needed to blow off steam and will now be content, will have a rude awakening if the nation returns to business as usual."[28] This section contains some of the most spirited individual dancing in the piece, with Sean Curran striking a barefoot tap that appears to send sparks flying through his head and upper torso, while his companions file somberly by. Arthur Aviles, who can affect a heliocentrism at any altitude, spirals his way around Lawrence Goldhubber, a man considerably larger than any other in the company.

As is common in pieces of this magnitude, we get to see phrases of movement more than once. Within the epic structure, however, repetition plays with the movement of time internal to the piece to create the sense of recurrence as an effect of memory.[29] The referents of the historical past are localized in the work, and the selectiveness of what recurs is given the full weight of a discovery without the apparatus to privilege what is now revealed. Upon Aviles' return to the aforementioned duet only moments after it first happened, his naked body is offered for revelation. Jones himself remarks, "Whom I choose to show naked first sets up the pariah syndrome."[30] It becomes apparent that this particular state of difference has less effect on his ability to move than on our condition of watching him. But then there is some recapitulation of whippings from the first act (while the crowd chants "dream a have I") and a series of falls from the supper table into the arms of the clothed mass. In this singular nakedness, some sacrifice seems to be afoot.

There is, as well, the implied sacrifice of race to sexuality—as if these identifications could be subtracted from each other—in the final seduction scene of Amiri Baraka's *Dutchman* (1964). It is staged here with Sage Cowles, the woman who had played Harriet Beecher Stowe, on the table of the Last Supper. Yet the apparent exclusivity of identities is established only to be undermined through the operation of the dance piece. In Baraka's play, set in a subway car, a young, well-dressed black man, "Clay," is at first amused by the sexual taunts of "Lula," an older white woman, until she brands him an Uncle Tom. Her reverie makes explicit that it depends on an appropriation of a blackness Lula seeks in Clay. He is incited to warn her of what may be appropriated from her people, who had never imagined their black objects, what Baraka calls "all these fantasy people, all these blues people," capable of such activity, including murder. "Don't make the mistake, through some irresponsible surge of Christian charity, of talking too much about the advantages of Western rationalism, or the great intellectual legacy of the white man, or maybe they'll begin to listen. They'll murder you, and have very rational explanations. Very much like your own. They'll cut your throats, and drag you out to the edge of your cities so the flesh can fall away from your bones, in sanitary isolation."[31]

But it is Clay who is murdered instead by Lula with the complicity of the public that has amassed around them. Now this public in question is composed of the enlarged cast, who begin to carry on their own kinetic business in various states of undress, seemingly indifferent to the textualizing in their midst. But their indifference leaves the other public in something of a bind over where to place their attention, given that the progressive nudity downstage has the potential to upstage the tragic act. The audience is being asked to make a visual decision that rests on Jones's division of stage and identities, one that could be consequential for commitments beyond the theater.

After Clay's body is removed, the stage is reunified in the development of undress that is sustained over the final thirty minutes of the piece. Indifference alternates with involvement. There are exchanges of kisses and embrace and selective rejection but without any immediate principle. Sage Cowles and her husband, John, give "go" commands to the throng who run through one another in a realization of the worst fears of those with an antipathy to crowds. In the density of lifts and tricks that this circulating economy of dancers makes possible, there is over time a loss of the ability of movement in its individual instances to serve as a punctuation for experience by producing in the audience that transcendental gasp, the "ah." There are enough dancers so that one mass can constantly replace another in the stage space. The audience gets acclimatized to both the exceptionality of risky movement and the evanescence of human surplus.

These dancers taunt those who fear losing art to the popular, that famil-

iar neoconservative complaint, as they efface the intentionality of choreographic form with shapeless mass and emit raucous whoops and heys in a
simulation of a sporting event that conflates players and spectators. This is a
kind of wilding without victims. It celebrates the survivability of the transgressive. Toward the very end of the piece, bodily difference is most exposed,
and the nudity that had earlier marked the deficient pariah for sacrifice has
now become an available surplus. Unison increasingly serves as a mobilizing principle. Hand slaps on the floor are propelled by a series of rolls, which
distribute to another part of the body the marching to bondage through
freedom that had opened the work when the cast first sails from Africa.
The slaps soon yield to spinning waves of bodies that disperse themselves
through one another. This formation itself breaks down as the dancers file
through one another. Exuberance alternates with a rhapsodic calm sermon
that finds the performers in various associations until they are all in the
same condition of gentle exposure passing by one another, stepping back
so that others may be foregrounded, and singing a few hymnal tones, until
they face the audience in stillness.

By now they have made the strange familiar and have normalized what
might once have been claimed to be so threatening, for in 1990, the piece
was performed in the midst of state-administered antiobscenity pledges.
The refamiliarization of the body in its manifest difference displayed on the
BAM stage here encountered that conjuncture which had sought to render
all its various productions intolerably strange.

In the very sweep of this epic, recognition of the shared grounds for
identity are joined with several streams of a narrative of emancipation. The
freeing of the slaves to choreographer-employer Jones's slavery of a different sort that occurs between the first and third act finds its reversal by the
finale in a liberation from the labors (of dancing) altogether. The "we" who
are "last at free," which remains strongly identified with African American
history, retains a certain ambiguity of identification at a different level in
the light of the work's epistemology of labor. Coterminous with this emancipation from labor, the cast in its fullness presents a socialization of nudity,
slipping out of costume, mask, characterization, and role as an escape from
narrative altogether. In practice, they offer a resistance to all the devices employed over the course of the evening to singularize dancers' identities or
divide the cast against itself, whether visually or functionally. There is no

speculation about what this promised land would look like; clearly any attempt to do so would reinscribe the piece in some further narrative. Rather, the ending suggests a dialectic between narrative and its other as what is constitutive of the historicity shared by dance and disparate social activities. The rhetorical strategy of shifting among narrative ploys to suggest the possibility for an internal movement could be seen as the terrain promised in Marx's unfulfilled account of capital.

On the other hand, it could be argued that Jones does present a particular vision of what lies beyond history (which for Marx meant within history, given that everything up to this point had only been prehistory). Jones's comment in one interview about wanting to "elevate the struggle" so "that out of the fighting we will triumph, that something great and beautiful will come out of it," is consonant with *Last Supper*'s own historical narrative which evokes that particularly class-bound sixties utopian form, the commune, onstage as the beginning of the beyond of the present.[32] Even with the association of nudity with the primitive (whether taken to mean uncivilized or communally self-sufficient), such references in contemporary political discourse have often become a code word for the very unruliness of opposition produced by the sixties. At the time of this performance the initiative of cultural representation could be said to have passed into the hands of the enemies of what the sixties might have produced. At least saying so made it possible for the Right to picture the Left as a force of reaction to those imagined to be politically unaffiliated.

In this complex conjuncture, *Last Supper* was an instance of what the Right feared most: a good (and therefore politically ungovernable) example. Because of the magnitude of the piece, symptomatic of a certain economy for dance, different sections were commissioned separately. Acts 1 and 2 were cosponsored by the University of California at Los Angeles and the University of California at Berkeley. The final section was developed at the University of Minnesota at Minneapolis, which forbade students to dance without clothes. The uneasiness of presenters was met by special sessions of the Association of Performing Arts Presenters. The president of this organization, Jackie Davis, referred to the piece in testimony before Congress about the NEA's social impact: "Ironically, The Last Supper, so susceptible to criticism from NEA bashers, came to epitomize the positive social influence of the Arts Endowment before Congress."[33]

Perhaps the more interesting question would be what makes this type of theory of historical stages (which has now been revised to suggest that history necessitates difference) rest so easily on the art of the stage. It may turn out, on the contrary, that a stage theory of history could be merely a theatrical one and that periodization itself could be only an organizational division within a scheme of representation, like the acts of this dance. And yet, at the same time, the piece has no doubt assimilated something of a larger historical sensibility, which it has applied to narrative, although the movement of this narrative proceeds in dance terms through the continual effacement of each instance of authorization (from the displacement of Harriet Beecher Stowe to initiate choreographic authority, to the lusty pursuit of command that disappoints controlling powers) that gives rise to narration. This relentless eclipsing of narrator and narration could lead us only to hypotheses about the conjuncture in which a piece such as *Last Supper* becomes possible, appreciating all the while the indeterminacy "in the last instance" between the moment of art and that of the world. To contour such a conjuncture entails figuring the choreography's own internal breaches and transgressions with those crossings of the line(s) — economic, political, and cultural (what gets articulated more concretely in terms of race, class, gender, and sexuality) — that have provoked such anxiety in the world. In the final section of this essay, I will address the social context for this anxiety more directly as one in which the Right has sought to privatize and depoliticize all manner of social and cultural activities that, like Jones's work, have crossed the line into the public domain.

Critique/Receipt

Hopefully, enough has been said of the work of Bill T. Jones and his company to suggest that dance practice can still boom in the nineties. Yet it should also be apparent that *Last Supper at Uncle Tom's Cabin/The Promised Land* operated actively against the ideology of a decline in dance and of the political imaginary by the manner in which a plethora of dancing and of politics was set into play within the same work, thereby narrating a more expansive view of what both could be. For contrary to the impulses of standard dance criticism, overreading assumes that what is critical in art is displayed most forcefully when it can reflect on its own exterior — which is what links the institutional materiality of art to that of society generally. It strikes me that the practice of (dance and cultural) theory has been deprived of an adequate appreciation of its own context. The play with the authority of representation in the composition and decomposition of the frieze image of the Last Supper in the second act evokes certain features of the critical reception for choreographic work more generally, while calling some of the assumptions of criticism into question. Inspired by Jones's work, I would like to rehearse a revision of how this context for reception is conceived of, beginning with a reconsideration of dance criticism as framing the immediate context for dance's reception.

That dance theory and practice could appear disjoined at all is perhaps symptomatic of the manner in which dance is most commonly represented through the conventions of criticism. Criticism, if not subject to overreading, can elide the intrinsic relation of dance and context by assuming the autonomy of the former from the latter, thereby effecting a politics of containment. Criticism is an authority that can police the boundary between the aesthetic and the political economy of art, often coded as the divide between art and life. For while critics may claim an impartial distance from what they view and despite any disavowals to the contrary, their words can be instrumental in the choreographer's access to grants, performance venues, and touring opportunities. Hence, it is precisely at the point at which the relations between art and life are most actively denied that their stakes for the choreographer may be highest.

At one level the play with authority, the effacement of command — barely legible in the men's septet "The Dogs"; more insistent in the game of musical chairs, references to sport, and playing with rules in the second act; and culminating in the final collective undress — speaks to the contemporary patrons of the arts whose authority is not supposed to make its presence felt on stage. Besides criticism, the NEA is especially significant as an absent or implicit authority when it serves as the institutional link between the patron of the old — the state — and the new — the market. What was tacit in these relations of authority was made explicit with government sanction of the agency under the 1989 law introduced by Senator Jesse Helms (Republican, North Carolina). His rider prohibited use of federal monies to "promote, disseminate or produce obscene or indecent materials, including but not limited to depictions of sadomasochism, homoeroticism, the exploitation of children, or individuals engaged in sexual acts; or material which denigrates the objects or beliefs of the adherents of a particular religion or nonreligion."[34] Jones, at one point, made a decision to embody his resistance to this climate in the dance rather than signaling it in the originally selected title for the last act "52 Handsome Nudes" (after a deck of cards owned by dancer Aviles). Reflecting on the previous title for what became "The Promised Land," he remarked: "But then sponsors began to get nervous. It was early 1989 and the beginning of the Helms thing. We didn't want any censorship before we got there."[35] On the other hand, presumably the choreography itself was the anticipation of such censorship in the midst of reception. By loading the dance with what censors had already defined as the source of their anxiety, Jones assimilated their response and incorporated a self-awareness of their very effort to limit the efficacy of the piece. Rather than suggesting any conspiracy with respect to this particular dance (one that received generally favorable reviews nationwide), I first want to look at instances of critics' response to politics in dance generally and then turn to some of the press given *Last Supper* in order to grasp how the trope of containment operates in the representation of dance to banish politics from art.

In a review meant to acknowledge the overwhelming presence of "content" in contemporary dance output, the byline read "Political Dogma Fades. Social Awareness Remains." Jack Anderson of the *New York Times* continues: "Choreographic urgency is admirable, but passion needs to be tempered with caution. Dancers should avoid confusing mere vehemence with communicating something clearly. The worst political artworks present such oversimplified images of good and evil that, even though they are inspired by real problems, they appear to exist in a fantasy world of slogans."[36] Another article written in the same spirit of surveying the dance terrain—an unusual exercise for these writers whose more common focus on a single evening's performance seems to limit reflection on the context for dance making to such occasional Sunday columns—was written a month before by Jennifer Dunning. She lauds the work of emerging African American choreographer Janine Williams as "a miracle of taste, guts and inspiration, despite moments when it seemed threatened by needless political baggage. On the subject of such baggage, a moratorium might be called on pieces dealing with growing up gay—eloquent though some of them may be. And drag has become a drag."[37]

It might be possible to agree with these critics about what constitutes bad political art and to note the particular difficulties dance encounters when it seeks to narrate politics. But these formulations seem to suggest something different: that it is the presence of politics itself that is excessive in dance, a surplus generated elsewhere and somehow uneasily grafted onto the otherwise autonomous aesthetic. That critics of the *New York Times* adhere to the sensibilities of modernism, with its sanctity of muteness, is surely no discovery. That they should see it necessary to descend from their self-anointed heights of objectivity to give dancers advice and warnings suggests that this very sensibility has now encountered something different. Precisely because it is so difficult to imagine Dunning complaining that she has seen too much heterosexual romance in a season, her comments seem to assume the possibility that dance might return to some normative point of reference from which it had only recently strayed.

This type of implied nostalgia can be associated with what Hal Foster referred to as a "postmodernism of reaction," one that repudiates the conventions of modernism only to uphold the status quo. "This repudiation, voiced most shrilly perhaps by neoconservatives but echoed everywhere, is strategic: as Habermas cogently argues, the neoconservatives sever the cultural from the social, then blame the practices of the one (modernism) for the ills of the other (modernization)." Even among these two dance critics the nostalgia for better aesthetic and social days can take different inflections. Dunning concludes, "Let there be the kind of hope with which dance seemed to be oversupplied not so many seasons ago." She refers to recession and AIDS as the thieves of that hope. But one must wonder whether such communities as that of the New York dance scene which have suffered the devastation of AIDS have been politicized by the fact that people are dying or whether the response has come because those who died were being held to be responsible for their own deaths. All this, while money allocated to the machinery of death ($500 billion to prosecute the war in the Gulf) contributes to the politics of scarcity that is said to afflict dance, as well as other things. Anderson, who in his review privileged Balanchine, Paul Taylor, and Alvin Ailey (in a 1969 revival of *Masakela Language*) as instances of "social awareness" against the "political dogma" associated with a list of choreographers who came of age in the last decade, nonetheless concludes, "So, too, the outside world—in all its complexity and contrariness and its possibilities for despair and glory—keeps bursting into dances." While Anderson is no doubt nervous about what gets in, his statement hints at a problematization of postmodernism in a different direction, whereas Hal Foster located its resistive possibility. This condition of the social "bursting into" the halls of modern concert dance signals dance's resistive postmodern turn, and it is the agency of those dancers who have most self-consciously taken on this transgressive move as their own that constitutes its politics.[38]

Yet even when *Last Supper*'s notices were extremely appreciative of the work, the tendency to eliminate the political from the aesthetic remains. For example, in the *Chicago Tribune* Sid Smith praises the piece as "an ambitious, dazzling, gutsy undertaking" but goes on to say, "In tackling so much, Jones all but promises God onstage for his finale, and the flesh parade is poignant and lovely, but hardly a philosophical breakthrough."[39] Paradoxically, ambition seems to be what keeps the dance from generating something of philosophical value, rather than being its means. Similarly, *Village Voice* critic Deborah Jowitt sees that the work "inflates the younger Jones's shock tactics, formal strategies, topics, and rage to the level of spectacle." She concludes the review: "You liked Bill T. Jones the man? Now see BILL T. JONES the world."[40] The scale of the work, the shift from personal expression to spectacle, lyric to epic, is here a matter of degree rather than kind. The world generated by *Last Supper* is textualized quite literally as a capitalization of the choreographer. It is precisely this displacement from individual to work—which is taken by the present writing to be an enormous critical resource—that Lewis Segal of the *Los Angeles Times* takes as its principal deficiency. Accepting as axiomatic that the dancer is the dance, Lewis observes that "without Jones, the work has no center—for essentially it's a quest for context," and that "we feel his absence acutely." Rather than writing from this problem of an absent center, he demands of the piece that it make this absence a presence: "But until it finds a place for one of America's finest dancers—the man who created it—it'll remain incomplete, a personal outcry without a person. In art, some people are irreplaceable and testimony by proxy is never the real thing." For Segal, then, the authenticity of art rests on its ability to personify what gives rise to it, assuming that these last are sources that can be personified rather than means of dancing. "Proxy" for him is an indication that a work might display more than the labor of its author. He affirms this in his comment that "the work itself seems assembled by committee rather than personally crafted."[41] It would therefore appear that it is the presence of collectivity that does violence or absents the author, rather than merely standing in for the "real thing." The creator as center, the dancer as choreographer as "voice," recalls what Foucault termed the "author function," "the ideological figure by which one marks the manner in which we fear the proliferation of meaning."[42] What this entails for the review just cited is that the attack on collectivity within the dance constitutes an effort to subvert its being "assembled by committee" as a condition of reception. The dance becomes an encounter between dancer and critic, limiting its production and circulation to a closed circuit. In a climate in which censorship has already named the kinds of reception it seeks to limit, this particular critical trope of authorial containment becomes its double.

Marked already by loss, by the absence of the one "left behind," *Last Supper* operates quite vigorously against the very institutions of reception that would deny what is philosophical in the breakthrough of its own politics. For the critics, Jones is an author and therefore a well-bounded site for the accumulation of cultural capital on which the practice of their craft becomes possible. By allowing what has concentrated in his name to circulate freely in his choreographic text, *Last Supper* provokes the critical fear that would deny the critics their own privileged means of accumulation. The critic's authority resides in an appeal to a system of classification that values dance in terms of where it places choreographers and dancers in that system. Naming the activity of dance after a choreographic personage allows the former to be elided in the latter. As such, whatever their critical disposition toward the work and whether, heeding Denby's words, they agree to find it "good or bad," these critics have reason to fear the textualizing of author in the direction of context. For this move would alter the existing terms under which their authority is constituted. When art refuses to accept the boundaries that are intended to separate it from life, the critic can become a self-proclaimed victim, for conventionally, the critic's authority is invested in policing that boundary.[43]

It is just this fullness of context that animates *Last Supper*. Part of that context was certainly the general anxiety over boundaries burst into and across, which the dance criticism of Anderson and Dunning joined. Jones was the one "left behind" in the Bill T. Jones/Arnie Zane Dance Company when Zane died in spring 1988. *Last Supper* was the fullest evocation in the repertory of his companion's absence. At the same time, Jones's own choreographic assent represents a negotiation within the political economy of art that was emblematic of a concentration of productive resources among fewer companies (not just dance) which characterized a globalizing capitalist economy during the 1980s and which left so many facing the very conditions of scarcity that his work opposes. It is this contradiction between the control of resources for accomplishing social needs (aesthetic or otherwise) and the proliferating articulation of these needs by those who demand resources which Jones confronts and which urges a reappraisal of the rhetoric of scarcity. The dancers' unruliness in the presence of authority underscores that dance itself is more than just gaming. For contrary to the impulses of standard dance criticism, overreading assumes that what is critical in art is displayed most forcefully when it can reflect on its own exterior—which is what links the institutional materiality of art to that of society generally.

(In)effective Boundaries

The moment in the third act when Bill T. Jones sits down with the local cleric marks a double movement between the sacred and the profane. Immediately before, when Jones is dancing to the words of Job read by the cleric, his body both narrates the text and is outside it, so as to constitute the means of profanation that in turn sacralizes the word and its voice. Sitting to give back the word to the voice not only displays the hubris of speech before the presumably unspeakable that pertains to religious faith and the real in history (recalling Jameson's phrase of a "prior (re)textualization" of what is fundamentally nonnarrative) but also profanes what is sacred in art, namely, that its distance from life be maintained. By effacing this aesthetic boundary, *Last Supper* produces its own version of the shattering of mimesis and effectively conjoins the figures of artistic production and the judgment of taste on which aesthetic reception presumably rests. Clearly, these figures are conjoined within the piece and not outside it, and so the piece problematizes the relation between art and life only by representing, not transcending, the divide. But even this interweaving of history and fiction with which *Last Supper* is so replete accomplishes for the dance what I had earlier termed narrative displacement.

The narrativization of what is generally left unsaid or unread allows for another level of context to become legible through the work: the linkage of the various institutional effects through which contemporary dance must operate. These institutional effects, which Jones and other artists have increasingly incorporated into their work, entail a grammar of cultural production, or postmodernism; regulating mechanisms for an arts economy whose apparatus of legitimation is the National Endowment for the Arts; and a principle of regulation (here, an overconfident political Right) that has of late found its strongest voice as an opposition to the very thing it regulates. These three domains could themselves be joined through a certain narrative displacement from the aesthetic to the economic.

One powerful myth that has operated in the concert dance world is that the sixties and seventies produced a dance boom that had by the eighties gone bust. This myth I take to be the ideological horizon that joins a conservative antiaesthetic, a policy of defunding, and a blaming of cultural difference for social decline. For now, I want to establish these institutional effects as a context for contemporary dance and will, in the next section, extend it more explicitly to the politics of other domains.

It is worth noting that the recent rightist assault on the arts is but the latest manifestation of a rhetoric that links art and decay to keep enemies at bay. Anticommunism too had its aesthetic front. Consider, for example, these words of Michigan senator George Dondero before his colleagues in summer 1949 attacking modern art as foreign "instruments and weapons of destruction": "The evidence of evil design is everywhere, only the roll call of the art contortionists is different. The question is, what have we, the plain American people, done to deserve this sore affliction that has been visited upon us so direly; who has brought down this curse upon us; who has let into our homeland this horde of germ-carrying art vermin?" [44]

Following in Dondero's footsteps, Jesse Helms has sought to purge the NEA of HIV-positive artists—living or dead. These efforts acquire added significance whose compound meaning is addressed in Bill T. Jones's figure of the naked pariah. The artist stripped bare, alternately avoided and supported, allows both dancers and public to work through the contradictory accusations of creativity as a force of social destruction. The notion that what is creative in art could extinguish itself is one version of the modernist imperative for eternal innovation. [45] In dance, a notion gained currency in the eighties that a creative expansion that had spurred the professionalization and proliferation of many dance companies had come to a close. This putative decline in creativity was associated with an economic metaphor of boom and bust that is meant to describe an unceasing oscillation of cyclical growth and decline in business activity. The use of boom and bust applied to dance, however, bore no such optimism of rebounded expansion. This was a dance myth that *Last Supper* sought to give the lie to, but the claims of the myth first need to be exposed. It is important to emphasize that this mythology not only seeks to contain the aesthetic impact of professional concert dance but also to eliminate from consideration popular forms of dancing that are particularly resistant to any notion of expansion and contraction given their firm placement as daily cultural activities.

As I've already suggested, periodizing is precarious business: the December 1945 edition of *Fortune* ran a story called "The Boom in Ballet." Suggestive of a very different body image, it showed a picture of a dancer, sandwich in hand, captioned "few ballet dancers worry about weight." [46] But *Fortune*'s perhaps premature discovery of boom also signaled a place to look for the limits to dance's expansionary tendencies. *Forbes* ("capitalist tool") featured a ballerina on its January 15, 1971, cover, which read, "The Performing Arts: But the Costs Are Soaring Too." Although recession and Reagan had taken hold in 1982, one piece in the *New York Daily News* declared, "Triumph for the City Ballet and the Dance World Booms." The article provided the following figures: between 1975 and 1982 the number of dance companies in New York City grew from eighty to some five hundred, involving over ten thousand dancers. Companies had enjoyed extended runs and increased audience attendance every year since 1977 at the premier dance venue, City Center. In 1981 there were roughly twenty-five hundred performances. The story hastened to add, "Financial trouble is everywhere. . . . government cuts and rising costs could imperil it all." [47]

Indeed they did. But this specific economic problem in the arts had long been recognized and was part of the impetus that gave the NEA its expanded funding, an issue I will return to shortly. Suffice it to say for now that if increases in productivity had always put the performing arts in jeopardy, then financial strain could only magnify with the so-called boom, and there is every indication that this was the case. In this regard, then, the bust was unlike the end of the putative business cycle on which it is modeled insofar as expansion is unprofitable and (therefore) market forces were indeterminate. So the bust was never about economic pressures narrowly defined (those constraints were always there) but connected more closely to institutional supports and ideology. It would seem that the ideology was mobilized to unmoor the former. Although it is tempting to say that there was a boom that went bust, I want to suggest that the assumptions which underlie this claim are untenable and to argue the opposite. The bust was what arrested the boom.

Hewing to the bottom line, the 1971 *Forbes* issue cited above asked, "Can the transistor save the arts?" At least one critic, Roger Copeland, answered in the negative. Writing in the mid-eighties he suggested that Baryshnikov's appearance in the film *The Turning Point* signaled the end of the boom that began in the seventies. For him, the antinomy of the boom was not economic but cultural: "The rising fortunes of American dance are directly, statistically proportional to the declining standards of American literacy." Dance, an object that can be consumed visually, without reflection is most like television and in that regard "a respectable form of anti-intellectualism." [48] Copeland is positioning dance theory and practice as aspiring to fundamentally opposed situations. According to his argument, the expansion of cultural production makes it impossible for intellectual activity to establish (cultural) values. If these values are seen as representing some putatively universal public interest, cultural production clings to a somehow merely private one. Hence not only is it difficult to imagine grounds on which dance (or any other cultural) theory and practice could join in a politics, but practice also is herein relegated to a private domain and therefore without politics at all. It is here that the discourse on dance was joined with broader currents of cultural contestation during the eighties. I would like to offer an alternative account of the conjuncture for the theory and practice of dance in the eighties that might refigure a conception of the boom before returning to the politics in/of dance in the present.

The standard study on the economics of the professional performing arts isolates dance from theater and concert music as experiencing the only genuine expansion during the sixties. [49] A more recent study documents the expansion of the number of dance companies during the seventies not just in New York but also nationally irrespective of the size of the urban center. [50] But the development in dance has been more than numerical, although its aesthetic dimensions and cultural significance are more difficult to measure.

Arguably, the possibilities and occasion for human movement have been explored with an intensity unprecedented in the United States, resulting in a dramatic expansion of the dance lexicon, for both concert and popular (especially African American and Latino) idioms.

Yet, as it has become increasingly specified and specialized in terms of human movement, dance activity has also pushed the boundaries between dance and other means of performance. The different solutions to the problem of minimalism associated with the explorations of pedestrian movement by the dancers at Judson Church and of Grand Union, on the one hand, and the subtle modulations of a choreographer such as Laura Dean, on the other, joined concert dance with developments in music and theater, such as those of Robert Wilson, both conceptually and practically. The Tanztheater of Pina Bausch and a host of other Europeans pushed dance past expressionism in the direction of self-representation that had been largely absent from the generally mute medium so that the dancer appeared as more than a body laboring under choreographic authority. The presentation of self in much contemporary concert dance initially emphasized relations of gender but soon came to embrace matters of sexual preference, race, and the political economy of dance. The dancing body was now placed in tension with its confinement to movement as something that specified it but also kept it sequestered from other issues. It was not simply that dance took on subject matter, for that had never been foreign to the first dance modernists. Rather, subject was unbounded by media and reached for social and historical context in a manner that had probably had no parallel since the political works of the 1930s.

The juxtaposition between the ordinary and the epic, between affect drawn through movement and drama achieved through the address of audience, amplified the tension between the space of the dancer's body and that of performance in a manner which sought to make connections with social spaces beyond the stage. The presence of this kind of material in so many pieces was indicative of how dance had reframed questions of the relation of structure and process in artistic work more generally. The interest, intended to be shared by the audience, in how the work was generated in the process of performance alluded to the forms of sociality that made dancing possible. Process was allowed to abut structure constantly, just as personal reminiscence increasingly found use in connection with historical reckoning.

That so many small venues that had once been public spaces were able to sustain dance performance (churches, schools, sites of abandoned industry) was indicative of how the vitality of the performing arts could contribute to a very determined project of urban renewal. At the same time, outdoor festivals, environmental pieces, and site-specific works served not only to congregate groups of people but also to raise questions about the conditions under which art was made available to its public. Surely this was not the first time that modern dance had raised such issues—one need only think of Isadora Duncan and Loie Fuller—but they were now being raised with respect to a different set of concerns about access to urban space as a newly problematic feature of society. Nor could it be said that current dance output has forgotten these concerns or its ability to touch them. The persistent search for connections between aesthetic form and social content that transgress existing boundaries can still be found in recent dance, Jones's included. This ongoing exploration raises the question of what could be meant by the term "boom" and whether it can be considered over or, perhaps, somehow arrested in its development.

Clearly, the most dynamic initiatives in dance were part of a broader cultural phenomenon, the extension of public life promulgated by the demands of various social movements. The specificity of a dance boom would have to be located in terms of the ways in which this context for the expansion of public life animated the relation between form and content in dance. But the clear expansion of dance activity also needs to be explained in terms of an infrastructure of support. Given the uniqueness of the economics of the performing arts—increases in productivity do not translate into the reduced unit costs characteristic of other industries—growth comes at the expense of a growing gap between revenues and expenditures. Without the support of a recording industry or the benefit of extended runs, as in music and theater, respectively, this countereconomy of scale is felt most acutely in dance. The solution, agreed on in the literature, is to find some mechanism other than the market to sustain growth.[51] But social investment within the framework of a capitalist economy scarcely occurs without struggle and mobilization. The initiation of the National Endowment for the Arts in 1965, prompted no doubt by an immediate sense of preserving the national patrimony, of which modern dance was undervalued kin, had its broader context in the implications for civility demanded by, among others, the movement for civil rights in this country.

These demands met a response in the establishment of an entire apparatus of state funding. The Great Society programs, while prompted by social movements, were the glimmer of decency in the apex of U.S. imperium fevered by wars hot and cold. The NEA was but one small part of a social hypothesis that claimed culture as necessary to a just society. The Great Society expansion was felt in dance circles beyond the university with the establishment of the NEA, and it was with a grant of $142,250 that Martha Graham was able to make her first national tour in fifteen years in 1966. As with other constructivist programs, government funding for the arts was viewed as a political palliative, not simply a celebration of the national patrimony. President Johnson, signing the Endowments bill on September 29, 1965, proclaimed, "For it is in our works of art that we reveal to ourselves, and to others, the inner vision which guides us as a nation."[52] As the Rockefeller-funded studies of arts economies meant to rationalize public support to help organize private giving put it, "leisure" could become an "individual and social problem" if not constructively "channeled" into arts activity. Douglas Dillon, a former treasury secretary and chairman of the Business Committee for the Arts, was even more direct in saying that "artistic performances of one sort or another are essential in handling the crisis of our cities."[53] Hence arts funding was a part of a larger strategic response to counter the popular mobilizations ironically dubbed leisure time (uncontrolled by work discipline) with a unifying call that art would civilize this nation (and others) and cover dissent with an aesthetic legacy.

At its height in the late seventies, NEA funding was aimed not only at the development of choreographers but at support of presenters and their venues and arts management as well, a field pioneered in 1962 by the Ford Foundation, whose arts director, McNeil Lowry, was instrumental in modeling what the NEA would become.[54] In 1967, the Coordinated Dance Touring Program was inaugurated, beginning with four companies and five weeks in two states at a cost of $25,000. Ten years later, this program had grown to 440 weeks across fifty states and was funded at nearly $2 million. The touring program allowed 30 percent reductions to presenters and generated a list of companies for them to choose from on the basis of fiscal solvency. The NEA even helped bail out the bankrupt Paul Taylor Company in 1976. The NEA encouraged the formation of companies modeled on businesses, requiring them to have boards of directors and to file for nonprofit status (501[c][3]), and by 1987 it was devoting 62 percent of its funds to dance companies as opposed to 9 percent to individual choreographers (of a total $8,723,750).[55]

Interestingly, state support for the arts began not as domestic but as foreign policy. The Division of Cultural Relations of the State Department was established in 1938 to open an ideological front in Latin America. Fifteen years later, the United States Information Agency (USIA) was established as a global counterweight to Communism's good ideas.[56] The USIA's arts initiatives were designed to "correct and humanize the image of the American people held by other peoples . . . disposed to look down upon the United States as a nation concerned only with the creation of material wealth and with satisfactions provided by creature comforts and ingenious gadgets."[57] Martha Graham was the first of the moderns to tour abroad in 1956 when touring was institutionalized under the International Cultural Exchange and Trade Fair Participation Act passed that year. She was followed by José Limón, Paul Taylor, Alvin Ailey, and dozens of others as funding for the program expanded precipitously in the late fifties from $5.0 to $22.8 million, despite State Department efforts to reduce it.[58]

Although the conditions for dance's global circulation were instrumental, this did not result in a singular official American art form. Rather, the message sent was of freedom of expression based on a manifest plurality of individual forms. Kennedy, early to recognize the domestic political capital to be gained by arts funding, also saw in it a counter to the Soviets, who "recognize even though they manipulate this desire, the tremendous interest people have in the arts." For him, artistic freedom validated national character: "In serving his vision of the truth, the artist best serves his nation."[59] The institutional infrastructure of modern dance was being constructed at a national level, and here the development of dance within the university curriculum was a crucial factor in support of touring, employment of teachers, audience development, and choreographic commissions.

Paradoxically, the promise of universal education meant as well that educational institutions would be venues that would be susceptible to demands that knowledge be particularized. With respect to dance, this context made possible the creation and expansion of academic departments and performance venues, seen broadly as features of a more democratic culture. By 1968, there were 22 independent dance departments and 110 campuses where students could major in dance.[60] The democracy here had to do both with allocation of resources for the development of social institutions and with the shaping of those institutions by and through participation.

As we are all well aware, this dramatic expansion has now undergone a draconian contraction. The contraction has been as much ideological (in the sense of an idea outside dance that is opposed to it) as financial and ultimately constitutes an effort to reform the polity and to limit public participation. For while it is true that many social programs have been reduced, the federal budget and its accumulated deficit expanded yearly during the eighties. Those who called for less government responded with greater state expenditures — but of a certain sort — simply put, to free economy from the demands of its public. Capital, the putative means and end of that economy, increasingly restless with the social costs of democracy, was looking for pastures beyond our shores, and the government was serving as combined realtor and travel agent. At issue for partisans of democracy was how a massive redirection of resources was politically managed and ideologically legitimated. The irony for modern dance was that just when it was best positioned in theory and practice to project itself nationally, the possibilities for such a projection were undermined by a shift in the relation of the state to the activities productive of public life.

The redirection of resources can be traced to the policies generated in the service of a highly mobile capital (deregulation, tax cuts, free trade, deficit monetarism — in short, the odd assortment of initiatives dubbed Reaganomics) and a countercultural assault from the Right that sought to pin social decay on cultural difference. Clearly it has not been the case that every or even most dance works have aesthetically addressed this social situation. Rather, the main impact that rightist ideology had on dance was to create a national climate for its reception that robbed performances of their own immediate context. The significance of the hateful pronouncements of Jesse Helms, Dana Rohrabacher, William Dannemeyer, and the like lay in their ability to bring the subject of dance and art generally from the specialized discourse of a criticism already predisposed to decontextualize aesthetic expression into a nationally public arena with a highly simplistic view of how context operates within an aesthetic. Hence, critic and conservative politician were complicit in maintaining the static divide between what is interior and exterior to the artwork that both *Last Supper* and overreading seek to undermine.

By claiming to value work exclusively in terms of its content, the very voices who brought the matter to the public made it impossible to discuss whether such work could be considered art, presumably their actual question, by denying the ways in which art brings content into tension with form.

The ability of those espousing rightist ideology to trade on the effacement of high and popular, the critique of specialized knowledge, and invocation of the public signaled an abuse of the very principles of democratization embodied in the social gains that supported the dance boom. Most important, the assault on public funding for the arts that took the explicit form of vows of self-censorship to grant recipients, discussed in the previous section, was part of an effort to redraw the boundaries between public and private life and draw art within the domain of the latter.

Here the two frequently used meanings of the term "private" were intentionally blurred: private in the economic sense of market driven and in the philosophical and anthropological significance of the sphere of domesticity—supposedly where all issues of sexuality belong. Hence the public funding of art was being reconceived as a matter for the private domain of the market in order to reprivatize issues recently politicized by social movements away from the domain that could guarantee them recognition and resources. Surely the NEA gets more credit from its detractors than it deserves for actually funding art. In the mid-eighties, federal funds constituted only 5 percent of the total of public and private support.[61] The NEA budget for 1995 was $167.4 million, which, controlling for inflation, is just over half what it was at peak funding levels in 1979 and a tiny fraction of the $9 billion raised privately for the arts.[62] By 1997, the budget had been slashed to just under $100 million, and the agency that had issued over 100,000 grants was slated for elimination altogether. Yet, as a mechanism for legitimating forms of art and for orienting the arts economy and as an object of public discussion, its influence is far more extensive. By the same token, the annual ritual of assassinating it ideologically may prove more important to the detractors of public funding than the NEA's actual elimination.

In the early eighties, when Jones and Zane were coming to prominence, cultural policy expressed through the agency of federal funding allocations signaled a turn from supporting emerging choreographers to established artists. Then director of the NEA Frank Hodsoll defended deep cuts to his agency by denying that anything of the vitality in the arts would be lost.[63] By the end of the eighties, appropriation levels had barely crept up to what they were at the start of the decade before declining again. They have continued to decline. For dance specifically, both total amount and number of grants declined (particularly given cumulative inflation of over 50 percent through the decade), from $9,122,202 and 398 grants to $8,964,738 and 355 grants. While, during the eighties, the amount of money given to individual choreographers more than tripled, this has to be factored against the impact of a decade of inflation and real estate speculation on the dance community, especially its ability to appropriate space—the very premise of its activity— for habitation, rehearsal, and performance. The relevant frame of reference for assessing these spending levels is the federal budget as a whole, which doubled over the course of the decade. Hence it was certainly not the case that the arts funding was experiencing a discipline reflective simply of fiscal trends in the budgetary process. Rather, funding was subject to an anti-economy. The only appreciable increases at the end of the 1980s were to the NEA's administrative budget (the numbers are $11.3 million in 1982 and $14.9 million in 1987, according to NEA annual reports).[64]

More significant, something with the look of a national cultural aesthetic was appearing in politicians' pronouncements about what could be considered appropriate form and content in the arts. This, of course, had its very concrete manifestations in the antiobscenity riders attached to choreography grants, and the overriding of panel-approved grants by then head of the NEA John Frohnmayer. These acts did not go unanswered. In 1990, $750,000 worth of NEA money was rejected by artists and organizations that refused to sign the pledge, and some of those who were denied, such as Bella Lewitsky and Tim Miller, sued the NEA. The pledge was rescinded.[65] The integration achieved between dance and performance art gave strong identification to performers such as Holly Hughes and Karen Finley. Finley had been chosen but declined to cohost the 1990 Bessies, the New York dance awards held at BAM, in light of the fateful triangle the event had formed with the likes of Philip Morris and RJ Reynolds-Nabisco and the art police (Philip Morris, one of the largest corporate donors to the arts at $15 million in 1990,[66] also gave generously to Jesse Helms). While arts activists from Get Smart passed out leaflets (rolled as cigarettes) on these connections outside the theater, speeches advocating further activism were made about them from within. Two months after the Bessies award ceremony (September 12, 1990), *Last Supper at Uncle Tom's Cabin/The Promised Land* opened on the same stage, drawing into its midst the politics of the dance community's own occasion for celebration and self-recognition. Its internal crossings of art and life, sacred and profane, its interweaving of history and fiction, drew from this exterior of politicized art.

A Utopia of the Real

The "promised land" referenced in Bill T. Jones's finale to *Last Supper* has multiple meanings that resonate with what Houston Baker Jr. has identified as the recurrent theme in African American culture and history of "freedom and apocalypse."[67] I want to focus on two avenues of interpretation for this promised land. It links the Reconstruction promise of "forty acres and a mule" meant to provide the means of subsistence that were intended to offer the material conditions to break decisively with slavery's exploitation, and the historical promise (with both sacred and secular expressions) of a world transformed, a promise that rests on a system for the allocation of social surplus very different from what a profit-driven economy can provide. Although the first promise was broken and the second remains unfulfilled, the joining together of a politics of subsistence and surplus has much to recommend it, as does recognizing the persistence of the conditions of enslavement under putative emancipation, especially the virulence of racism itself. Jones's powerful synthesis hints at how production and reproduction, public and private, might be located in the same dance and mobilized against the pervasive politics of scarcity and on behalf of a utopian conception of a more livable social totality. Here, again, I want to import some of those dance insights into an exploration of the staging of theory and practice in contemporary politics.

One of the contributions to emerge out of feminist theory has been the demonstration that the relation between public and private spheres is itself a political construct. This reconceptualization of separate spheres ideology has made it possible to problematize the presumed identification of women with the private and the private with the apolitical.[68] The fundamental distinction between socialized production (where the resources and capacities for making society lie) and social reproduction (the renewal of those capacities) retains logical and structural significance but cannot be neatly grafted onto mutually exclusive domains of public life, with its market-driven instrumentality, and domesticity, with its associations of moral and affective substance. Further, politics that emerge during the 1980s undermine any simple binary opposition that would differentiate public and private spaces.

The ideological thrust of the rightist movements that emerged during the eighties maintained the binary of private and public so as to deny political claims on the basis of race, gender, and sexuality as purely private matters inappropriate to politics. At the same time, the Right attacked the very privacy that it saw as harboring identities that deviate from its vision of moral order. The attack on these other bodies occurred in the same conjuncture that a highly mobile capital was fleeing its own sites of socialization, an economic formation also known variously as deregulation, privatization, and free trade. One theoretical implication of these rightist politics is that the material and political basis for separating the public and the private has been complicated in ways that jeopardize the effectiveness of this strategy of containment. Limiting what could be legitimately considered political was intended to ameliorate the contradictions of privately owned production and socially constituted needs of reproduction.

The hypermobility of capital (the disinvestment of productive resources in pursuit of higher rates of return) has a depressing effect on wages and social services and surely complicates the ability to maintain separate spheres. The consequent unevenness to capitalist development is of a sort different from the clearly bounded zones of inclusion (first world nations with their relatively privileged laboring populations) and exclusion (third world, capital's as opposed to capitalism's presumed exteriority—which until recently had been figured as the second world) that have characterized colonial development to date. The assumed condition of labor for the first world was that, despite its own differentiation and stratification along lines of race, gender, and unionization, real wages would rise with national wealth or gross national product. As such, labor in the first world could maintain an interest in the expanded circulation of capital and in imperialist expansion. The eighties saw certain secular leveling in wages framed within an overall immiseration of wage labor irrespective of occupational strata (as indicated by the layoffs or "downsizing" that became so prominent during the late eighties and nineties, which was itself an adjustment for the centralizing corporate mergers a few years earlier).[69]

Indeed, the global recession of the late eighties and early nineties evidenced the extent to which circuits of capital flow through the consumer/ service nexus were now depleted of realizable demand.[70] The flight of capital and downward pressure of wages in the first world meant that workers were no longer enlisted to the same degree in the expansion of capital through their collective capacity for expenditure. The society of consumption that had provisionally conjoined the immediate interests of labor and capital had lost some of its economic utility. The absurdist claims, disseminated largely in print media, of rising consumer confidence (an index of the willingness to go into debt) driving an economic recovery are symptomatic. If the deflation of labor's means to rescue capitalist overproduction (the excess capacity of supply over commodifiable demand) through consumption declines in the first world, it also reconfigures labor in/as the third world. While the third world is where capital has newly (again) landed to appropriate surplus which that labor will never use, it also has the effect of driving a wedge between the category of labor and that of population as such. Typically, third world labor in a global economy is labor whose wages are insufficient to purchase the commodities it produces (and often those commodities are not even marketed to that labor). The low-wage maquiladora, the free enterprise zone, and the North American Free Trade Agreement (NAFTA) all represent capital's ability to penetrate the geography of the third world to establish an internal boundary of production activity against the requisites of social reproduction.

The freedom alluded to in these highly fluid economic formations is none other than the freedom of capital from the demands of its situation, either in terms of taxes, organizations on behalf of labor, or political institutions (such as the national state) where that labor could redress economic disruptions. The more dramatic impact, however, rests on those whose bodies are not the object of multinational capital's desire, that population already expropriated from the land and its means of subsistence which constitutes a global level of urbanization that now ranges between 50 percent and 80 percent. Where forced migration to the cities had, at one time, fueled industrial capital, now such migration is an effect of deindustrialization on a global scale. The chief consequence is a surplus population reflected in unemployment figures of from 40 percent to 70 percent not uncommon in third world cities and precisely within the range of unemployment experienced by African American males aged eighteen to twenty-five in U.S. cities and within the range of workers laid off in those industries of the former Soviet Union considered to have made the transition to the market.

Slavery, which had once been a means to appropriate populations into the global circuits of capital, is now usurped by more insidious forms of social control that operate to exclude people from societal wealth. This transformation in the generalized economy of desire for African American bodies from forced inclusion to coercive exclusion is fundamental to the turn that racism has taken in the United States. What complicates these changes is their very unevenness with respect to the African American population itself. Both morally and materially, the life circumstances of black people in the United States are emblematic of what is going on in the country at large. Hence, contrary to the well-placed concerns that black politics be treated as wholly exceptional to some imagined mainstream variety,[71] the polarization visited on African Americans crystallizes the national condition. The success of the civil rights movements of the fifties, sixties, and seventies resulted in what Manning Marable has called the "second reconstruction."[72] The Civil Rights Act of 1964 and the Voting Rights Act of 1965 signaled a meaningful realignment of the social and political compact for access to labor markets, higher education, and voting booths. These reforms had their distributional effects, which were quite palpable by the mid-1980s. In electoral terms, the number of black government officials increased from one hundred to eight thousand from 1965 to 1995, with particular prominence as mayors of the major U.S. cities—yet blacks still represented only 2 percent of all elected officials. Economically, by the mid-1990s, one in seven black families earned above fifty thousand dollars per year, while a third lived below the poverty line, with half the black teenagers seeking employment unable to find it and nearly a quarter of the black males aged twenty to twenty-nine in prison.[73] Against the claims that blacks somehow menace white security, four-fifths of the roughly twenty thousand homicides committed in the United States are intraracial, and black men are seven times more likely to be murdered than are their white counterparts.[74] Finally, in terms of media representations, the extremities of murder and incarceration rates are daily contrasted with the adoration toward the successes of a Bill Cosby or a Michael Jordan or the obsessions with the ambiguities of an O. J. Simpson, on whose body this polarity is itself mapped. It is on this divide of collective devastation and individual emancipation that the mythos of America is being reborn as offering ever more selective mobility, along with increasing dread of abject abandonment. While the polarization indicated here has a firm demographic foundation, the imaginary of race itself as bipolar is more firmly ideological and serves, among other things, to reinscribe a racial divide among those others who fall outside this reductionist model.[75] Surely this is only the most recent version of a tale continually retold in U.S. history. One significant difference here is that what was the essential functionality of slavery to the accumulation process that (under)valued all black bodies for their laboring capacity is now transformed.[76] The present ideological partition of the African American population divides it into a portion rendered extraneous to the accumulation process altogether and another whose bodily talents themselves are said to be a source of accumulation. Needless to say, what is also left out of this particular binary is the actual majority of African Americans who work for wages, typically at some fraction of the national average for their given occupation or still limited in access from relatively better-paid positions.[77] The jostling between the appearance of these represented minorities and the silenced majority bespeaks a certain ideological violence underwritten by coercive practices. What was once a source of surplus labor is now the renewed basis for what Marx termed a "relative surplus population."[78] The rage of being enslaved to these circumstances is most typically treated as part of the character of those subjected to them. It is these permutations of slavery and the sacrifices they bring that are exposed so effectively in *Last Supper.*

Once, the market had been figured as the site of the simulacra for the body's universal desire (universal in the sense of assimilating every instance of a body, no matter how different that desire might be). Now, the global market is constructed to exclude whole universes of bodies. Against its real dependence on cheapened labor, the third world is figured in first world political discourse as a trap, a place that forces of modernization can get stuck in. What could be said to connect the question of when to intervene in Somalia with that in regard to Bosnia is not so much the belated admission of oil interests in Somalia but that the disposal of (surplus) bodies in Bosnia had not fully run its course. In the fiery Los Angeles spring of 1992, we could similarly ask how the found innocence in the abuse of one body occasioned the desire for the abuse of many—namely, the narrative (which was shared by all the presidential candidates at the time and echoed by defense attorneys and police chiefs a year later) that more coercive forces were necessary to solve the problem that the uprising displayed.

Despite the formulation of a term such as "new world order" and the intensification of myriad forms of racism on which it relies, this enthusiasm for coercion has yet to find an ideological expression anywhere near as pointed as anticommunism had been. What is more apparent is that the divide between labor and population introduces the grounds for a new episteme of bodily discipline, where surplus bodies encounter a rhetoric of deficits. This rhetoric can be introduced to cleave race, gender, and most recently age over who will get more of less. The scarcity effect that this produces justifies no end of autolimitations on desire, precisely what Jones — by refusing the cleavage of identities against themselves through their shared display of a common capacity for movement — seeks to counter by transforming a condition of scarcity (such as the initial nudity that signals the "pariah syndrome") to one of surplus (communal undress that makes way for diversity).

All this is to say that the body gets privileged in this political conjuncture of surplus desire unleashed from the boundaries of market and in the coercive strategies meant to recontain them. These body politics (on the stage and off) migrate across that oversimplified divide of class/state (or old) and new social movements/identity politics.[79] The migrating body as a globally socialized condition is the counterpoint to the mobility of capital. Granted, most of this migration occurs within nations — from country to city — rather than across national boundaries — an estimated 120 million people globally, yet in both cases the industrializing drives cannot be readily disarticulated from transnational investment flows.[80] This migratory body is constituted through the crossing of borders (like the *Last Supper*'s migrations into and from slavery, the interruption of speech and movement, and the prolonged passing from a regime of exclusion into the communal of Jones's last act) and hence made sentient of its loss of a locational specificity and its spatial dispersion.

I have no doubt labored a point, not only to show the labor of politics where so much effort has been made to disappear it forcibly but also to hint, as Jones's dancers do, at a labor that emerges against the grain of the market. For while emergent politics first associated with the 1960s that continue to develop in the 1980s and 1990s make demands for material resources (for control over both conditions of production [jobs and labor mobility] and reproduction [from health to sex and healthy sex]), they do so in a manner that does not rest easily within the prevailing language of consumption. The array of social movements that cause the Right such anxiety imagines a politics of the body in which desire cannot be contained by the simple transit between markets for labor and for commodities but rather, as *Last Supper* ultimately insists, in which desire is generated in transit. At the same time, these deterritorialized flows that overspill economic and cultural boundaries are themselves generated out of a socialization process that focuses on the formation of collectivity rather than individuation. Ever changing axes of association bring people together in ways that constantly reconfigure the spaces of social life and not simply the objects that surround a person. The proliferation of myriad categories of collective identity is wholly consistent with the segmentation of markets (greater aggregate sales through the constitution of target groups rather than mass markets) practiced by the most recently capitalized sectors of the technoculture. Yet, with all these politics, what we see is the organizational effect of socialization of emerging affiliations, without being subordinated or even included in capital's aim for group formation—the production and consumption of commodities. Through the political economy of representation that traffics in the experience of the exotic, it is possible to appropriate the imaginary lives of those very subcultures that are then excluded from the formal economy altogether in the hyperactive and destructive mobility of capital. Jones's staging of the mobilization, affiliation, and reinclusion of these masses performs against this exclusionary edifice of representation and for a society where what is excessive, where the production of surplus, acts on behalf of those who produce it.

The disarticulation of socialization of labors and circulation of commodities may turn out to be the most profound contradiction of what the decade of privatization produced. Such disarticulation is less surprising, however, than the rhetoric of privatization would concede. It should be recalled that the freeing of capital from the now constraining effects of what were once considered by those same capitals to be helpful regulations was and remains a state-directed project that proceeds through laws, treaties, and ordinances with a still more extensive and global scope. It is the very centrality of the state that leaves the depletion of the material supports of the public sphere confronting less the administration of social welfare than the state's repressive apparatus. For this reason the supposed disappearance of the state as an institutional mechanism of social regulation generates its own narrative of the return of the repressed, for the calls to eliminate or shrink government bureaucracy allow the scale and scope of state intervention to expand to unprecedented heights. That what returns is precisely repression is amply evident to all those engaged in a politics of deprivatization, of decensoring, or, to return to the dance, of necessary exposures of bodies to more than they are expected to bare. These various body politics face the dilemma of demanding less of one kind of state and more of another or, metaphorically, that the dogs be called off (once, like Jones's slave catchers, we notice the foibles of the gendarme's relation to authority).[81]

Even if we were momentarily to segregate the U.S. exterior from its interior markets and somehow bracket the forces marshaled in the repression of anticapitalism from Cuba to Vietnam, it remains a quandary why so many troops were needed to put down dissent in the streets and universities of this country, if consent were so firmly intact. Instead, what can be said about the eighties is that the discourse of consent collapses so that repression finds its way into those spaces thought able to police their own desires, especially family, domesticity, sexuality, and corporeality per se (bodies that, so to speak, stick to themselves).[82] This extension of rule by repression is rendered all the more complex in that the discourse of coercion properly effected through the state apparatus is ventriloquized by putatively private interests formally outside it, what could be called the New Right. In practice, the New Right's own confusion of public and private facilitated the circulation of its influence in the corridors of state power. The effort to limit what can be considered public, now enjoined by neoconservatives and neoliberals alike, gives a double meaning to the term "privatization." It is both a sell-off of social capital to profit interested corporations and an effort to deny political recognition to that whole range of voices and interests that had historically been considered part of the domestic purview of propertied white men. The scope of their ambition to regulate political economy through an attack on what they consider to be aberrant cultural expression has only increased and remains perhaps the most forcefully articulated idea in U.S. politics.[83]

Among social movements, the body is not always represented as the subject of the politics under consideration. Yet dance that is full of these politics offers not only the reflexive display of the body as a site of politics but something of the methodology of the social through which a political site is produced. The question that dance figures most forcefully for the debate is, What becomes of the status of the body when the conceptual divide between coercion and consent, public and private, state-centered and identity politics is complicated? This question does not assume that dance could be generative of a politics elsewhere but that it might provide a more comprehensive grasp of those conditions under which politics is already inscribed but scarcely legible through existing figures of analysis. Let me return to *Last Supper* to rehearse how some of these connections in a given work could be made available as a more general narrative for the reading of history.

A Reception for Overreading

Last Supper at Uncle Tom's Cabin/The Promised Land moves, like this essay, through a range of narratives that suggest a complex array of temporalities for theory and practice (sited/cited/sighted in the same textualized event — essay and dance — but dependent on different scales and sequences of time). Four moments can be discerned very schematically (to avoid overstating their separation) and are ordered sequentially but in practice permeate both dance and essay as a movement. To begin, both dance and essay use a particularized narrative (that of *Uncle Tom's Cabin* and the descriptive account of the dance itself). Each then moves to a contextualization of the reception for that narrative (the play with authority, especially in the second act, which anticipates the tropes of criticism that seek to contain the politics of dance which are themselves discussed in the second section of this essay). Next, essay and dance offer a contextualization of the grounds and constituent features of that narrative. The oppositions of sacred-profane/slavery-emancipation in the dance and the presumed oppositions of art and life, representation and practice, all become problematized when their normativity is dislodged. Finally, both works undertake a reflection on the possibility for theory itself with a renewed appreciation of the context for practice. The final act of the choreography presents the possibility of dancing beyond the dance into the promised land, a certain utopia of the real, and the politics that might emerge beyond the conceptual division of old and new social movements are explored. Hopefully, the cumulative effect of these moments would point toward the prospects for overreading dance.

Like self-critical theory, Jones's piece arrives at the point of grasping its own conditions of possibility in the display of the social body as the very product of the evening's work. In it, a virtual inventory of crossings was signaled — from slavery as private property (under the whip of Legree or the jail cell of Allen's rap) to freedom (of and from dancing) in the publicity of the social body; from the profanation of the sacred (the ready appropriation of a private religious language in Jones's duet with his mother or the local cleric) to the deprofanation of the secular (in the reverie of communal nudity);[84] from cross-gendering to degendering, racial transgression to deracialization, dance labor that circulates across style to the end of that labor; from masking, with its intimation of something private, to the loss of that ground for split representation. Each of these is foregrounded during certain times in the piece, but they all circulate throughout it, indicating a complex and differential economy of narrative temporalities in which stories that reference different scales of historical time and experience can be told and exchanged.

And yet, if the piece managed to locate each of these positions and trace through their politics as an account of transformation, it also demonstrated the totalization of context (that is, the process by which the contours of the whole social formation are made legible) that made these various specificities possible. That is, the dance itself provides a context within which to imagine the social and historical horizons where apparently disparate politics emerge and the conditions under which such politics might coalesce without disappearing into one another. The dance narrates together the times of many historical tales which span different scales of time (Christianity, slavery, civil rights, sexual liberation, rightist triumphalism) and which suggest a means to narrate the historical context for the dance and for contemporary politics as well.

By the very fact of its completability, the performance could represent the tension between the local and the global carried through the mobilization of bodies against the domineering presence of choreography itself (necessary, no doubt, to assemble the constituent elements and sustain a work of this scale). Yet to speak of the dance's representation this way is to identify not its internal narrative but rather what ends its tale serves. Dance cannot generate a narrative of context, a history, unmediated by that context. Rather, the theorized particular (made palpable through performance) is the only site in which that larger frame is made coherent. Even in a work as strongly narrative as *Last Supper*, the refusal to be only narrative helps navigate a way through the stories that conventionally get told about the present and also points beyond those common tales.

Overreading suggests a closer affiliation between form and context than was previously thought to be the case in much cultural criticism and history. The particular move toward social and historical context that dance signals (perhaps unexpectedly for some) winds up mapping the traces of its own possibility. This is why it may be worth the effort to fight the rhetoric of bust that signals lowered expectations for everything from the dance world to the American dream, even while struggling against the displacement of material resources that make the production of dances and dreams so challenging. If, even in its own excesses, a given work of dance generates a larger fund of aspiration than it can sustain in a single performance, it retains the capacity to bail itself out of the arresting strictures of the bust or breakdown in its own system by reappearing under a different guise. For while a given performance ends, it frequently recurs on another occasion, marking a continuity in the desire to see more than a moment can provide, which is itself a crucial resource for ongoing entanglement with the political. A single work can thereby serve to join the figuration of diverse social mobilizations in a dance before they can fuse in practice. The concreteness of bodies moving onstage, which serve as the agents of this confluence of ideas, is, as Marx observed in the *Grundrisse,* the result of the "concentration of multiple determinations."[85] What is assembled through these movements are not only specific bodily forms but also the very capacity to make momentarily present the whole context of determination itself and, with this, the ability to generate other contexts.

Offering a theory that combines the politics of production and reproduction, labor and identity, public and private, all of which supposedly divide new and old social movements against each other, however, provides no guarantee of the oppositional strength that those combined forces can wield globally. Theorizing combination does not render each instance of practice a realization of the theory. Nor should the impulse to combination detectable in a single dance work be misidentified as a totalizing framework that exhausts further readings of it. Rather, a desire for totalization is part of what makes reading inexhaustible. The process that figures the context within which diverse political impulses are combined, or totalization, is but one gesture within Jones's "promised land," but one with the capacity to amplify the shared context for social transformation that may be scarcely legible from within a given political expression. The terror that a gesture of amplification might become the only gesture, that totalization would monopolize and restrict the proliferation of social energies rather than, more modestly, coordinating difference, has sometimes operated in contemporary discourse to threaten the imagination of what is other than the present.[86] Yet in dance there is a certain insistence that the forces of combination that give a sense of context never ossify into a fixed framework of totality, a rigid image of the whole. Further, the diversity of influences that are displayed in any instance of movement keeps alive the tension between concrete particulars and, under the sign of choreographic authority, the totalizing moment.

This amplifying gesture of totalization, one could say, is the utopia that winds up being particularized momentarily but concretely in performance. Performance is utopian precisely in its intimation of an entirely different world that flashes through this one. This is not a utopia that one could move into but a passing state that takes the fleeting movement toward emergent possibilities as its own. While the archetypal utopian community had to retire someplace where no others could see it, the politicality of dance (which is surely not all of it) places utopia on display with all its possibilities and limitations. By making more of each instance of dance (or any other activity) than it could possibly claim for itself, the desire is expressed for an economy other than the one productive of endlessly regressive cycles of scarcity and deficit. It is this desire, this promised land, that partners theory and practice.

3   The Composite Body of Dance:
Re(w)rapping the Multicultural Nation

"Why waste your time, you know you're gonna be mine." The nation calling? Or just the music to a fitness warm-up? As the tune changes, the
assumed shapes matter. In what follows, I explore whether some of the linkages between "nationalism" and "multiculturalism" that would transform
the prevailing usages of those terms can be exposed through two very specific cultural practices—hip hop moves taught in an aerobics class, and rap
music video. While the politics of rap are far from unproblematic and have
been subjected to some very incisive and instructive criticism,[1] I will entertain, through the embodied promise of hip hop, a certain "structure of
feeling"[2] that is generative of national difference. This search for an emergent *societal* sensibility, couched in nationalist terms, is significant precisely
at this moment of a hegemonic reconfiguration in the ideology and political
economy not simply of the United States as a nation but of the entire global
system of nation-states as well.

In my analysis of multiculturalism, I am privileging the category of race
because of its centrality in the constitution of national identity in the United
States. I do this with the awareness that as multiculturalism has been main-
streamed, its conventional uses have greatly confused matters. As a watch-
word in the circuits of media and policy, multiculturalism has alternately
been deployed to reduce all cultural difference to racial categorization; to
displace the political economy of racial divisions with narrowly defined cultural expressivity; or to omit racism from consideration of the national
polity altogether. I seek to avoid both the reductions and the elision by
sustaining the tension between the specificity of a particular historical formation (in this case race) and its operation within the whole field of cultural difference (here, multiculturalism). Acknowledging the dilemma of
continual (mis)appropriation of the critical vocabulary of an oppositional

political project by forces hostile to its politics, Wahneema Lubiano reminds us, "We cannot give up the ground because of what they can do in the name of the ground on which we have chosen to fight."[3] Hopefully, elements of a nationalism and multiculturalism that efface the power of this nation-state's racist imaginary may begin to emerge from these two nonreducible but related moments of an internally differentiated hip hop culture.

The articulation between nationalism and the global framework of nation-states, posed by the ideological confluence of foreign and domestic policy, will serve as the point of reference to join two questions concerning the conceptualization of nationalism. First, if nations are historical and not natural phenomena that must constantly reconstruct their basis for existence as human communities, what principle of societal association gets asserted in the process? Second, what are the practical means for communicating and insinuating this historically bounded assertion of societal order as nation in the everyday lives of the populace? The first question assumes that nationalism is ideological without specifying the content of that ideology. The second suggests that ideological form must be realized through some material communicative practice and technology. That neither the specificity nor relation of ideological form and content can be assumed from the fact of any given nationalism opens up possibilities from which politics spring. In the case of rap and hip hop, the analysis of "form" and "content" (to the extent these terms remain conceptually distinct) of a particular expression may produce diverse images of nationalist politics.

One could say that multiculturalism of a certain sort is at least as old as nation-states, particularly if the exclusion of some cultural difference that resides on national ground, but is considered alien to it, is taken as a founding moment for a national polity. Yet the present manifestation of multiculturalism represents a recognition by the state itself of a certain discrepancy between the fictitious unity proclaimed by the nation-state, and the multiplicity of identity which that state must now contain if it is to retain its legitimacy as the warden of a national entity. In this regard multiculturalism marks and divides a double relationship. From the perspective of the state attempting to police a national monoculture, it is the refusal of any given identity to be contained within the center, to abide by the institutional boundaries by which the state allots recognition (a predicament from which social movements themselves are by no means immune, insofar as recognition and other material resources are mutually constitutive). From the perspective of those multiple identities, it is the insistence on the unruly polyvocality of difference that hints at what is formative not of nations but of society. Between these two perspectives lies the politics of recognition — the state seeking to determine the form of what gets recognized, versus the multicultural forces that are themselves agencies of self-recognition.

In the present context, multiculturalism is not only the name given to cultural diversity but also the terrain where opposing ideologies of culture are in contention. When multiculturalism is deployed as a negative point of reference (a bad other or an ontological threat) to consolidate the new order, it is as a discourse and as a political economy of racialization. This political economy wields race in word and deed as a principal means for dividing society, seeking legitimation in no small part by treating the divisions within society as natural consequences of the differences among cultural groups. By means of these racial divides, those who are as authentically domestic as any others are linked to the foreign, both in terms of their origins and therefore fidelity to the national way of life and in terms of some putative cultural association to whatever ails peoples in less resource-full parts of the world.

To reimagine nation along more fully multicultural lines, I propose a conception of body not as a stable presence already available for appropriation but as a composite entity mediated across a conflicted space of the imaginary (literally the representational domain where images appear) and the performative (the practical means through which imaginary forms are enacted). Dance both appears in the conjuncture of imaginary and performative spaces and puts the constitutive features of a composite body on display. For dance is both a bodily practice that figures an imagined world and a momentary materialization through performance of social principles that otherwise remain implicit. In particular, hip hop moves are constituted across very different kinds of space laminated together to configure a composite body. While the electronic media provide a mapped virtual space in which bodies can circulate, these composite bodies always seem to be getting away, disappearing in the moment of reception only to reappear in altered form in that virtuality.

The idea of a composite body may invoke associations with the bionic synthesis of flesh and machine or the cybernetic hybrid that rejects the dualism of nature and culture.[4] Whatever its debts to these notions, the image of a composite body operates on a slightly altered conceptual terrain that seeks to grasp the very motion of cultural processes that emanate from different sources and never fully come to rest. It is a body that is not one but multiple, not a being but a principle of association that refuses the neat divide of self and society, of the personal and the mediated, of presence and absence. The composite body is less an empirical type than a heuristic for thinking the physical constitution of complex social relations. Although all dancing bodies come to us live and already mediated, these two dimensions of bodily composition are quite vividly on display in a practice such as hip hop. Here, the debts to both immediate enactment and the images from distant airwaves are more difficult to deny than they may be with those arts of dance that are sometimes said to spring directly from a singular body of origin. For multiculturalism as a critical perspective rather than a government policy, the composite body allows us to focus on how difference is associated among those assembled in the nation, rather than being forced to sort out one body from another.

In this chapter I examine two moments in the larger process of production of this composite body: its dissemination as image in the rapper Ice Cube's music video *Wicked* (1992) broadcast on the music television channel MTV's weekly program *Yo, MTV Raps;* and a seemingly discrete site of reception for hip hop, an Orange County, California, fitness club aerobics class that I attended twice each week for some five months in 1993. These are juxtaposed to the conventional means through which an image of the monocultural nation is constructed—namely, the nightly television news broadcast, which relies heavily on racial representations, particularly, of crime, that are set off against other segments such as sport and entertainment.

My purpose here is not to take *Wicked* as representative of rap music video, nor to take the aerobics class as typical of how the nonblack population relates to hip hop culture, nor to graph the effects of the former on the latter, for I suggest that the relations of racial appropriation are more complex than any simple model of cultural translation would allow. Rather, my aim is to specify how instances of popular culture are situated in and figurative of a certain multicultural and national context, a context that mediates their relationship but one in which, for the most part, persons who attach to practical instances (songs, videos, dance or fitness clubs) never actually meet except in the present scene of writing where I attempt to imagine their connection. This connection based on things that never actually meet, what I describe later on as "weak links," applies not only to the music video that is never heard or seen in the aerobics class but also to so much of what passes through the largely impersonal space of the nation. This, then, is a study of how impersonal or mediated forces—those which never meet face-to-face—produce concrete effects. The understanding of mediated relations, irrespective of the medium through which they pass, is crucial if the idea of society is to have any purchase.

For myself, I am tracing the contours of my own composite body through this one mediating link, because the study of culture in capitalist society is precisely the study of such mediations. The spirit of this inquiry is to consider my own suspicions about the demonization of nationalism (which as an internationalist of a certain stripe I am susceptible to) and multiculturalism (of which I am a partisan in search of practical affiliation) to see what may be repressed in them. By reflecting on my own process of incorporation into the body politic, I am mapping the scene of what mobilizes my affinities and affiliations within the multicultural nation.

Nationalism and the Global Order of Coercion

As the seemingly uninvited guests of the new world order, a barrage of nationalisms (ideologies, movements, political formations) have been tearing at the claim that we are living through a happy, if hasty, consolidation of global society. As with the Communism of old, there is still a specter stalking, but unlike Marx's formulation in the *Communist Manifesto,* this specter appears to be not just haunting Europe but also disquieting its old colonial haunts. While these nationalist impulses may threaten to fracture the unifying consciousness of a new *global* order, it should be clear that they are the negative point of reference for a particular *nationalist* project, that of the United States, which takes as its own interest the role of capital's global guardian. For the United States, at least, anticommunism animated the ideology of how America came to be seen in the world, but anticommunism was also intended to make it impossible to speak of labor's domestic desire in political terms that were fundamentally opposed to capital. I would like to suggest that nationalism, when it is encoded for consumption at home as multiculturalism (though more can be placed under this sign), effects a similar slippage of foreign and domestic policy. What is at stake politically in this slippage, however, are the principles used for encoding the policy toward foreigners with precisely what the state finds difficult to manage domestically.

Yet multiculturalism can also name the aspiration for a postracial constitution of difference. By postracial I simply mean that the structures of institutional division by race would yield to a societal context for identification in which associations formed by people through all manner of activities would be mutual and self-constituting. A postracial politics does not preclude an ongoing cultural or historical significance for racial or other categories of identification. Rather, this postracial politics acts against the history that made racial classification such a fundamental aspect of colonialism. Further, it is implicitly internationalist in that the attainment of national sovereignty as a defense against divisive and appropriative incursions to which a population or territory is subjected would no longer be necessitated for the articulation of any people's process of identification and differentiation.[5] What complicates this discourse is the tension between the historical formulations of race as tied to the biological and ideas of culture as linked to some notion of civilizational destiny. One risk of multiculturalism is to efface this history by subsuming race to culture, where the latter is simply an attribute shared by all members of a national polity.

The global proliferation of nationalisms against the singularizing national project of the United States already indicates that the time when nationhood could be imagined to be sufficient as a condition for even limited societal and cultural development may have already passed. For now the one (nation-state) is attempting to excise the (national) others from its own body politic by weaving an attribution of societal decline through a narrative of crime, race, immigration, and scarcity. Rather than providing a model for development as such, these emergent nationalisms offer a newly displaced perspective on the relation between cultural and economic development. Taken together, the global emergence of so many nationalisms can be read against what is conventionally seen as *their* splintering impulse to figure a different principle of composition, association, and ordering of people in the world. To promote a more comprehensive understanding of present circumstances, it is not helpful to assume that every single instance of nationalism can be recruited to a counterhegemonic project (one that opposes what is coercive in the global order). Rather, it is the task of critical analysis to raise questions about the field within which the whole range of nationalist phenomena emerge, in an effort to locate what might constitute adequate terms of opposition.

Beyond the particular identity claims that are made for social groups, something of the context for identity lies entangled amid the repressed. Hence, precisely at a moment when nations and national boundaries are being violated on an unprecedented scale by forces as varied as markets and armies, questioning nationalism can reverse the moralizing binaries of international politics to reveal the identification of dominance. From within the United States, the spectacle of disorder attributed to those without globally legitimated state power has been offered as an object lesson whose truth (that so-called tribalism will succumb only to a rationalizing — read external — force) can now be applied with equal vigor to the domestic population, whether by better policing communities or incarcerating those who deviate.[6]

The representation of coercion as a force of reason is central to the current ideological conjuncture (though hardly new). Time and again, media images of violence perpetrated by those most subject to the disordering effects of the system are substituted for any portrayal of the coercive power of the system itself.[7] To the extent that this substitution is accepted ideologically, it assumes the place of a popular desire for state intervention to redraw society along racial or national lines. The problem of this generalized desire for coercive intervention (even if, like all desire, it remains unfulfillable) to reinforce boundaries (whether of nations or neighborhoods, domestic spaces or private properties) that have supposedly been transgressed underlies so much of the racialized narrative of crime. (Although this narrative is decidedly gendered as well; consider, for example, the daily discursive allotment of street crime to black men in the public sphere and a version of domestic crime attributed to the very existence of pregnant teenagers and welfare mothers — typically portrayed as black and unwed.)[8] This incessant overrepresentation of crime — even as crime rates decline, whereas incarceration numbers increase — provides the ideological grounds for the isomorphic identification of foreign and domestic policy along the newly redrawn racialized lines of those who savage society's order and whose presumed wildness can be tamed only by applications of state violence.[9]

Disentangling Multiculturalism

Within the United States, multiculturalism is treated, by its critics and among some of its proponents, as a nationalist expression (black, Chicano, Puerto Rican, Hawaiian) without the power of a state that can undermine the claims to cultural sovereignty that support the prevailing political order. So too, critics and proponents can contest the notion of a single, monolithic culture that bounds and bonds the nation.[10] Clearly, the challenge to the idea of a uniform national character has many inflections and tendencies. Some appear to present a mirror reflection of what they oppose, particularly if it is said that a nation is composed of many cultures, but each is essentially and internally the same.[11] Yet the views which I find most valuable and which dispute the claim of a national monoculture accept diversity as residing both among and within cultures. National culture is conventionally understood as a set of collectively identifying attributes shared by a group of people. Following from this perspective of culture as a set of common values, one could presumably discover America in the features of a typical American. But, surely, such a procedure would produce a portrait of exclusion, a face of one that would leave others outside it. Once the definition of culture as a common content that defines a population is accepted as credible, the result is likely to be a conception of identity that is as rigidly homogenous.

If national culture or cultural attributes are instead defined with respect to the socially and historically constituted context in which they are generated, the United States can sensibly be spoken of as one such context in which identity and difference are defined. The matter of how people fit into that larger social setting, however, is by no means settled by invoking the name of the country where people live. The problem in need of explanation is how processes of identification operate within the national context to establish the range of diversity through which people come to know themselves and act with respect to others. If multiculturalism makes any sense as a force that transforms nation-states rather than one that conserves either the privilege of or discrimination against a particular cultural grouping, it is as the theory of that national context and not as an assortment of supposedly discrete minor monocultures held out against some putative national majority.

To realize the critical possibilities of multiculturalism, one must first appreciate that the meaning of the term is far from settled. It then becomes possible to enter into a contest over the various conceptual deployments of the term within the scene of national politics.[12] Given the increasing currency of its corporate, administrative, and monocultural manifestations in public discussion and institutional practice, simply flying the banner of multiculturalism is no guarantee of a critical and renovative politics committed to both diversity as national identity and substantive inclusion in the design of social life.[13]

Part of what makes the use of the term "multiculturalism" so complex in contemporary discussions is that the grounds for embracing or rejecting it differ so dramatically. Multiculturalism has developed into an entire discursive field capable of classifying positions (of both proponents and opponents) as conservative, liberal, and radical.[14] But these positions clearly do not compete in some grand supermarket of ideas. Rather, multiculturalism as a concept circulates within institutional and discursive arrangements, such as media, schools, and legislatures, that eclipse the very political differences the concept was intended to mark in the first place. More specifically, the state has acted to convert the demands of social movements (from civil rights onward) into entitlements that can be disbursed individually, upon verification of the citizen-subject's identity. Surely, this attempt at decollectivization has cut in both directions, as more and more kinds of demands can be directed at the state for redress. Hence discussing multiculturalism can itself generate enormous slippage of just what identities, issues, and frameworks are being considered.

Surely, such confusion is promoted when culture is defined exclusively from the perspective of commonality rather than as the very incorporation of diversity, as, for example, when culture is taken to be what demarcates one group from another or one kind of practice from others considered political or economic. If culture is taken simply as a certain type of practice or an identifying boundary of a group, then culture can be constructed as external to political economy. Once the discursive and institutional division of practices and groups is accepted, it is possible to define one culture as normative and see it as contaminated by another, to take culture as an autonomous sphere of the life-world (from which cultural values issue) which can be colonized by the instrumental reason that dominates the capitalist political economy, or to suggest that culturally inflected politics replace structural transformations of society altogether.[15] Each of these positions may critique multiculturalism for different reasons, but they all accept the conception of culture as an array of activities shared by a group that set the group apart from society as a whole. The picture of society as one that is composed of cultural groups (or communities), on the one hand, and social structures, on the other, recalls the sociological conceptions of *Gemeinschaft* (community) and *Gesellschaft* (society) that were enlisted by Ferdinand Julius Tönnies and Emile Durkheim, and many who followed in the twentieth century, to account for modernization itself. Community is here invested with an archaic status as the repository of traditional particularisms that are surpassed by the universal rationalization wrought by modern society. Community can then become an object of nostalgia, rather than being the associational aspect produced within contemporary society.

At the most general level of understanding, culture is the principle of association present in all forms, sites, and expressions of social practice, not simply a particular type of practice. Culture animates social movements and political parties; it is what moves people in the workplace and at home, what drives the experience of love and death. This conception of culture relates to a sociological perspective in which the production and circulation of value (economic) and the regulation and articulation of contradiction (political) are, like culture, aspects of all social activity. The workplace may be a privileged site for the production of value, and the dance club, a scene where identity is noticeably mobilized — that is, it is meaningful to speak of economic and cultural institutions — but the practices that these settings organize should be grasped as all sharing economic, political, and cultural dimensions.

It follows from this understanding of how society works that multiculturalism cannot be seen merely as the diversity that delineates one group from another but as the contest over how diversity mobilizes the entire process of identification. Part of that battle concerns how multiculturalism is recognized as a political force, one version of which focuses on what gets recognized as a legitimate cultural entity. The politics of recognition can then take for granted the stability and legitimacy of the institutional forces, namely, the state, which is in the unique position to grant recognition to those presumably without the means to recognize themselves. Recognition is a resource possessed by the state rather than a cultural capacity generated by those demanding recognition.[16] This officializing version of multicul-turalism is appealing to conservatives and liberals who enjoy government prerogative insofar as the state remains sole arbiter of what and who re-ceives recognition. Hence, whether the debates center on the curriculum, civil rights, health care, or employment, diversity will always end up being contained within the regulatory apparatus of the state. For the state, diver-sity will be treated as a problem to be administered and managed, like all others, whose importance is measured by the funds disbursed to solve it.

The homogenizing powers of recognition (by which the welfare state, such as it is, individualizes structural and historic inequities as social prob-lems of disadvantaged persons that can then be rectified through govern-ment administration and assistance) attempt to confine multiculturalism to the monocultural protocols of the nation-state. What is omitted from dis-cussion is a different politics altogether — that is, the contention over what would count as recognition. If the means of recognition are not assumed to be monopolized by the state, some of the powers of granting recognition to multicultural practice could be transferred to and through critical analysis. With this transfer of power, principles of association may begin to emerge that compromise the claim to universal recognition vested in the state's self-legitimating authority to arbitrate all difference within the nation.

National Minds and Bodies

National states have only ever been composed of many distinct cultural groups and identities. And yet national identities are themselves projected, to both citizens and foreigners, as if they made up some coherent whole, a unity. Given the actual cultural diversity within national borders, such claims of unitary identity can only be fictitious (that is, cultural inscriptions with political effects) or, in the words of Benedict Anderson, "imagined communities." For Anderson, "fiction seeps quietly and continuously into reality, creating the remarkable confidence of community in anonymity which is the hallmark of modern nations."[17]

Because nation, as a geopolitical unit, is stamped with the highest value in the global currency of identity and marked with the greatest freedom from external sources of exploitation, struggles articulated through multicultur-alism as an oppositional form of self-recognition through difference can themselves take on the calling of national formation. This observation seems consistent with Paul Gilroy's claim that "the politics of 'race' in this country is fired by conceptions of national belonging and homogeneity which not only blur the distinction between 'race' and nation, but rely on that very ambiguity for their effect." [18] As in other articulations of culture and political economy, the United States appears to follow Britain (Gilroy's "this country") down the road of imperial decline. But the very different global projection of the United States would seem to indicate that racialization here is more than a national effect. As such, this racialization raises the possibility that formations like "black cultural nationalism" are something other than the "inversion" of their hegemonic counterpart that Gilroy suggests.[19]

It is not that a politics of racial exclusion could counter the global effects of capital in an era of decline in the system of national states. Rather, analysis of nationalism cannot simply begin from within. Any call for separation must be read in the context of, first, a prior penetration of global forces (the trajectories of colonialism and imperialism) into the terrain of a given population and, second, a subsequent flight from or expropriation of what is valuable in that terrain, both of which sustain ongoing relations of underdevelopment. In this regard, the collective self-centeredness, or centrism, of certain cultural nationalisms cannot be seen as equivalent to the centers of state power that organize hierarchies of identity along racial lines, for that centrism is an effect of a racializing hierarchy and not generative of it. Such rhetoric of centrism must be placed within a multicultural frame to indicate the attempt to assert ground within a field of difference from which an identity could be voiced. Juxtaposing one conception of nation to another exposes the violent complicity of the state in the process of racialization and points to some other location from which the imagining of community could take place.

While the state concentrates violence, even terror must seek some distance from what it terrorizes. This is one reason why the sociologist Max Weber understood the state as the monopolization of the legitimate means of violence.[20] Because state violence can always be applied to a population, legitimation would seem to rest on the ability to imagine that violence will be applied elsewhere, generating both the anonymity of association and "remarkable confidence" in community that Anderson described. He also appreciates that imagination must have a means of constitution and expression and that it must link together a desire for association, an acceptance that power is exercised, and an experience of the movement of that particular form of society as the only possible means for the passage of time.

In chapter 3 of *Imagined Communities,* Anderson locates this massive and multiple process of ideological coordination in the ability for the representation of collectivity to circulate within a given population, creating a means of participation in the process of national self-reflection. He calls the political economy of information that supports the apparatus of imagined communities and precedes electronic mass media by several centuries "print-capitalism." Accordingly, cultural production in general and the production of the written word in particular become both a site of capital accumulation and a means of its extension. This capitalization of culture assumes that the control over writing that had delimited the state from the rest of the body politic and had defined the state's hold on truth now passes into a more general circulation of the written word, through books and newspapers, that will serve to recognize the necessity of the state. As a strategy for constituting state power, writing shifts from an interiority to an exteriority, from a self-containing technique monopolized by those directly affiliated with the state to a more general ideological economy that stands formally outside the state in order to justify it.[21]

Here Anderson has gone a long way toward bringing cultural processes into the center of political economy, as well as articulating the materiality of cultural forms with something like a mode of production. But he seems to take the persistence of nationalism as evidence that the cultural processes work in the way he describes, hence introducing the possibility of granting to nationalist ideology the unifying effects that it seeks for itself in practice. One question that can be raised is who and what is excluded in a given instance of print capitalism's circulating representation. Anderson claims that the experiential dimension of the nationalist project is most clearly consolidated in the novel.

Yet, one might ask how well this theory of nationalism travels when applied to other parts of the globe and whether theories generated from situations that have experienced colonialism can deepen an understanding of nationalist yearnings in the United States, which, after all, was once itself on the other side of the colonial divide. For example, John Rowe and Vivian Schelling, writing about Latin America, have puzzled over the efficacy of such forms of nationalist ideology (even as they are quick to identify the nationalism of Latin American literary output) for countries with vast non-literate populations or where mass literacy comes after national formation. They have pointed instead to popular culture, from religious figures such as the Virgin of Guadalupe to political ones like Simón Bolívar, as the circulating images for collective self-reflection.[22] Roger Bartra, reflecting on Mexico, understands well the cultural effectivity of the state project when he says:

> The nation state is the most traveled and at the same time the most impenetrable domain of modern society. We all know that those black lines on the political maps are like the scars of unremitting war, plundering and conquest; but we also suspect that, in addition to the state violence upon which nations are founded, there are strange, age old forces of a cultural and psychological nature that trace the frontiers separating us from strangers. These subtle forces, subjected to the harshness of economic and political oscillations, are nevertheless responsible for the opacity of the phenomenon of nationhood. Among other things, this opacity obscures the profound motives that lead men to tolerate a system of domination and, by the forbearance they display, to give a seal of legitimacy to injustice, inequality, and exploitation.[23]

In the twentieth century, cinema, television, comic books, and video constitute these "subtle forces" arrayed against the unnuanced presence of a "system of domination." Among Bartra's contributions to the discussion is an appreciation of how nationalism circulates between the levels of the popular and the dominant. It is crafted out of a "handful of stereotypes codified by intellectuals, the traces of which are, however, reproduced in society, creating the illusion of a popular mass culture."[24] For Bartra, nationalism is sustained by a certain antimodernist impulse that gets thrown up in the face of modernization. But for him this antimodernism is ultimately an imaginary figure that is impossible to sustain, and its collapse hints at an anticapitalism that the nationalist intellectuals (of Mexico at least) had refused.

People such as Anderson, J. A. Armstrong, and Anthony Smith view nationalism as more tenacious, the latter two especially because they trace it to cultural formations that antedate and are sustained through capitalism.[25] Whether or not one can find more continuity than reconfiguration in these nationalist tropes over time, the question of whether one can see the nation-state as containing a single nationalist ideology remains problematic. As Aijaz Ahmad suggests, we may be better off picking our nationalisms on the basis of their particular politics in a global context that renders nationalism a central idiom of historical shifts of any sort (a point that would now seem to hold for multiculturalism as well). "The issue of nationalism is much more difficult to settle, because nationalism is no unitary thing, and so many different kinds of ideologies and political practices have invoked the nationalist claim that it is always very hard to think of nationalism at the level of theoretical abstraction alone, without weaving into this abstraction the experience of particular nationalisms and distinguishing between progressive and retrograde kinds of practices." [26] With respect to postcolonial situations, Partha Chatterjee has grasped the double bind of seeking national autonomy by securing a place within the system of global capital. According to Chatterjee, political expressions may critique the language of Enlightenment discourse while succumbing to its effects. He notes, "There too the fragility of the forced resolution by nationalism of the contradiction between capital and the people-nation is shown up." [27]

For the United States, the most politically interesting and complex nationalist expressions have emanated from those quarters closest to postcoloniality, especially from the African American community. Spike Lee's film *Malcolm X,* based on the life of the figure with the greatest contemporary resonance for issues of black nationalism, illustrates the intricate relation between the form and content of nationalist ideology. I would insist that the entire racist formation of the United States and the Reagan-Bush-Clinton racializing terror (from their fiscal policies to their campaign pronouncements) has to be included, along with the agency of cultural personae such as Lee, to account for Malcolm X's ongoing appeal among diverse sectors (and for different reasons) of the African American population. [28] In a recent collection of essays on Malcolm X, editor Joe Wood pointed to a reappropriation that proposes a counterhegemonic reception:

> We need to put Malcolm to better use. Malcolm, in the end, gave us no coherent ideology, but he did leave us a site for Black political discourse. Recently I asked Justice Thurgood Marshall what he thought of Malcolm, and he said, "All he did was talk." The Justice meant this ob-

servation as a complaint, but I see it as Malcolm's most appealing characteristic. He stands for Black talk about Black thinking; we use him as a starting point. We seek, as Malcolm did, to name ourselves, and we begin, as Malcolm did, with the Black mask given us. We take the baton from Malcolm: we take our humanity for granted, and we realize that our community is made up of people of all sorts of colors, genders, classes, ethnicities, sexualities, etc. We have always known that African Americans weren't the only niggers on this earth, and now we invite all other people who are oppressed to join us. . . . "Race" is a dying category; Whiteness, and the Blackness it makes for itself, is dying too. We will seize the day and make a new Blackness.[29]

The promise of Wood's comment is that blackness could be understood situationally rather than constitutionally. A nationalist project built on the former premise could only operate against the dominant language of nationalism offered by the latter term.[30] Implicit here is that nationalism would have to become a front of multiculturalism by recognizing difference as its constituting principle. Gianni Vattimo puts the matter well when he discusses the immediacy of encounter with "other worlds" that become possible in "a society of generalized communication and the plurality of cultures." As he says: "Other possibilities of existence are realized before our very eyes, in the multiplicity of 'dialects' and in the different cultural universes opened up by anthropology and ethnology. To live in this pluralistic world means to experience freedom as a continual oscillation between belonging and disorientation."[31] While we could wonder what language these "other possibilities" are dialects of (I would call it socialism) and whether "plurality" could refer to a present society so dependent on exclusion, Vattimo nonetheless can be read as pointing out what has become socialized under the current circumstances. He then adds the caveat that "we ourselves still do not have a clear idea of its [freedom's] physiognomy."[32]

I would suggest that physiognomy has been altogether too absent in discussions of freedom insofar as they assume the form of a nationalist project. A conception of nationalism as an embodied affiliation might temper the separatist impulses of national liberation (flights of freedom from the old order aimed at taking some possession of territory rather than a potentially more radical collective self-possession) with a fluency of movement on a terrain shared with others. Moreover, it is curious that in an ideological form often noted for its display of irrationalism, the analysis of national-ism's technologies would assume such a strong cognitive basis.

When we look at nationalism's strongest articulations, it is not at all apparent that reason is what holds the nation together. Although the en-forcement of boundaries may keep others out, there remains, beyond the question of legitimating the state, what keeps those within in touch (at least virtually) with one another, for even an imagined community must main-tain a sense of itself. Unlike the image of a national border, which presum-ably contains a static void, the real forces of society are constantly in motion. Yet the recognition of this social motion's materiality is scarcely recognized in the literature.[33]

It is as if the once vibrant notion of nation as the body politic had lost all its kinesthesia. Some of this may no doubt be the effect of choreogra-phy's slipping out through the palace gates, thereby rendering the relation of dance and state, body and nation, more opaque. But it may turn out that even if dance has lost the political instrumentality of its courtly manifesta-tions, it remains a place to locate the practical embodiment of nation. I will now turn to theorize this possibility, bearing in mind one of Homi Bha-bha's very suggestive formulations with the hope of applying it beyond the practice of writing on which his analysis depends: "The nation reveals, in its ambivalent and vacillating representation, the ethnography of its own his-toricity and opens up the possibility of other narratives of the people and their difference."[34]

Dance Nation

The double relationship of multiculturalism and nationalism—the state's containment of identity, which multiculturalism refuses, and the unruly polyvocality of difference, which it promotes—has certainly been present in dance.[35] In the most general terms, what precedes and follows dancing is the ongoing capacity for the differentiation of physical activity, namely, what is constitutive of the cultures of dance and dancers. It is this aspect of self-constituting differentiation, the creative energies assembled across dancers' bodies, that points to the capacity of dancers to make instances of society. Dance labors typically go unrecognized by the state and may be self-recognized exclusively in terms of making dances and therefore in a manner that minimizes their political efficacy. This unrecognized capacity for society that results from the encounter of difference is, from the perspective of those who create expressive forms, what might most properly be termed "multiculturalism." From the state optic, they neither are recognized for this capacity nor are means of representation adequate to promote their interest.

Popular culture (here conceived in terms of its circuits of expression rather than any determinate aesthetic content that would differentiate it from art more narrowly) can be said to be where production and reception of knowledge and aesthetics come together for the majority of the population. Here the state appears absent (according to current free market rhetoric), despite an uncanny willingness to prosecute signs of difference as if they were sources of social ills (for example, 2 Live Crew, the "obscene" rap group) [36] or as if they represent the world (as in the news coverage of the Gulf War). Nonetheless, it is in mass media and popular forms that the multicultural presence is most fully represented. Yet these abundant displays of difference (although certainly much difference is excluded from the most accessible venues of commercial representation) are often taken to be the very indicators of and explanations for social underdevelopment. Specifically, in the strident tones familiar to the disciples of reform for the laboring populations over the last two hundred years, the pleasures of popular culture are said to have eroded the work ethic (to say nothing of the social wage). In short, no matter how much difference is displayed in popular culture, for the disciplining gaze of production, it cannot amount to much. Suffice it to say that a consumer-driven economy runs into serious trouble when profitable acts of consumption are attacked as immoral. But this apparent immorality in the marketing of cultural forms sundered from a concern with their content, to which corporate agents express such hollow bafflement, reflects the very disarticulation of production and circulation that Marx identified so clearly.

It is important to identify a multiculturalism both of form and of content. Emblematic of such content is the emergence of hip hop culture among young African Americans and Latinos over the last two decades. While initially apparent in street forms such as break dancing and in clubs where contemporary rap developed out of the work of disc jockeys in the seventies, these expressions quickly found representation in mass media. The capacity of these circuits for appropriating images from emergent styles, again without respect to their use or context, is characteristic of commodified culture generally and, insofar as it results in extensive distribution, signifies capitalism's democratic promise. Yet appropriation presupposes control over some means of production, in this case cultural production. With respect to black popular culture — itself forced to confront a whole history of cultural appropriation — the claims to ownership over traditions of stylistic innovation come tinged with the politics of racial domination. Beyond the compensatory dimension to these cultural economies for those excluded from other circuits of capital, the demands and consequent capacities that are features of all cultural creativity attain a concentration and social reflexivity that informs particular aesthetic constitutions of blackness. In this regard, the generative capacity for innovation cannot be subsumed to the control over the dissemination of cultural output, what gets seen and heard in the marketplace.[37] In this larger respect, the trajectory of hip hop is unexceptional; rather, it is the context in which appropriation occurs where any novelty in the process must be assessed.

Indeed, within a few years of the appearance of break dance, it was performed before President Reagan at a national arts awards ceremony. By the end of the 1980s, it had left nary a trace on the streets. As Alan Light remarks, "Maybe it was just too obviously contrived to last, but the breakdancing sound and look quickly fell into self-parody — much of it was dated by the time it even got released."[38] Yet other dance styles continued to emerge from hip hop culture, in a generative capacity for style that was not exhausted by the incessant appropriations and commodifications. On the contrary, because hip hop emerged at the same moment as that visualization of sound, the music video, the image of African Americans especially was now expanded in the figuration of youth more broadly. Simon Jones has appreciated the constitution of youth culture across racial lines, which effectively "unleashed a new phase in the popularity of public dancing":

> From its very inception, the production and consumption of the "new" music was the site of a complex of power relations linking both black and white musicians and consumers to the entertainment industry. Those relations turned on the contradictions of using forms inherently opposed to white hegemony, and forged out of the experience of racial

oppression, as sources of meaning and pleasure. At the heart of them lay a fundamental tension between white youth's struggles for more responsive and articulate modes of cultural expression, and black musicians' struggles against white cultural and economic power to redefine their music. The result has been a unique cultural dialectic white appropriation and black innovation which has supplied one of the inner motors of popular music's evolution.[39]

While diverse in their own right, these images of youth generated through hip hop often suggested an ungovernable economy of motion, a pleasure in speed that does not find measurement in productivity, a celebration of the capacity for celebration. It is not that these qualities are adequate to specify hip hop moves, for these features can be found in other dance forms. Rather, they pertain to some of the generalized features of multiculturalism with respect to its refusal of containment through commodification and disappearance through appropriation.

This last claim would be particularly suspect if popular African American dance were confined to music video. Although MTV displays hip hop as part of its programming content, hip hop is a form of multiculturalism that occupies a range of public spaces. The rapid editing techniques used to represent contemporary popular dancing in video suggest bodies that are continually spliced, fragmented, pursued by the frame, and consummated beyond it. The resulting visual density of these videos assumes a kinesthetics of reception among bodies whose pleasures are taken through these mediatized paces. Indeed, these dancing bodies are composite bodies, part mediated image, part club-based referent, part Walkman interiorization. Given the emergence and reemergence of multicultural forms in the already represented spaces of popular culture, the body is never available for dancing as the authentic, original experience suggested by certain notions of modernism. This compositeness troubles the kind of originary tale told above in which hip hop is wrested from its humble beginnings to be selectively digested by the culture industry. For contemporary black popular culture is already inside of and penetrated by electronic media. Consider the following from what is generally taken as the most authoritative cultural history of hip hop:

> Street culture has always been a good sales pitch for pushing vicarious thrills on the market. For a brief pause in all the phoney realism of

Flashdance, the hyped up dance movie of 1983, one of the sources for Jennifer Beals' overblown dance routines comes to life. Like a revisitation of Bill "Bojangles" Robinson teaching Shirley Temple how to tap, the heroine takes in a few seconds of The Rock Steady Crew doing their robot routines in the park to the accompaniment of a huge portable tape box.

The music on the box is a hip-hop anthem — Jimmy Castor's "It's Just Begun" — a hard dance track from 1972 which fuses one-chord riffing, a Sly Stone pop bridge, fuzz guitar, timbales breaks and an idealistic lyric applicable to any emergent movement, be it dance, music, politics or religion. It gives an impression of the breadth of Jimmy Castor's music and its reflection of the New York mix, encapsulating an involvement which dates back to the beginning of rock and roll. [Castor himself had his start in music with Frankie Lymon in the 1950s.] [40]

One could go back to the formation of slave culture and its articulation of nationalism, as Sterling Stuckey has done, to trace influences that confound origins.[41] But as an intervention into a world saturated by mass media, the observation by Rush Communication's Carmen Ashhurst-Watson that rappers used turntables as instruments after music programs were cut from the schools is quite useful for thinking about the conditions of hip hop's emergence.[42] By the early nineties, some of the physical manipulation of recorded music displayed in scratching had become computerized in the relatively affordable sampling machines. And yet this reappropriation of the ability to sample material from across the cultural spectrum simulates, through its own capacity to construct an imaginary terrain, the very powers of the complex media-market-state constitutive of nation. This simulation creates a virtual community expressed in one volume of "hiphopology" as "nation conscious rap," a cultural emulation of what states accomplish without the powers to impose a sovereignty of exclusion by reason of territory or citizenship.[43] Hence, although there is nothing novel in the fact of cultural reappropriation, these current manifestations are constituted out of a penetration of national and global airwaves, that may insinuate a larger scale of imagined community than was available to the song and dance hybrids (jigs, tap, jazz, rock) of earlier times. Further, these prior appropriations occurred under the star of a framework of nation-states that was still in ascendance. With today's cracks in the edifice of national sovereignty increasingly visible, the pathways of appropriation may have changed. This only raises the stakes for cultural borrowings, whether in the direction of more strident exclusions and prohibitions or in the service of new grounds of affiliation.

That multicultural bodies are composite bodies, constituted across sites that are themselves fundamentally different from one another, hints at what is so disruptive about multiculturalism to any effort at appropriation or containment. In this regard, multiculturalism presents a radical difference of form and content, as the above example of hip hop dancing suggests. If this radicalism of cultural form is to be made available to politics, it might be useful for fuller reflection on those social relations made palpable through dance.

As I suggested at the opening of the chapter, I want to adopt a conception of a composite body as mediated across a space of the imaginary and the performative in order to rethink how nations are imagined. As imaginary, the media provide a mapped virtual space in which bodily identities can circulate. As performative, composite bodies elude any simple representation or appropriation. Before moving on to the workings of the composite body as it is figured in hip hop culture, I want to indicate the national geography of race in the ideological technology that the composite body is up against. For all its limitations, the most comprehensive figuration of nation in the media is the evening news. It could be said that the limitations of the news belie its principles of operation.

The very redundancy of the news, its repetition of formula, and its marking of the day's end provide a stability of representation that constitutes a field from which being called or interpellated into the nation becomes possible. The problem that this interpellation poses is above all that of scale. How can the enormous expanse of nation be reconciled with the privatizing limits of the citizen body? Insofar as it is a technology of national ideology, the news functions to invert the order of that national scale by reversing the spatial values of the globe with the internal temporality of programming. In effect, the smaller the scale, the longer the coverage. Twenty minutes of "local" news, two minutes of national, one minute of world, and the separate voices that mark the time of sports and weather typify the ratios of coverage in a half hour punctuated by the different spaces of advertising.

Taken together, the broadcast could be said to provide viewers with a map of their own emplacement in the world that also reduces that world in and to a single stroke. Sports reporting, too, narrates what are projected as local affiliations in the field of the national, and weather literally maps the process whereby an eye is placed on the national space as it converges on one's own backyard. The content of those twenty minutes of local stories, the unspeakable crimes brought to you live, are perpetrated by entities frequently described as savage, wild, or tribal.[44] The civilizing voice of the news anchors one at home by effectively racializing the space of the private so that irrespective of one's own racial identification, the domain beyond the private is a space of terror for all to fear.

This space of terror is, of course, the public sphere, where no demands can be made (we can only seek protection from it) and therefore no politics are possible. While the news is putatively local, the spatial hierarchies of affiliation, the very conformities of the genre across locality and network, establish it as a technology of nationalism. Negatively by the spaces its sanctions, as much as positively by the security offered through a placement in a virtual space, news locates the citizen body in the national field. The crime story, rather than being an account of what economic forces are doing to the country, becomes the most abiding figure for narrating the nation.[45]

This imputes a great deal to what the news signs and almost nothing about how it signifies to people. While its nationalizing strategy may be perfectly legible, the efficacy and effectivity of this strategy are more difficult to read. Nominating the news to lead the national imaginary does not mean its authority will be elected or its rule followed. However people attend to the news, they are implicated in the very transgressions it proscribes. For they do go out into the very public space that the news images as impassable and impossibly dangerous. They are unglued from the set. They even circulate unevenly through television's own offerings. This very unevenness suggests that on the same surface there can be a variety of reflections that permit different imaginaries of the virtual space of nation. Presumably these also set the composite bodies in motion in different ways (to say nothing of introducing different principles of composition).

One of the commodity forms to emerge in the uneven development of print capitalism is Music Television. Its emergence derived in part from the very weakening of a certain configuration of the technologies of nation extant at that moment—network television and the music industry. As Lisa Lewis has argued, the appearance of cable television had already signaled a

move from mass to segmented markets in the emergence of demographically driven programming.[46] This, in the midst of what Ernest Mandel called
the "second slump" of capital (the global economic downturn of the mid-
seventies) but which could be viewed in less economistic terms as a conjuncture formed internationally by the U.S. defeat in Vietnam; the oil crisis
created by the response of the Seven Sisters (energy multinationals) to
the Organization of Petroleum Exporting Countries (OPEC); capital's flight
from labor and the cities and the connected decline of labor's standards of
living; Reagan's first presidential bid; and so on.[47] Demographically targeted
marketing could be seen as print capitalism's attempt to recoup culturally
the fragmented critical publics of the 1960s, now redubbed the baby boom-
ers. The panic in the music industry over declining profits established the
other component for the creation of MTV in 1981. While commodification
was hardly new to rock and roll, its doubling in the music video had a certain appeal in an industry that had to focus anew on its own problems of
realizing value (selling its products). Yet with production now coming from
outside the conventional television studio system, the permeability of programming to the vagaries of the popular only increased.

Although MTV began with quite narrow and exclusionary musical selec-
tivities, its own marketing drives introduced certain openings so that the
forces of internal differentiation would belatedly yield programming even
for such African American popular forms as rap. Rap, in the words of one
of its prime movers, Public Enemy's Chuck D, is already the equivalent of
"black television . . . a network for communication."[48] Rap, it turns out, is
as internally diverse as any other cultural form. Among its variations, however, are some of the more critically minded instances of popular culture.
The particular instance I want to examine here is Los Angeles–based rapper Ice Cube's music video *Wicked*. It is intriguing both for the imagination
of a (dancing) body for nationalism and multiculturalism and for the way
it functions intertextually (as television so extensively does) in relation to
music videos generally and the claims broadcast news makes as history-in-
the-making.

Positively "Wicked"

When a record is put on a turntable to play, there is a tangible space between
cuts, a ring of silence, that separates and frames each tune in that field called

listening. Compact discs seem to have turned that opening into an edge, a perforation that nonetheless serves as a distinguishing mark between what are assumed to be discrete aesthetic units. The way a music video is inserted into its field of reception lacks the temporal seriality of its aural counterpart. Beginnings are difficult to discern. Because one is already looking and at a box that makes implicit (although infinitely interruptable) claims on focus, the start of a video seems to have already happened when one attempts to notice it. The density of change in the visual field renders the perception of difference difficult to identify as a marker of an autonomous aesthetic object. Music video in its broadcast format takes advantage of these circumstances for viewing to present an aesthetic form that emerges intermittently from its cultural context — that is, whose form and content force the periodic display of that context. This is not to say that all music videos begin in the same way but that they share a problem of beginnings as what gets them started.

The origins of Ice Cube's *Wicked* lie way beyond what is perceivable on the screen, no matter how much repetition it is subjected to. Indeed, the elusiveness of exactly where it is coming from invites a certain repetition of viewing that mimics some of the work's own internal tropes. The kinesthetics of performance and reception are thereby joined in ways unanticipated in other media. The first words — more indecipherably textural than textual ("boom, boom, boom, zoom-zoom . . . 007, James Bond") — are churned out at an incredible pace. In grainy footage, a young black man is visible being pushed into the back of a car. Two white youths run across the screen. A searchlight scans a neighborhood. A black man holds his head. A jet flies over. Black boys run through rubble. The jet again. A man wears a T-shirt that bears the message, "L.A.P.D. 'We Treat You Like a King.'" "Wicked" is the first signifier to achieve full audibility. Barely seven seconds have passed. This is the pace kept over a little less than four minutes. A lot of ground is covered. You're expected to stay put.[49]

I kept putting it on. Dozens of times. The speed of the video splintered the illusion of cyborg fusion between myself and the video screen. I would attempt to catch a detail (like what the T-shirt said) and hit the pause button only to miss the picture. The labor of intellectuals was here mired in the machine and forced to confront its manual dependencies and inadequacies. Trying to stop the flow put me out of time. This temporal conundrum is a process Sean Cubitt has uniquely attributed to video, the "timeshift." Whereas television presents the prospect of national simultaneity whose real time is demolished by videocassette recorder, with timeshift, TV is no longer a slave to the metaphysics of presence.[50] Because a mass-broadcast video recording cannot be watched for the first time, the spectacle of viewing is shifted out of the eternal present from the immediate authority of the symbolic to the "variable capital" of the imaginary. As such, video (here in significant departure from its documentary functions and conventions discussed in Chapter 1) bears a certain resemblance to history, because it "remembers the process, the hard work of forgetting" but also "has the potential to be less a medium of forgetting and more a medium through which is recorded what has already been lost, the memory of absences which once motivated desire, or which can still promote anxious, guilty or—modified—nostalgic emotions now."[51]

There is something curious in this militancy of the detail, an understatement in a style noted for its overstatements. But such would be the problem of trying to view the video as if it were simply the words of the rapper, namely, from the perspective of auteur. Yet *Wicked* is distinctive for the persistent disappearance of Ice Cube into the fabric of video and sound. This movement of the rapper's image is amplified in the motif of pursuit that runs through the piece. The early insinuation of crime and apprehension takes its twists and turns in a confrontation with the discourse of blame to the point where Ice Cube as both suspect and investigator is placed in circulation. While the two white punks (they are stylistically denotative of what they connote in the narrative) of the opening take hammers to a building, we hear, "Looking for the one that did it / cause you know you're gonna get it." The "it" in question is particularly mobile.

The two whites are the most recurrent dancing figures in the video. The white boys confound dance and destruction; their kicks that break the glass windows of a vacated building are literally moves in hip hop vocabulary. This doubling of form and function calls into question the social innocence of the dance step, which relies on its relation to an activity—unlike the movement gesture of modern dance, which retains its position with the so-called autonomy of the aesthetic and therefore has no effect other than its own expression. Some of the movement of the two white dancer-hoodlums is more like a self-inflicted hurl of the entire body and so lacks the coolness that comes from keeping the full explosive power set in motion within the body. It must also rely on the work of the video that surrounds it to give it its cool.

One of the most contrastive absences in Ice Cube's video is the display of female sexuality (this from a performer who had once directed the full wrath of his anger on "bitches") or the body of woman as dance against the arm gesticulations of the rapper. Ice Cube does gesticulate here, but he places white men in the structural role of the dancing feminine, leaving these men with the culpability ascribed to woman in so many rap narratives. While certainly not a refiguration of the feminine, the absence is worth reflecting on in the context of such intellectuals as Angela Davis and bell hooks, who have engaged Ice Cube on these issues, and given his ongoing willingness to participate in conferences and public affairs programs. The mutual respect this cross-participation displays for all too often segregated public spheres is suggestive of the potential that lies in a deeper exploration of the practical conjuncture of culture and politics.[52] While women are still at great distance from self-representation in his work, the anger that had once been directed at black women is displaced without necessarily being dissipated. Hence whiteness is feminized in the kind of impossible desire seen in MC Hammer's hit video *Can't Touch This,* in which women are made inaccessible to the star by dancing on a part of the set that is separated from him.

Later in the video, in one of many reversals of who must run and who must hide, or of the expected figures of panic, Ice Cube and friends chase the two whites through the streets. In similar moves, a middle-aged black women snaps a young black man's gold chain and keeps him at bay with a pistol as she backs away with her shopping cart. Two masked men are involved in a beating. One mask is of Reagan, the other, an almost subliminally occluded Bush. The former vice president is visible behind his mentor only in an instant of one of many searches for evidence with the remote control that the video invites. It is precisely this type of investigation that articulates and enlists the composite body through the work of reception. The presidential delinquents subject a cop to a fire hose. A fireman torches a car. Two women stomp on a man who is down. "Kick-it, wick-ed, see what they done," goes the refrain. Near the end (like the beginning only an approximation, a direction, not an endpoint, nor an endgame), the cadence remains but the words become, "We're wicked, we're wicked, but we run this town."

Through the thicket of images the question of culpability has become more complex (who is responsible for what, and what is the agency of responsibility?) so that a visual display of something like a structural account is produced in the movement from persons to the relations of effects. Certainly Ice Cube has not totally abdicated from the culture of personality that lends attention to his voice. But in the context of the highly instrumentalist discussions of the efficacy of rap, his willingness to take himself out of the (video) light affords a reappropriation of the conventions of star focus to other ends. The ethos he constructs banishes the good to a division within the wicked, a running from destruction and toward power, that also introduces a double entendre into the identity of who the "we" are that "run the town."

For if *Wicked* sketches an urban landscape or, for that matter, a nation, it is one defamiliarized out of the myriad clips of representational cliché. The slippage between city, or inner city as colony, and nation is particularly significant both for black nationalist movements such as the Nation of Islam and for the state project of containment. The former treats the urban core as its national terrain, and the latter sees in that same territory a looming threat to public order that could spill over into other precincts. The principal trope of visual terror in the coverage of the Los Angeles uprising was screened as the transgression of the inner colony's borders into the nation proper, the so-called multicultural riot. In the video, this black flight appears to have already occurred in a vacated landscape, for this is a town which people inhabit but which no one can live in or work in. There are emptied buildings but nothing like homes, and closed storefronts but no traces of capital, except perhaps the fly-by jet that exists in a different plane. From within the terrain of the video, it is possible to see capital but not touch it. This visual context gives a certain irony to the line, "Take your job and stick it, bigot" that immediately precedes an image of two boys on a bicycle, one sitting on the handlebars with a shotgun. No job is offered, and the employees of the state (police and fire personnel) don't seem to be doing theirs.

It is worth mentioning that these kinds of spaces vacated by capital are common settings for rap music videos.[53] In the two hours of rap programming in which this particular airing of *Wicked* appeared, EPMD's *Headbanger* video stages a confrontation with those on the other side of the camera in an abandoned warehouse, a scene also used without any denotation of violence in several other videos that night. Digable Planet's *Rebirth of Slick (I'm Cool Like Dat)* trades on capital's flight, making room for the avant-garde in a New York, SoHo-set deindustrial nightspot. In an interview that follows, a band member claims, "We've carved out our own slice of America."[54]

Yet as the popularity of rap across racial lines indicates, the pies of culture and economy remain stubbornly distinct in this country, so that even successful cultural projects (like the joining of hip hop and bebop that the *Rebirth of Slick* video references) are segregated from the failure of increasing segments of the population to occupy their proportional segment of political and economic resources. In this regard, the insurrection—past and future—referenced in *Wicked* is a figure for the burst bubble—in this case, not the ruptured economic miracle of Los Angeles or Tokyo but the hyperspace between them. If Rodney King was a spark, it was ignited in an emptied gas can that was full in the mid-eighties, when Los Angeles was the nation's leading manufacturing center and transpacific trade surpassed exchange across the Atlantic.[55] All this is to say that features of mapping do not specify a particular vision of social space. This becomes palpable only at the level of a principle of assemblage of the visual.

So just what is the space mapped in Ice Cube's video? The alternation that appears early on between the view from the street and that from the sky (the helicopter searchlight) evokes the marxist geographer Neil Smith's notion of "jumping scales," which suggests a strategy for suddenly enlarging what appears as a merely local social and political instance.[56] Other mapping devices appear in the video, as it were, from above. They are literally taken from broadcast news, a medium claiming to remain above the fray it depends on capturing if it is to have content. One is a sampled image of a map of central Los Angeles, placing a dot on the hot spot. Another is an icon of that index, an aerial shot of the freeway that displays cars in motion without indicating where they are going. These two shots construct planes, perspectives, or scales that are joined momentarily when a jet is shown flying downward, and a soft impression of the word "crash" flits by. One is reminded of the accounts of people firing at aircraft during the uprising, or of the fleeting reference to 007, also the flight number of the Korean Airlines (KAL) jet shot down by the Soviets in 1983, in the first mumblings of the video, now allowed to have growing coherence. If the networks shoot footage, the feet just might shoot back. In this exchange as in so many others, the sign breaks up or crashes when it hits its multifarious uses.

But there is also the hint of a crashing of the presumed distance between representation and referent when broadcast news assumes responsibility for mapping the imagined community of nation. Not only because of its sampled content but also because of its hypermobile format, *Wicked* acts as the double of the news. "We're like reporters," Ice Cube had once remarked, but rappers are also unlike reporters in that they appear as already situated in the event rather than as merely passing through or over it.[57] In an interview on MTV, the rapper hinted at one connection between the video of the Rodney King beating and his own: "It's been happening to us for years. It's just we didn't have a camcorder every time it happened."[58] Lacking the omniscient vantage of the panopticon, *Wicked* suggests that total surveillance—what network helicopters, following their police equivalents, project—is not necessary to document the effects of state. If, despite its claims to be the scene, the news pretends that its visual underrepresentation of events is complete coverage, this video, in the very activity of viewing it, denies any such comfort of sufficiency. It breaks up the self-emplacing ground of the local, implicating an elsewhere and a need to know something else in each passing display.

In this regard, for all its references to mapping, the video is also something other than a map. For all its historical references to musicals and the coterminous and articulated histories of rock and television, as a genre within television, MTV is closest in form and function to a commercial. The aesthetic resemblances result in part from similar techniques of visual sampling and the compression of production values into a few moments that if budgeted for prime time could provide hours of programming. Unlike that programming, whose content needs only to reproduce the activity of viewing it, commercials and MTV aim to make a particular point, which is that a certain commodity must be bought. Further, while it has many stories to tell, music video is visually defiant of narrative. Music video corporealizes sound. It is no accident that the biggest pop music stars of the eighties, Madonna and Michael Jackson, are kinesthetically robust in a way that makes the shimmies and shakes of such predecessors as the Beatles and the Stones (though not, significantly, James Brown or Little Richard) appear incidental by comparison.

Rap is the art of tearing into the endlessly sampled surface of popular culture, and it exposes the edges of production in the sphere of consumption. At its best, it treats the silencing barrage of noise to particle acceleration. Madonna certainly puts popular culture on display by using her body as a screen on which the desire for infinite transformation promised by stardom is projected. Michael Jackson, as a bildungsroman of the star system, is that transformation. His has always been a voice whose agency is the body, his spindly legs like a filigree, a note that plays itself.

Jackson is even filtered through *Wicked* in a variety of ways. In geometric terms, Jackson's seminal video hits, *Beat It* and *Thriller,* constitute a sphere to which *Wicked* is a tangent.[59] *Beat It* is a soft, multicultural *West Side Story* blanched of its tragic moment. Dance heals the wounds of racism, and Michael teaches the steps. Like *Wicked,* it complicates the discourse of blame that suffuses the race-crime complex, but it imagines a moment prior to conflict when blame can be suspended: "It doesn't matter who's wrong or right, just beat it." That conflict is taken as *Wicked*'s interiority with which it seeks a break. Another iconic Jackson video, *Thriller* touches on this interiority but psychologizes it as the other within. In a film within a fantasy within the short film, Jackson, after asking the woman he is with to be his "girl," confesses, "I'm not like other guys, I mean, I'm different," and promptly proceeds to turn into a werewolf. The woman, now shown in the theater terrified of this flight from commitment, leaves, and the two find themselves outside on the street when Jackson launches into song and dance. The street they walk down, it turns out, is Union Pacific Avenue in what could (still) be described in the early eighties as industrialized East Los Angeles. The scene (in video and life) quickly becomes deindustrialized, as the couple walk past a graveyard, where Jackson confronts and then becomes one of the foreigners, again changing face and sending his girl in flight, this time to an abandoned Victorian mansion, where, in danger of imminent gang rape by these dead others, she is awakened to the comfort of her suburban couch by Jackson himself, who in the parting shot flashes those other eyes.[60] These eyes, embedded in their skull, with a bangle of hair, bounce in one double-exposed image of *Wicked* before we see that they are on a T-shirt that Ice Cube is wearing. Bobbing up and down, he appears to be giving the Jackson image a shake to see what will come loose. Against the ersatz mobility from the vacated urban scene, Ice Cube defiantly stays put. He won't dance his way out of this one.

But I would argue that unlike Madonna or Michael Jackson, for whom video places their dancing on display, Ice Cube's video work is itself the dancing. It takes its territorializing reach as the reincorporation of an otherwise fragmented cognitive map back onto the social body. It twins its visual jumping of scales with rhythms double-timed within other rhythmic figures, setting the underlying tempo into motion. Taken together, music and image press beyond the borders of representation, while dragging some of the representativity of the video into the virtual space of reception. If TV news is a window on the world, music video is a door that opens in, filling the privacy of one's living room with a world's worth of visual economy. While a piece like *Wicked* is too thoughtful to be free of worldly images, it takes aim at a body in a way that its more spectacular video cousins cannot. But the body it takes aim at is not confined to the particularized space of reception but rather imagines joining other bodies in a variety of ways. Just as *Wicked* itself is a condensation of a vast urban space held taut in Ice Cube's voice, these very parameters of the social are what are loaded onto a (given) viewer's rocking body, joining it with its virtual society of reception.

Yet this crossing between the image and the body is none other than the dynamic of popular music-dance forms as such. Here the high-low model of cultural dissemination (and dilution) is not collapsed but effaced in the impossibility of fixing a single direction of dissemination/appropriation between the box and the street. It is this ligation between body politic and imagined community that generates a media/performance crossover between social practices and their representation. Particularly with rap it is difficult to say who's whoing whom. And yet this seems to be precisely what has provoked so much anxiety about rap (whether Ice T's *Cop Killer* or Ice Cube's *Wicked*); from the perspective of moralizing authority, representation and practice are collapsed in a different direction so that the word becomes the deed.

The studied conflation of image and referent came not only from the likes of Reverend Wildmon and Tipper Gore but also from within the Reagan administration (as well as the campaign trail of candidate Clinton). In detailing the opposition to popular music, Serge Denisoff relates the following: "Surgeon General C. Everett Koop told a southern medical school audience: 'Violence and pornography are at a crossroads now. One place they are crossing is in these rock video cassettes that have become so popular with young people.' He warned that youngsters have become 'saturated with what I think is going to make them have trouble having satisfying relationships with people of the opposite sex . . . when you're raised with rock music that uses both pornography and violence.' "[61] This mythos of the power of simulation makes for much entertainment, but it is clearly not the ideology of people like Ice Cube, who insists that his work is about "raising questions." But it also carries a certain transitivity—not of emulating its depictions but in joining in the movement of connecting what has become separated by the virtual economy of terror. This virtual economy of terror is imagined as the divided space of the nation by the likes of broadcast news and other ideological technologies affiliated with the state.

Weak Links and Strong Dancing

Certainly, a single video (no matter how many times it is viewed) cannot carry the weight of imagining community in some still emerging multicultural nation. Nor is it apparent, either in terms of production or reception, in what sense a music video—that most intertextual of forms—is ever single. What is most problematic, however, is how the textual multiplicity of the video appears in the social realm bearing those connections that array the composite body. The way a rap national imaginary proliferates within the boundaries of the nation-state complicates any picture of reception that might assume a one-to-one correspondence between video and virtuality.

Without doubt, an ideological technology, whether novels, news, or music videos, will have strong and weak effects. As such we should take seriously what can be learned from *Wicked* about disturbing the apparently local instance with the global context, a rerun of that old favorite, the particular and the general, so that its cultural resonances will not be contained by reference to a monocultural nation. There is no simple correspondence between an artistic voice and the people it invokes or addresses, as if one fit neatly inside the other. Without denying that a video such as *Wicked* can have its strongest effects of identification among those whose lives find a visual resemblance to it, the work also admits of a kinesthetic sensibility whose weaker effects have a more comprehensive reach. Privileging these weak effects may go further than a study of the obvious strong resemblances to enunciate how hip hop's composite body constitutes a national sensibility in ways that run counter to the dominant imaginings.

It is perhaps at the point of its weak links that nationalism can most properly be called multiculturalism. For it is away from the merely demographic segmentation that the ambitions of an uncontainable polyvocality are felt. The conception of cultural difference as the basis for identity shifts from a strong constitutional divide between groups to a weak situational relation in a given context. If the politics of such weak effects are themselves difficult to imagine let alone predict, we might be able to say the same for the dominant forms. It would have been difficult to predict this nation's resistance to its putative interest in imperialism with respect to Vietnam or Nicaragua and surprising how shallow the effects of agreement turned out to be in the case of the Gulf, where the political limits on engaging in sustained warfare (though not waging war) were never far from the discourse of state military planners.

It would seem that rap lies at great distance from these examples until we recall that it is precisely the specter of warfare, the hints of a principally, but not exclusively, racially based genocide in the talk of generalized sacrifice, that society is currently being subjected to. It is here more specifically that *Wicked* imagines a kind of countertalk to the news. Although so-called gangsta rap displays this situation directly both visually and lyrically, other forms of hip hop expression, thought to be thankfully softer, may turn out to share a more profound affinity at the level of the kinesthetic out of which the composite body is assembled. Rap in its totality can more usefully be understood in terms of common sensibilities in its musical form than in continuities of lyric content. These formal affinities become particularly significant for thinking about politics enacted by fewer people than those who are affected by the changes wrought, a situation closely associated with the scale introduced by modernization itself. Rather than assuming the liberal model of majoritarian politics, we may have to recognize that actual political mobilizations invariably draw on what turns out to be a minority of the population. What may therefore emerge out of a study of the weak links drawn by composite bodies is an appreciation of the context out of which mobilizations themselves are constituted and to which they refer. Rather than the study of who political actors can claim to represent, the focus on weak links asks how political activity is connected through the mediations of a cultural kinesthetic of a composite body that is unequally shared with those not considered to be activists. The gain of this question is to offer context as a materiality actually assembled out of the real social fabric, the composite body politic. If an ideological technology such as hip hop is to be seen as more than the provenance of a particular cultural group and as a structure of feeling for embodying a multicultural nation, the weak links that mediate the affinities between seemingly disparate identities must be foregrounded.

Let me suggest one unlikely network with an even more uncertain out-come in which hip hop traces connections in a multicultural nation, namely, the fitness club. If disco opened the pop kinesthetic in the late seventies to a live encounter with the vinyl surfaces that would get torn asunder with the development of hip hop, aerobics had made those bodies come clean a decade later. At its most sanitized, the circulating sexuality of the disco was transferred to a 900 phone-sex number. The proliferation of fitness clubs in the eighties indicated a transfiguration of bodily publicity that encased each body in a machine or subjected it to the rigors of the workout.

As a countermove, we might see in the aerobics class a distant cousin of the jook, what Katrina Hazzard-Gordon calls the "dance arena" that pro-vided a space where differences within the African American community were negotiated. The eighties were not the only time to see popular dance move from indoors to the streets and back inside again in the form of the house party. Hazzard-Gordon reminds us that in the 1940s in a move that anticipated the civil rights movement, black dance left the jook joint for the streets where gangs filtered through the block parties.[62] The fitness club cer-tainly lacks the economic supports of mutual aid that the jooks provided and offers little respite from discriminating effects elsewhere. The images of the perfectible body emanate from beyond the pulleys and weights where the work-to-fit body is manufactured. The unrelenting music that accom-panies each stroke of the fitness regimen attains its greatest functionality on the dance floor of the aerobics class. The making of bodies uninterrupted by other kinds of social division constitutes the club's tacit kinesthetic democ-racy.

Although I grew up amid sport and sought many venues for dancing, I had always resisted this move into the aerobic until, in what seemed a safely temporary stay in the Southern California of my youth, I found myself a member of the Irvine Family Fitness Center. There, as indistinguishably elsewhere, in addition to the various instruments of corporal adjustment, is a full complement of aerobics classes and their derivations. Among them was one called funk but inflected with hip hop. At my first class, well over a hundred Anglo and Asian predominantly female bodies obediently fol-lowed the steps of the instructor—usually the lone African American in the room. The image of this face-off fits neatly within the visual rhetoric of race that has come to dominate the airwaves, where the nonblack masses attend to their own pleasures by watching their black idols at play (despite the highly problematic recruitment of Asian Americans into the mythos of assimilation).[63] These particular demographics seemed consistent with the notion that aerobics is already gendered as a scene of bodily transformation under the regimen of the gaze. That such a setting would be a site for the reception of hip hop, with its nationalist associations, introduces certain confounding prospects into the construction of nation that are themselves generally absented from political discourse.[64]

The teacher, it turns out, despite assuring us that she assembled all the combinations herself, also went into Los Angeles to take hip hop classes with those who were really down. There, by her account, her teachers' bodies could be found somewhere on MTV, but her fellow students, clad in baggy pants and oversized jackets, were all drawn from the 'hood. Such sheathings, of course, would never do in the fitness club setting, where shiny skins that look like they were newly molted are de rigueur. There also seemed to be little doubt in the teacher's mind that transforming the flesh took precedence over doing hip hop in order to reflect on the broadest possible contours of its national kinesthetic. Surely, this most bland of assimilative processes was no more radical than adding fruit to frozen yogurt. Like fruit, steps can travel. But it is interesting to reflect on the shape those aerobicizers were getting into. It is probably fair to say that nothing actual is ever typical, and ethnographic description carries with it the burdens of specificity. Here I will attempt to specify a practice of composite bodies based on some five months of attending these aerobics classes. My aim is to explore what sensibilities might emerge in this unexpected site of reception for hip hop. It could be placed somewhere between the privatized space in front of the television screen, where the demands on the body are difficult to discern by way of its response, and the mythological 'hood itself, where the presumed identification with the representation of hip hop may get in the way of noting its effects. Let's see what I learned.

The faithful gather on the sidelines of the long, mirrored hall. They await the completion of the class before theirs. There is a moment of congestion as the two waves of bodies filter through each other. The earliness is intended to secure the class taker the most desirable placement in the room. Some come early so that they are assured a place in the front center and others in the back corner. Based on conversations and greetings, people seem to know each other but only a few others. For the class as a whole, corporeal knowledge is assembled in anonymity. Given the width of the room, it is difficult to see everyone so that even at this scale the community must be imagined. The reference for this imagination is the instructor, Teri Kotinek; the interval of five to ten minutes between classes scheduled in the same studio allows for an anticipation of her arrival not entirely unlike that found at a rock concert. That she comes in with a handheld microphone and greets the class in the larger-than-life tones of an entertainer (her credits include a stint on *Soul Train*), while being buffeted by the driving music that she slips onto the tape machine, quotes the excitement of the concert (or, more precise, a live television show) as much as it references an aerobics class.

She builds on this sense that something is about to happen that people can get swept up in while she offers a process of enlistment in the mutually created event that will follow. Invariably she surveys those in attendance to ascertain who is there for the first time. She offers a mixed message, enticing frenzied output while admonishing people to "go at their own pace." Beyond juridical considerations of torn bodies, this last phrase, which she will often couple with an exhortation to fuller expenditure, signals the impossible but ongoing conjuncture of the demands that this community fulfill its ideal imagery with the constant slippage or pacing of a particular body through the pictured ideal. Against the enveloping tide of synchronous movement and stereochronic music, going at one's own pace as a common strategy for taking the class hints at the differentiation generated by this socializing process. Despite the common commands, bodies may come out moving more differently from one another than they went into the class, for difference of a certain sort lies amid what they learn.

The initial synchronizing gesture erupts out of the alignment of spatial polarities, the face-off between teacher and students, desire and mirrored demand. The initial rocking side to side with arms punching the air is simple enough to accustom one to getting the movement without having to see it; it calibrates what will become the central fact of dance and music and establishes the strong lateral emplacement in the space that aligns bodies with the structures of dancing. The architecture of the room is such that visual depth based on frontal reflection in the mirror (some four bodies deep) is more superficial than the invisible linear pull of thirty bodies across. The choreography adheres in its Cartesian precision to these two forces of visuality and viscerality.

At least several times during the class, Teri will interfere with this opposition, selecting those who can't be seen to demonstrate a phrase of movement or routine. She is clear about her didactic principles in this: "I selected these people because they all do it differently. She does it hip hop. This one does it with technique. And this one just does it." She also plays with hierarchy in the course of her teaching, offering different variations for "new" and "advanced" (which I sometimes hear as "dance") people. Having introduced this distinction, she then makes fun of those who would adopt it as their own. "Now look at these people laughing like they think they're advanced people. No, just kidding." Whenever she disses someone, whether that person is inside the class or outside, she will add "just kidding" to put the point in play. This relation of inside and outside is itself interesting, for all her references to popular figures, which she places in the familiar (for example, Michael for the young Jackson brother), name the anonymous forces which place demands on the body and which are rendered familiar and offered in miniature within the space of the local. These references also help break up her own discourse as composed intertextually of the authority of techniques for the perfectible body with the pleasures of popular culture. These two texts are structurally related as well in the organization of the class per se.

The first half hour is represented as the "warm-up," a movement phrase which accumulates out of a series of moves that she shows through constant repetition and which remains basically the same each class. In the second half, she teaches a "routine" whose newness to all is intended to level differences in familiarity and aptitudes for movement and allow the focus of the class to slide from getting in shape to getting into hip hop. Yet, from the very beginning of class, she herself offers hip hop as the means to a style rather than simply a fit end by opposing her authority as teacher to that of performer when she invariably takes liberties with the very movement she has presented. Hip hop proceeds as the very movement away from its pedagogical conditions toward its performative promise. Rather than speaking a language of performance as that which is other to technique, she offers something else to compensate for the urge to follow her technical imperatives too closely.

To modulate any fixation on getting the steps right, Teri provides commentary on the context that has brought people to the fitness club which draws out and on the contradictions of the situation. One evening, before offering us a special extra segment of the class to work on "abs" (the sculpting away of the body's center as an offering to beauty), she delivered a testimonial on the vagaries of anorexia and a homily on the beauties of a size 12. Another evening, in a pitch for a benefit for a community organization in Long Beach that assists persons with AIDS, she asked the room what they "had done for AIDS" in the last year. Here she made the connection between the (re)construction and the ravishment of the body that was presumed to divide the class from its outside. The curious syntax of doing something "for" AIDS, like multiculturalism itself, introduces the class into a field where difference became the figure that made the imagination of community possible.

Thus far, the account has been a teacher-centered one, assuming that she was the medium for introducing hip hop where it would have been presumed absent. The shift of focus to those who take the class is one into the heart of the problem of weak effects. Even a casual glance around the room reveals a range of affinities with hip hop, from professional associates of the teacher who occasionally take the class to those evidently knowledgeable of the music, to those who clearly hip hop on their own, to the interested neophytes and novices. Dancing together, this diversity is assembled. In the last minutes of the class, difference is put on display. The dense packing of bodies in rows and columns that affords the immediate supports of emplacement is loosened a bit. The group is divided in two, and performance is given the status of a mutual offering common to many practices of black dancing including hip hop where one half performs while the other watches and then applauds. These last moments signal the end of restraint that comes from the problem of pacing through an aerobic situation.

The faucets of sweat have already opened and closed several times, and the heartbeat has raced and settled. The aerobicized body has been made pliant to the point where it need no longer attend to its own aerobic situation. For in these last minutes when the phrase is learned (such as it will be) and available in its entirety as an activity, the roomful of people is suddenly in a position to draw on its own local history. The same process of vamping that initiates the class now serves as a kind of gating device out of which the dance will spring. The accumulated phrase generally occupies something in the vicinity of a minute's worth of dancing, enough to provide the thrill of navigating one's way through its landscape.

For me, the experience of dancing hip hop is that of a process of rhythmic self-containerization that, at the moment it has put its fourth wall into place in the endless obligation of four-four time, provides a way out into another space in the making. Part of this has to do with the process of assembly of bits of movement that are one measure long. But part seems to lie in the pleasure of hip hop's own syntax, which establishes the patterned expectation of breaking with itself, a desire for indeterminacy of outcome that rests on an initial move toward repetition. If break dancing itself had formed in the spaces the disc jockeys opened up in the records for instrumental passages, hip hop's own increasingly dense layerings disseminate these spaces throughout the music. In these classes, unlike earlier forms of hip hop movement such as electric boogie, we never touch. Rather, the sense of connectedness to others in the room is made available in those moments (offered in practically every measure of the music) during which the body breaks out of its recently acquired containment within the square space defined by the steps, in the direction of what lies outside it. The little box the body had made for itself is broken in order to inhabit an area just left vacant by another dancer. That outside then becomes the anchoring point for the next constituting move. It is this ready availability of exteriority that joins the dancing bodies.

Against the rather diffuse openness is the persistent linearity of how the dance moves in space. Viewed from above it could be said to be confined within a screen not unlike a television. Viewed from within, the composite body dimensionalizes effects not available on a screen. Beats are incorporated that are never seen. The fissures of rhythm in the composite body allow it to break in several directions at once. Finally, there is the question of the movement itself, its deceptive simplicity. Rarely is there more to the choreography than steps with alternating feet in the horizontal dimension and jumps in the vertical. There may be more demanding coordinations, such as a hitch kick, which requires sequentially placing both legs in the air, but these are the exceptions within the vocabulary. The demands of the steps themselves come in the speed with which they pass, the precision with which their reorientations are executed, and, most elusively, whether the body in question looks like it is dancing them.

Dancing the News Away

This account has already anticipated, as has the teacher, the unmeetable demand to look anything like her. But precisely in this impossibility a fairly wide space is opened up between the correct sequencing of the steps and the sense of dancing them. This is where dancing itself touches on its imaginary, for it is only from the perspective of the entire dance edifice (here what fills up both time and space with motion) that it is possible to assess whether one is getting it. For this "it," or what we could call "style," is what joins langue and parole, lexicon and syntax, presence and absence, in short, the totalizing frameworks for the imagination of community with instances of performing the danced connections that would make the composite embodiment of community possible. Because the body in question emerges from beyond the mirror in the electronic reflections and splicings that hip hop moves circulate through, the irreducibly composite affiliations take their place on the aerobic dance floor as well.

No doubt, style comes late in this game, but the notion that hip hop is the key to these folks' bodily salvation approaches something of Raymond Williams's structure of feeling, bringing an embodied desire for racial difference in through the back door of a county constructed (under the ancien régime of spatial apartheid in Southern California) to be free of racial difference. That is not to say that the desire for blackness long activated in the white imagination that takes the former as a transgressive rapture that always returns to its place is not also in operation, but simply that other forces are at play.[65] Put another way, one could ask whether in the appropriation of otherness that has been profitable in myriad forms over centuries of capital, you ever really get it for free. Here, dance insinuates a difference from what the body had been to now enlarge its capacity for being. It inserts into that model of sameness contained in the obsessive gaze in the classroom mirror an other truth of body's ideality, one that never quite fits and helps to break up the authority of the ideal. Style contends somewhat uneasily with perfection in that getting the style down makes it appear as if you are looking at someone else in the mirror. No doubt, the constitution of a gaze always bears such complications, only now the divide between body and image is converted back into a difference to which dancing itself is the negotiation. There is also another sense in which dancing negotiates the mirror, namely, that in the very industrialization of fitness that packing over a hundred bodies into a room displays, getting "the routine" is not routinized behavior for most, and therefore people must glance at one another not simply to make hostile comparisons but also to try to get it right. Value returns in the use people find to make of one another. Hence the authority of perfection is used at least partially to subvert itself. Those bodies may go out into the Orange County night with a wedge of complicity with the culture they are normally called on to oppose, before turning on the evening news. Given the rapacity of racist narratives broadcast on any given night, checking the facile absorption of the savaging tales may require a bit of a running start. The bodies leave the fitness club not only aerated with multiple racial inflections but also with a complication of the gaze that is less likely to look into a mirror (or television screen) and see a simple other. This body of one coupled with another is put into circulation through the social kinesthetic without passing through the impossible first step of consensus. As part of a structure of feeling that supports a disposition to politics prior to the experience of a shared predicament that might incite people to action, consensus in the newly imagined multicultural nation is not necessarily a requisite for mobilization.

Perhaps even so mediated a transfusion of another corporeality could offer a counterweight to that fragile unanimity within the body politic. This prospect could be joined with the problematic status of my own political and cultural authority of representation. I speak now of the risks entailed in speaking for others. I would hope instead to effect a movement counter to representation, in allowing other kinds of practices to introduce silences into my own affiliations with certain subject positions interpellated specifically with respect to dominance. Whiteness is possessive, but it is not a possession; it calls but does not offer an already consolidated response. While whiteness may emit a persistent drone, its call may also encounter a busy signal.

If dancing can momentarily silence that me whose ascribed situation has historically been deployed in the effacement of difference, with the commands of an other, then those very noises become complicit in interfering with my own privilege to speak the world. This is an interference that would well serve the discourse of nation, for all its aspirations to assert the monologic voice of the patria against the possibilities of all others taken together.

The only globally realized, capitalist nation-state insists that it be heard as an already consolidated and singular voice.[66] Against this consolidation of order, it is possible to introduce a certain silencing of those standard representations of self (in terms of gender, race, sexuality, as well as the class and national privileges of global capital) that are affiliated with dominance.

Paradoxically, the silencing of those particular voicings affiliated with dominance through other means of identification among those who have but a partial stake in the whole apparatus of domination may go far in permitting the mobilization of practices of difference to emerge. For this re-affiliation to blossom into a different kind of national kinesthetic, one that is properly multicultural, the desire to be the other must transgress that partition which is said to divide the cultural from the political.

What has been registered here are simply two moments in the imaginary and performative from which the composite of what I call my body is emitted. That I would dwell on the timeshifts of Ice Cube's video and all those aerobic steps could in no way stand as an inventory of where any body has been. Nor can it suggest a project of aligning a national sign with its embodied referent. The challenge for grasping the distance between these two moments is not how to identify the body that they typify but how to map the national landscape they imagine—that is, to imagine a kinesthetic context in which what is different between the production of a black nationalism and a national fitness craze might be joined. Ice Cube's video incessantly jumps scales; it breaks with the spatial frame it inhabits rather than occupying a space over which it claims sovereignty. The violence done to a body to make it fit into a putative national ideal is itself made crazy or split by that very body's desire to be an other. The subjection to this order of difference is typical of what and how contemporary bodies are composed within the diversity of spatially engaging practices, or "heterotopia," we all inhabit.[67] This topos is a multicultural landscape without fixed boundaries whose referents must be constantly and sentiently mobilized.

The multiple affinities to racial and other identities that are drawn to hip hop are precisely what compose a heterodox national body. In actuality as opposed to virtuality, the nation too is itself composed of countless such tenuous connections. Against the confidence that all these weak linkages might be held together by a solitary narrative of nation, such as that proposed by the evening news, this diffuseness of the composite body can introduce some very productive doubt. Between that desire to cast oneself against the flickering screen and the desire to emerge from the other side of the aerobic mirror is a bodily space that admits of an unconsolidated diversity that I would here champion as properly multicultural. If the imaginary proposed by the news posts a nonnavigable divide between bodies of innocents and criminals who are essentially different from one another, the surfaces of hip hop that emit identity hint at a different principle of bodily composition that circulates across national media borders.

Whether or not I ever moved to those pictures on the myriad screens and mirrors in this cultural landscape, there is no risk that I could become one with them or fuse into any one of them. The beats that fuel my desiring machine mark a structure of feeling that has no purchase on singularity. They make no claim to be *the* news. But to begin to recognize those disparate spaces where I am not structured in dominance, I must do other than listen for the sound of the monolith. I must be moved myself through the nations (and not simply the notions) of others. Silencing that autonarrative that claims such omnipotence, the walk that separates my two hip hop encounters stretches on to alloy itself with the desires of others whose pulses I can just begin to feel. The heartbeat of America? No. These are the rhythms of a body that dances to a different composition.

Modern dance technique is often enshrouded in the myth of an individual creator, whose urge to be free of convention gives rise to new expressive forms.[1] This trope of freedom through self-transformation is at the root of the claim that modern dance is one of the few distinctly "American" art forms.[2] To create this mythology of the national self, (American) modern dance is most frequently juxtaposed to (European) ballet to signify a break with the cultural influence of colonial powers. This cultural break occurs more than a century after political independence but adapts the latter's revolutionary rhetoric to an aesthetic domain.[3]

From this perspective, the establishment of modern dance is treated as evidence of the belated emergence of an authentic American character. The distinctiveness of modern dance from other dance forms can therefore come to stand for the freedom of Americans more broadly, a name for a national universal that grants equality as a birthright. But because this is an equality of opportunity and not of allocation, the explanatory emphasis of modern dance as a trope for national character is placed on access to means, not assessment of ends. Inequality in society can therefore be attributed to differences in individual competency rather than to differential treatment within and by the social order.

It is the assertion of a practical competency that springs from an individual creative genius but can be applied to all that marks the primacy of technique as what grounds the modern dance aesthetic, namely, "that making stage work is inseparable from teaching an approach to dancing."[4] Modern dance can be seen to situate the technically accomplished self as the foundation for a universal American identity. Based on talent and hard work, this self can transcend both cultural diversity and a hierarchically divided social structure. As such, modern dance is enlisted ideologically in a larger political project where the language of national identity serves and complicates the formation of a (nation) state.

Like all mythologies, the story of modern dance turns out to be many stories. To call modern dance American is a particularly freighted misnomer, not only because it standardizes the relation of self to society as a national brand but also because it suppresses recognition of those other places that have been forced to share the same name. The seemingly innocent wordplay collapses the name of the colonizing power within a hemisphere with what it colonizes. For, outside the United States, among certain Latin American intellectuals, "Our America" has come to designate those who struggle for national and hemispheric identity in the shadow of the North.[5] Hence, what is taken from others, both within and outside the United States, goes by the name of "the land of the free." In this respect, the very powers that allow for the omission of the many by the one, that continue to colonize America in its hemispheric totality, are mistaken for the guardians of independence as a national ideal.

On closer inspection, modern dance tells this story and suggests an account of why the history of colonialism remains incomplete, in this hemisphere and the rest. In this tale, which exists in tension with the mythos that I described above, modern dance develops as a very complex matrix of appropriations of different movement sources, not the least of which are dance expressions generated by those subject to the colonization and enslavement that enabled the United States to form as a national state.

While others such as Isadora Duncan preceded her with nationalist pronouncements,[6] and many others followed in the constitution of the form, Martha Graham is the quintessential modern dance self whose body gave birth to a technique for being American. Yet from her own perspective, it is the bodies of others that constitute her "sources." She alludes to this process of appropriation (the possibility to "adopt a dance" of "another people") in a statement about her technique that argues for African and Native American dance as "our two forms of indigenous dance." She goes on: "These are primitive sources which, though they may be basically foreign to us, are, nevertheless, akin to the forces which are at work in our life. For we, as a nation, are primitive also—primitive in the sense that we are forming a new culture."[7]

In the course of just a few words, Graham assimilates them and us under "we." This we is, in turn, an amalgamation of what is primitive and what is modern under the singularity of nation. The politics and the institutions needed to affect this fusion go unnamed but not unreferenced. For Graham here argues that the development of dance technique is but an instance of those powers that enable national formation. Hence, she suggests a more programmatic theoretical tie between American dance technique and the state that sustains this capitalist nation than she makes explicit in the quote above.[8] For at least one facet of nationalism strives to adhere the identity of a population with the administration of that which divides that population against itself, whether in terms of class, race, gender, or sexuality.

Graham, by connecting the development of modern dance in the United States with nationalism, in effect makes two claims. Such a linkage first implies that this nation was initially formed by taking as its own what is foreign to it and that it did this in a way which masked its own origins in violence by identifying the newly born with the (recently subdued or adopted) primitive. Second, her words indicate that dance reveals how these "forces" operate.

This chapter is an effort to take seriously the dual claims of this dance pioneer who reminds us that national self-discovery is an ongoing process that occurs in the space between technique and the state. Such spaces are not always easy to recognize, particularly if the colonization that sustains the national state is taken as unproblematic and complete. To identify what moves the more subtle features of appropriation on which nation building and dance making rest (and continuing the analysis of appropriation begun in the previous two chapters), it makes sense to turn to a setting where the efficacy of pioneers such as Graham may still be felt: a university dance technique class. But her influence does not stand alone. Distinct, though related, principles of modernist dance movement, which I will abbreviate as torque and release, circulate within a class of students and among instructors who rotate teaching during the week. In the studios where dance is taught and learned, the legacies of technique cross with the institutions of self-formation. Even more, bodies are held together by the unrecognized authority of the state, their progress is marked, but there are also powers generated here that remain unstated.

The question that the study of the dance technique class helps explain is how, despite a decline in the percentage of the population for whom the prophylaxis of participation in the political public sphere may still be directly offered by the state, an imaginary affiliation with the nation-state's regime of authority may still get produced. Even given the coercion of institutional subjugation and of exclusion from available social goods, this consent occurs through authorities not formally associated with the state. These guardians of technique mediate the rift between what local bodies produce and the general condition of a sustainable social order that those bodies may credit with the possibility of their own production.

Stating the Dancing Body

This ethnographic study of one dance technique class is intended as an occasion for theoretical reflection both to illuminate how the state operates to secure the legitimacy of its command over the nation and to explore the resistances generated in that process. There is no doubt that modern dance choreography (Graham's own work included) has, at times, been critically disposed toward existing political arrangements.[9] By separating technique from choreography, I want to focus on dancing itself as a political practice rather than on the politics of its aesthetic. This is not to suggest that dance classes are somehow free of or prior to any aesthetic; quite the contrary, I will argue that modern dance has often aspired to a universalizing aesthetic. Rather, a politics of the aesthetic can assume a formal unity to its object that takes for granted its internal relations of production and grants the observer who makes this aesthetic claim a status of objectivity.

The stably separated binary of observer and observed, of subject and object, is reminiscent not only of conventional positions within aesthetics but of discussions of technology as well. Bruno Latour, one of the more prominent contemporary writers on issues of society and technology, cautions against viewing these two terms as if they were "ontologically distinct entities." Instead, he recommends treating technology as "the moment when social assemblages gain stability by aligning actors and observers."[10] Hence the durability typically attributed to the presence of things is here reinscribed as a feature of a form of domination that renders subject and object as identical to each other.

Dance technique, whose initial relations of domination and authority appear founded on the very separation of subject and object and of observer and actor that joins conceptions of aesthetics with those of technology, ultimately unsettles what is facile in each of these oppositions. Thus dance, as a site where domination and its subversion are actively negotiated, may avoid certain of the traps of thinking relations of power through technology that forge a nonnavigable divide between the transcendent freedom of progress and the alienating instruments of subjugation.

Bodies can be treated like machines, but then, like machines, they must be produced to produce. While the study of dance lends itself to the sense that Latour makes of technology, the shift in emphasis to technique, where what is objectified must be put into practice by an active subjectivity, may go further in realizing and generalizing his aims. The more restricted meaning of technology as the study of techniques makes plain that even the use of machines comes about only through practical human applications, hence discussions of technology are always already about social relations. Further, by treating as inseparable the domains of science and art, dance technique may display more clearly the powers of their irreconcilability.

The formalization of teaching and learning dance is but one technique, or disciplined practical competency, among many in capitalist society through which the contest over the articulation of the state and its subjects takes place; it is, however, one that is particularly useful in terms of what it displays about that contest. The articulation of technique with the political economy of capital is made quite forcefully by Michel Foucault:

> If the economic take-off of the West began with the techniques that made possible the accumulation of capital, it might perhaps be said that the methods for administering the accumulation of men made possible a political take-off in relation to the traditional, ritual, costly, violent forms of power, which soon fell into disuse and were superseded by a subtle, calculated technology of subjection. In fact, the two processes—the accumulation of men and the accumulation of capital—cannot be separated; it would not have been possible to solve the problem of the accumulation of men without the growth of an apparatus of production capable of both sustaining them and using them; conversely, the techniques that made the cumulative multiplicity of men useful accelerated the accumulation of capital.[11]

For dance technique, with its productivities that amass steps for the trained body, the structure of the university curriculum—from grading to successively numbered courses—may mark one of the most explicit sites of technical accumulation.[12] But, particularly in the college classroom, the "accumulation of men" may encounter certain disturbances in what frequently amounts to a virtual city of women.[13] Dance technique can be considered a political practice precisely to the extent that it represents a moment where bodies that are primitive with respect to their subordination to a given authority develop the means to move for and against that very authority.

In this dialectic of appropriation, technique is doubly complex. On the one hand, the gain of practical competencies in a particular technique (be it one that is explicitly licensed, such as driving, or juridically inscribed, such as home ownership) provides a framework that both enables and limits participation. It is not that there is some specifiable threshold beyond which participation can no longer be tolerated. Rather, the fact of participation as what makes things happen within society is always problematic from the perspective of regulation, which is the functional terrain occupied by the state. At the same time, the ability to claim credit for promoting that participation which exists as a feature of what is productive in society, and not of regulation per se, is fundamental to create the legitimating consent necessary for a particular population to be governed by any authority.

Consent is not consensus or mutual agreement but a general assent that the rule of law marks the conflicts through which people locate themselves. To the degree that acquisition of techniques frames the participation that produces consent to be ruled, technical accumulations effectively conceal the hold on the body—coercion—that is the state's ultimate recourse to regulate society.[14] Institutions of coercion, such as the military, are generally absent from most citizens' daily experience. Yet the manner in which all sorts of techniques (dance among others) take hold of the body suggests a more insidious and pervasive presence of coercion. This coercive presence is concealed in what would be taken as otherwise benign and voluntary institutional sites of consent, from workplaces to agencies of social welfare (broadly construed as schools, hospitals, and social services).

On the other side of this double complexity, the direct exercise of coercion by a state against its own citizenry is far from unproblematic and not simply for reasons of legitimacy. The social body that the state seeks to hold and wield can also stand against the state and loosen that grip. It is not that the state stands as one social body against that of the citizenry but that the state is above all a nonproductive mechanism, a device of regulation, whose existence depends on the appropriation of what other bodies produce (whether for revenues, performance of functions, or applications of force). Hence, the notion that the state is without a productive body generative of participation suggests that coercion itself is not simply a force directed against bodies but a bodily capacity that could be directed against the state.

The breakdown in the U.S. fighting machine in Vietnam might be understood in these terms.[15] So too could the long history of resistances to the draft (as evidenced, for example, by the thousands who participated in the bloody New York protests against the 1863 Federal Enrollment Act), whose degree of resolution under the guise of a professionalized armed services has yet to be put to any persistent test.[16] While the soldier may be clearly defined with respect to the ambiguity of coercion, the citizen is less so. The direct linkages between military and state are dispersed and mediated in everyday life, in which the implication of the state with coercion is not so much distant but immanent and concealed. So, while the demands of state authority are carried in the institutionality of daily life, that authority is seldom named as such. As a consequence, where the state appears as formally absent, the role that putatively civic institutions play in the mediation of its authority tends to go unrecognized.

If the words of Martha Graham can alert us to the relations of appropriation on which authority rests for dance and nation, the examination of dance technique can expose what is problematic in these relations. In the dance class to be studied here, Graham is an absent presence like the state itself, a force made palpable through its exertions on the shape that technique takes. So too, dance technique serves as a site where the state is thought to be absent but in practice exists as a mediation of the state's relations of authority. It offers an instance of institutionalized social life where the otherwise concealed relation between coercion and consent (the hold on the body and the legitimating powers of participation, respectively), are palpably articulated, indeed, taken as an explicit and accountable object of reflection and development.

While sport and fitness activities certainly take hold of the body, the bracketing of the dance class from other dimensions of dance practice (rehearsal and performance) places the relation between authority and technique on display in a uniquely reflexive manner (to schematize: coaches command technical performance, aerobics teachers offer their bodies as technical mirrors with little self-reflection, and dance teachers reflect technique in their verbal and gestural commands). Yet, because of its self-reflexivity of the relations of authority, a dance class also registers the conditions under which the legitimation of authority fails. In class, the first steps toward the failure of that legitimation are taken. These occur in seemingly incidental but visible moments when authority is superseded by what any functioning institution depends on for its own existence, namely, the practical competencies that are both socially organized and released through technique.

Although Martha Graham died in 1991 and Hanya Holm in 1992, the architectonics of their pedagogy is still practiced in many dance studios across the nation. That they did embody a claim for absolute authority over what could transpire in a given space (and spaces colonized throughout the world where people can say, for example, that what moves their bodies—what they do—is something called Graham technique), in the form of a demand for productivity in others, concisely states a body politic (as discussed in the previous chapter). Competitive games are governed by established rules that are meant to assure a certain disjunctive result. But the indeterminacy of aesthetic outcomes (what does it mean to win in art?), especially in the ideology of modernism, privileges means (techne) that must provide their own ends (in this case, dancing). Where this convention operates most fully, teaching is not done by example but with the word, for technique is a vocabulary that carries choreographic will and insists on the apparent translatability of what is otherwise untranslatable between different media of expression.[17]

The ability to organize an entire symbolic domain under the authority of a single signifier is also consonant with what is here being called the state. That the dance technique class bears relations of authority that are stated as such cannot account for how technique itself comes into being within the space of the studio. While named after an individual choreographer, the naming may already be weakened by the time the teacher summons the class to order. More generally, modern dance is an attribution made to a body of competencies, the naming of which momentarily arrests the movement of those competencies on their own terms.

Even if the relations of authority remain intact over time, the auteurity has already been displaced onto bodies that are only referential of it, especially in the university setting (one, however, that is stated in its own right and whose own curricular requirements foreground constraint over the freedom that might be associated with selection in a dance class market such as New York). But the teacher is also, more often than not, referential to other dance techniques, and more profound, dance must of necessity reference other corporealities, for it cannot render the body newly born so that it could give rise to technique as such. The capacity for transformation, the machinery, so to speak, must already be inscribed in the dancer's body long before a choreographer gives her first technique class, thus while dance may be uniquely reflexive among techniques, it by no means originates or terminates the means to subject the body to authority. Yet here dance foregrounds the problem of authority in a manner that makes the latter available to contestation.

By denying that formal power derives from an appropriation of productive forces that are external to any given authority, it is possible to maintain the appearance that power has been successfully consolidated by that authority. The apparent autonomy of the dance class from its physical and political world rests on the denial that the appropriation of what others produce even takes place. Instead of being one instance of the more general relations of appropriation that govern society, the dance class can seem wholly exceptional, consumed in its own world. But, as I have been arguing throughout this book, dance is in and of the world, in a very special way that can make global dynamics all the more legible. In this case, dance technique exposes something of the fragility of legitimation more broadly. But precisely how legitimation is threatened is difficult to imagine in the abstract and now warrants a turn to that certain space of dancing where I will address the above questions ethnographically.

Dancing to Learn

The room is full, densely packed to the point where there is already the feeling of scarcity. Nothing much has happened, but there seems to be a deficiency of space. But this is a density unlike a crowded subway or an elevator. The deficiency is in relation to demands which these bodies could put on their surroundings and which in fact are being put on them. Out of the doubt as to spatial sufficiency comes a sudden shift that finds each of the bodies aligned with the others in synchronicity of movement. The room now accedes to its specialized function as a dance studio once the teacher's self-assertion calls the class to order. The neat rows of potted dancers, fronds upward, have yielded their immediate sense of spatial inadequacy to the authority of that single figure who stands with the reflection of the many behind him. The wall of glass is as uniform as the ground on which they stand, but seen through him it becomes a surface of their self-estrangement.

I am taking this class as an auditor, a corporal listener who promises to tell. Besides the teacher and the accompanist, I am the only male. From where I typically stand in the back corner of this large, packed studio, it is difficult to see the teacher, and so his instructions are always mediated for me through the bodies of others. Like other technique classes I have taken, the initial phrases of movement, designated as part of a warm-up for the body, are fairly consistent from one class to the next. These phrases do more than serve to prepare the body for an activity that has not yet begun, enabling it to be poured into a certain mold that the warm-up itself helps to construct for the body.

This reformation of the body, its internalization of a subjection to certain coordinates, or coordination, does not occur without resistance, and I, at nearly double the age of many in the class and a decade's remove from when I last engaged in this particular regimen on a daily basis, am of a body that admits of a rather extreme version of such resistance. Complicating this further is my own ethnographic gaze on the activity that is mastering me. Hence, what is already apparently interiorized in the bodies of others is still hovering about me, which is to say that I am aware of the degree to which I depend for my own movement on my affiliations with others, who are more accessible visually and kinesthetically than is the teacher.

There is something of the fluidity of accomplishment termed "getting it" that reveals its pedagogical means only when it breaks down, namely, when a mistake is made. There are times when the mistake can be localized, as when the bulk of those in the room move in one direction and some few in another. And yet, if I am following someone who is herself discrepant from others in this respect, I experience the double shifting of assimilating that person's movement along with the uncertainty into which it is now cast. Clearly, there are different orders of mistake and different ways in which mistakes form part of the pedagogical order. Early on in the class, mistakes can be entirely functional or nondisruptive if, say, a variant of a familiar movement sequence is not done to the proper counts or done on the right side of the dancer's body instead of the left.

Such variations of the variation are things that we already have names for. But to take the evenly spaced markings of time, or counts, that are meant to coordinate the movement in the room, there is clearly the kind of internal variation that Ferdinand de Saussure said was constitutive of the linguistic sign when he asserted that a given signifier could be recognized only as a relative difference rather than a pure presence.[18] It is this passable range of difference that technique is intended to regulate with respect to the body's capacity for movement.[19] Mistakes, then, are not absolute values but depend on a certain economy on which the class itself is structured. During the class, which passes through certain phases, various demands are made on which of the student body's capacities are to be placed on display.

Hence, it is only when a movement sequence is framed as something new that the question of whether the class is getting it or not even gets posed. Given the persistence of certain coordinations over the course of studying a given technique, what appears as new is immanently relativized in part through the function of the mistake. This opens up a pedagogical moment in which the teacher is no longer acting as if students acquired movement through visual mimesis, or the mimicry in their own body of what they see in another. Instead, by breaking down the components of the physical phrase, it becomes possible to speak of the more general principles through which the movement as a whole is constructed and of how the movement itself is learned or referenced. The teacher says, "You have to stop looking at the mirror when you do this, because if you don't it will be impossible to do the movement. Imagine that there is a mirror on the ceiling and that you see yourself as you make the final gesture." This statement is more than a tip about what to do when a movement phrase places the body in a position where the focus of the eyes shift from horizontal to vertical. It also indicates how mimesis becomes virtualized as a figure of the imaginary that stands in for the authorized image of self. The ability to see the correct(ed) image of self wherever one is looking is key to the experience of getting the movement, which perhaps makes it possible to have the movement at one's disposal as well.

This crucial shift from other to self and from a real reflection to an imaginary one points to what is modern in this dance, namely, the fixation, the obsession, with getting identity that frees it from its fixed place. This is what Michael Taussig refers to as "mimetic excess" or "mimetic self-awareness, mimesis turned in on itself, on its colonial endowment, such that now, in our time, mimesis as a natural faculty and mimesis as a historical product turn in on each other as never before."[20] For Taussig, the divide of self and other is reinscribed through colonial conquest. The creation of this culturally displaced other made possible the ascription of the savagery and barbarity of the violence of the colonial self to its object. The necessity of the history of colonialism as such is thereby attributed to nature (naturalized). But since that necessity must be made through the successful subordination of the other, looking for the other is identical with a destabilization of the self.

The culture of mirror in the dance class is founded on this mimetic economy. The twist, however, is that for the dancers, the other is initially the very image of correctness, of "getting it," of perfection, that is sought in the mirror, which represents that authority which colonizes their bodies by seeking to repress what is primitive in them. This command over what can properly be seen of the self attacks the body but is also, when generalized from the mirror to appear anywhere, what allows dancers to "attack" the movement, in the sense of moving as if they already had the authority or approval of correctness that they sought. Letting go of the mirror allows mimesis to proliferate. The process of acceding to the rigors of training a body to dance creates consent to the treatment of those bodily sources of a nature that must be colonized so that it, too, can devour the space around it (an attribute of the confidently trained dancer). Attacking the space, which could be taken as a dancer's nature, should be understood not as the start of colonization but as its continuation through other means.

This class, like many others, is structured so that movement which is initially contained within a space of the body is taken into the space immediately around the body so as to culminate with this body in motion traversing the space of the studio. In the course of ninety minutes, dancers move from stationary positions into the practice of a traveling movement phrase that is often performed in small groups while others watch. That is, it is structured very much as a sort of modernist progression of expanding horizons for the colonization of space, although this progression occurs only through repetition. Typically, phrases of movement across the dance floor (maximizing the linear space of the studio by dancing along a diagonal that transects the space from one corner to the other) accumulate by introducing a basic pattern of steps and then adding turns and aerial vocabulary in subsequent crossings. In this way, learning the movement occurs once one is already doing it, as the final version of the phrase in all its complexity is already motivated in the initial steps toward it. If the class is structured to support a certain myth of progress whose trajectory extends beyond the class to the promise of a career, it is but one of the myths and one with its own ambiguities.

The centrality of mimesis in Taussig's account of modernizing colonization depends greatly on the work of Walter Benjamin, whose own imagery for progress is worth quoting at length here:

> A Klee painting named "Angelus Novus" shows an angel looking as though he is about to move away from something he is fixedly contemplating. His eyes are staring, his mouth is open, his wings are spread. This is how one pictures the angel of history. His face is turned to the past. Where we perceive a chain of events, he sees one single catastrophe which keeps piling wreckage upon wreckage and hurls it in front of his feet. The angel would like to stay, awaken the dead, and make whole what has been smashed. But a storm is blowing from Paradise; it has got caught in his wings with such violence that the angel can no longer close them. This storm irresistibly propels him into the future to which his back is turned, while the pile of debris before him grows skyward. This storm is what we call progress.[21]

The wreckage of the dead in the dance class is the image of the dancer herself in space that she must discard if she is to continue to weather the storm. She progresses through the self-savagery of her own aspirations to attain the perfection in a mirror that recedes as she approaches it. But the pile of discarded possibilities is also the foundation of an extreme self-criticism that is generated through dance training so that she can blow her own storm not from paradise but toward a horizon of doubt defined by valuing that which is out of reach.

At the same time that this kinesio-cognitive activity of self-reflective learning is going on, however, the opportunity exists for dancing full out to occur that is, in certain respects, less watchful of the self. Going across the floor is both the telos of the class and its just reward for the dancers. The surreptitious copying that had characterized the earlier phases of class now becomes an explicit pedagogical principle, not only because two dancers are selected to go first and therefore model the phrase as dancing but also because the students have an intermediary period before this occurs to learn the phrase during which they explicitly enlist one another's help. Since the teacher will tend to indicate the movement rather than dance it fully, it requires someone in the midst of the room to emerge as one who corporealizes it. This person may or may not be one of those selected by the teacher to lead the pack but through her own activity gets featured in this instance as a model.

This too may have an influence on what the phrase ultimately becomes, hence shifting the authority of movement from teacher to dancer. At this point, therefore, mistakes can have a role in renegotiating what the phrase of movement will be for the movement toward the final accomplishment of the class in ways more directly and reflexively embodied in the students. Students will also make demands on the teacher for clarification that highlight possible discrepancies between the choreographic idea and the practical functionality of the phrase as dancing. Such shifts may be noted by the students when they call attention to the fact that the phrase has evolved as it has emerged through their bodies, as in the statement "But this isn't what you gave us before" or "Oh, so you've changed it?" This last statement keeps the teacher in his place but reminds the student of where the ultimate capacity for correcting the mistake lies.

Corrections made by the teacher usually take the form of personal attention in which the teacher instructs the class through the body of one of its members. While this may appear as a pedagogical synecdoche, the one dancer standing in for the whole, it also marks an economy through which dancers accumulate the teacher's favor. The point the teacher makes on this woman's body is not simply substantive; she is also made exemplary by being an instance of what receives attention. The struggle to incorporate the correction prolongs the ordeal of being instrumentally molded by the teacher's hand, but it means that she is now the one that momentarily directs the duration, though not the terms, of appropriation. This sort of lesson differs from the mastery of coordination on which the class is initially founded and marks a reversal in the logic of how mistakes and corrections could function in the authorization and disruption of technique through the means of technique.

In the technique class, the mistake is the hinge that mediates the relation between the figures of repetition and progress. It is the acknowledgment that change is possible in relation to the recurrence of certain patterns, patterns that sustain authority while they indicate something of the powers of change over which that authority has command. This intricate display and this process of mediation are evident in the state as such. Its incorporation of the universal will relies on both repetition and progress, the recurrent applicability of law as repeatable standard, and the claim to legitimacy of any given administration to pursue and deliver the most efficacious path of progress.

For dancers, the law is said to mark their training, the repetition of daily practice that, over time, will yield measurable improvement. From the perspective of this happy consciousness, instrumental and substantive rationality, means and ends, delivers the harmonious relation of repetition and progress. The prospect of progress is instantiated in every gesture, every exercise, every class attended. But, paradoxically, improvement within a technique is marked by greater fluency in its repetition, the pleasures of dancing being sustained through the ease with which the dancer moves through the inaugurating commands of a phrase to make it her own. When this pleasure is identified with the law, the name of technique, the affective consequences are something akin to a nationalism in which the civic movements of a population credit their own capacity to a state account.

But to the extent that the pleasure of dancing emerges precisely when technique is surpassed, the affiliation with the process of naming can never contain the desire it establishes. Both the state and the dance class seek to assimilate this contradiction within the figure of progress itself. While good government can be a goal for one whose deep political schisms are said to be resolvable through adjustment in administrative techniques (cutting bureaucracy, for example), the perfectibility of technique is not sufficient to sustain a discourse of progress. The government must appeal to a development of society and not just to the perfection of the state itself, if its populism is to appear convincingly as an ideology for the people over whom it has authority. In short, the rhetoric of ends through which the figure of progress is displayed must derive from beyond the state itself.

This problem gets articulated well in terms of the limits of technique in the dance class. When dancers are saturated with the technical, they can be requested to "forget technique." References to being "an advanced dancer" are generally made qualitatively, as, for example, the ability to embody images that would animate a given dance phrase in certain terms that here credit the already danced deed through its approximation to a word. A teacher remarked to the class, "I'm very impressed with your ability to use the images I'm giving you today." Substantively, the images reference what is outside the studio—eucalyptus trees after a rain, the sun reflecting on a wave, the feeling of warm sand on the skin (the university is in southern California). In this case, all these references to nature, familiar as they may be as authentications of movement, also serve as a form of naturalization of the body's own technical accomplishment as a pure, uncoercive interiority that could generate only consent to such commands.

While naturalization of what is politically contingent into something immutable is common to the legitimation of authority, it is not the sole means of reference for what technique could be in the service of. In one class, we are instructed to dance a routine movement pattern of alternating steps with "mambo hips" after doing some steps called "mambo" as preparatory to the modern dance phrase itself, as if this source beyond the studio, even when bracketed within it, were to animate what transpires there. This example recalls Martha Graham's formula of appropriation of "sources" for modern dance that would grant popular Latino forms the status of the indigenous. Beyond such incidental encounters, a well-known African American choreographer who teaches at the university employs the synthesis he developed of modern and African dance during the fifties in the technique class. And yet, in its own internal structure and its classification within the dance curriculum of the university, this class, called "Modern III," is not referenced in terms of its multiple cultural influences but, as we shall see shortly, is instanced in more than name only by its technilogic.

On the other hand, although the music is synthesized and synthesizes various rhythmic influences, including African, it does reference an entire field of dancing, of which these young (predominantly white and Asian American) people also partake, that is appropriative of African American culture, namely, popular music and dance more broadly. While the students await their opportunity to try the African-influenced modern dance phrase across the floor as part of the formal dance class, they break out in African-inspired dancing in the margins of the class (literally in the line in which they await their turn). The margins of the class, both spatially and in terms of its interface with other movement activities, specify that place where the technically driven class projects its own sources as part of its exterior, as a range of dance activities and opportunities that are not directly aligned with the authority attached to technique. Yet as is already apparent, this exteriority of physical culture, manifest in the popular dancing that occurs in the margins of the class, is also already appropriated within the formal movement of the class, thereby effacing any simple distinction between art and popular culture. It is this practical effect, that dance technique could lead to further dancing not simply in a professional context on another stage but also as an end in itself in a space generated by dance, that carries the figure of progress that is developed through the class furthest into society.

Splitting Authority

It is not so difficult to imagine that a given technique is drawn from and disseminated to multiple sites and activities of dance. But when actual dancers are being referred to, it is also important to appreciate the multiplicity of techniques, dancerly and otherwise, that reign in their bodies. Examining how disparate technical sensibilities are embodied in the same dancer could be of assistance in imagining the larger question of how any body gets multiply composed, where this multiplicity nonetheless allows for a practical continuity in that person's movement.[22] As with the composite body discussed in the last chapter, there is no single source for physical identity. Yet, in the dance class these various sources are already within the performative mode and make much more oblique references to mediated images. In a formal nod to the desirability of such diversity as constitutive of a dancer's training, the technique classes at this university are taught by different teachers on different days. Within a field called modern dance, substantial continuity no doubt exists between the two teachers that establishes the conditions for differentiation of technical competencies among dancers. The differences between the two teachers establish the parameters for the breadth of that field, in its historical, multicultural, aesthetic, philosophical, and pedagogical dimensions. To map each of these dimensions would take us further into the intricacies of modern dance than the terms of this chapter call for.[23] For the purposes of contextualizing the particular diversity of this dance class, it is useful to sketch certain affiliations between the emergence of modern dance and its techniques, with the universalizing project of colonialism more broadly.

Where nineteenth-century ballet tended to displace women's labor onstage onto the prior image of an exotic other that could not carry the weight of intention and hence could not work, the women who inaugurated modern dance restored this relation of act and meaning. The dancing of Loie Fuller, Isadora Duncan, Ruth St. Denis, and Maud Allan provides an image of agency that had previously been denied women on the stage. Yet this very celebration relies on an appropriation of the exotic other as the source for dance that is identified with the Romantic ballets of the nineteenth century. Like the figure of the Orientalist ballerina, the modern dancer Isadora Duncan is represented in standard accounts as an originality, a singularity without history. An appeal is made to Duncan's essence as a performer to account for the emergent character of the dancer's work. Her contemporaries provided emotional or poetic responses to Duncan rather than describing her work, hence suggesting an opposition between a rationalist mode of science and an intuitive mode of human and cosmological nature. In her own work, Duncan denies having been subject to any influence, suggesting her own experience as her only inspiration.

Yet, Duncan had studied the movement systems of the French professor of declamation François Delsarte (1811–71), which he claimed was a fully scientific approach to the body. Delsarte represented not simply a technical influence for the emergence of modern dance but also, with thousands of practitioners of his method, part of the larger physical culture that provided the context for the development of dance. Like the folk dance movements in education of the late nineteenth century, the practice of Delsartean exercises permitted Victorian-era women's bodies to congregate in the public domain.[24] Under the guise of elocution and pedagogy, speech was referenced by a perfectible body that occasioned a public gathering of women at the height of the ideology of privatized domesticity. The aestheticization of this feminine public sphere both defused the challenge presented to the conception of women and, as Duncan's self-presentation made clear, rendered the politics of women's appearances difficult to contain.

The problematic character of any interpretation of Duncan lies in an opposition of nature and science, conceived of as an obligation of analysis that divides dance's essential sources from the activity of dancing. Modern dance constituted a set of universal foundations that could transcend the very cultural differences that it appropriated. Duncan claimed that the "primary or fundamental movements of the new school of dance must have within them the seeds from which will evolve all other movements."[25] Thus the motion of veiling and unveiling, culture/science and nature, is inscribed not merely outside but also on Duncan's body as a body. That is, it both reveals and is an act hinting at a desire to reveal.

While Duncan sustained a coterie of disciples who have sought to perpetuate her work through her ideas about movement, hers is not the most influential genealogy in the history of modern dance. The institutional base for the emergence of concert dance lay more strongly in the ability of Ruth St. Denis to shuttle fees and fame from vaudevillian tours toward the development of what was then termed "legitimate theater" and the support of the Denishawn schools (and company) formed with her partner Ted Shawn in Los Angeles (1915) and then New York (1921). Orientalism was no doubt the bridge between these two performance idioms, the colonizing continuity between the high and the popular. St. Denis first toured what she considered her own choreography in 1909–10. She traveled with ten "Hindus . . . labeled 'colored' in Jim Crow America."[26] Six pieces were performed: *The Yogi, Radha, Lotus Pond, Nautch, Cobra,* and *Incense.* These Eastern materials were subject to Western relations of property before they were ever performed. The initial incarnation of her concert pageant, *Egypta,* was copyrighted in 1905. In her colonizing gaze, nature elided her cultural situation: "All the motions one needs to study for dancing can be found in nature."[27] This linkage between Orientalism and national embodiment of the "primitive" underlay the claims made by Martha Graham that opened this chapter. The imagery of the veil receives attention in writing on Duncan and St. Denis.[28] In the latter case the modernist impulse is connected to the more "universal" Orientalist roots of Western dance.

In the spectacles of nineteenth-century ballet such as Filippo Taglioni's *Revolt in the Harem* (1833) or Hippolyte Monplaisir's *Brahma* (1868), the Orient is appropriated in the service of a single colonizing gaze that disciplines gender, race, and class in the ballerina's romantic loyalty to the heroic male figure who authorizes her labor. Modernism psychologizes this appro-

priation as an interior division of the self into consciousness and the unconscious. In this myth of modernist "absolute self-creation," [29] Orientalist
content is replaced by an aestheticized appropriation of the artist-as-origin.
The external "real" or concrete veil and its hint at a nature beneath is replaced by an internal territorialization of self, one part of which is populated
by the exotic other as the labor of the creative process.

These Orientalist tropes in the antecedents of modern dance recur in the
work of Martha Graham (for example, *Cave of the Heart* [1946] and *Part
Real-Part Dream* [1965]) and can be read more obliquely in the attribution of Merce Cunningham's aleatory choreographic techniques to "Eastern
philosophy." But their iteration is perhaps most significant in founding the
universalizing claims of modern dance technique as the acculturation of a
given exotic nature. Louis Horst, who became Graham's musical collabora-
tor after the two left Denishawn in the mid-1920s, said of the dance modernists that they "recaptured the relation that the primitive has to the body — an
intimacy with the muscle tensions of daily movements which have been lost
to modern men." [30] It is in the claims to be a set of movement principles for
any occasion, transcendent of any given situation, that the repressed figure
of science returns through modern technique.

The scientific is an omitted influence that circulates under the guise of an
unmediated relation between nature and the body. For example, in denying
that she has founded a "school of movements," Martha Graham asserted,
"I have simply rediscovered what the body can do." [31] Here the artist's own
body is but an instrument for the discovery (with all this term's colonial
connotations) and subsequent adoption of what the universal body can accomplish. Nature is given the force of an absolute reality that instructs and
authorizes the body. But by attributing the Oriental other as that which lies
closer to nature, it is the power of colonization that ties the Western nation
to the self that is hereby secured. Consequently, the appropriation of labor
itself can be naturalized as what founds the Western nation. This reversal is
apparent in Doris Humphrey's statement, "The adventurousness and restless spirit of a still-young nation certainly permeates everything about us;
we are notorious for being less leisurely than most other peoples in our
ways, and more demanding of variety." [32] This aestheticization of the work
ethic as an imperative of modernist innovation was written in 1959, and
already the primitive that gave rise to the modern is now posed against it.

The primitive, the archaic, is that which resists the sheer efforts aimed at self-making the body under the name of an other and which transpires in the dance technique class as well.

It should now be clear, however, that this resistance does not go away but is the foundation for constituting this modern self and its national culture of labor.[33] Yet if the history of modern dance is viewed from the perspective of its process of appropriation rather than from that of its product, the self generated through technique is not that of a singularity but of a diversity of forms.[34] This diversity is more fundamental than that suggested by the curricula of private dance schools earlier in the century. In putatively discrete classes termed Eastern, religious, or folk dance, these generic names homogenized internal differences among the subaltern cultures that were presumably the authentic sources of these classes. Today the names applied to dance classes in colleges and universities conceal through their own administrative categories the internal differences that compose such contemporary generic techniques as ballet, modern, jazz, or ethnic.

Under these conditions, the ideology of modernism can persist even as the form and content of its techniques change. The resistances attributed to the primitive or archaic forces that belong outside the studio are now agents of the disparity between the diverse principles of movement which organize any body and the singularizing figure that authorizes which of those movement principles is appropriate. The singularizing authority arrayed against an internal diversity that it names and appropriates constitutes a kind of contradiction in the theory or ideology of modern dance technique and its practice.

Dancers, in the class I attended, and others confront the gap between the diversity of influences that reign in their bodies and the plurality of named styles and techniques, each of which, at any given moment, claims the status of a singularizing universal — that is, as technique it asserts itself as a grammar for every utterance.[35] Among the resources that dancers develop in the course of their study is the deftness to negotiate this contradiction. At the same time, this antinomy is sustained no doubt by dancers' ability to allow their bodies to serve as a site of accumulation for the fully mastered self. It would be tempting to end the account of the dance class with this fantasy of self-mastery as a compensation for an impossible division of the body into separate quarters of command, but dancers learn far more than to assume this mask of identity: they also learn to mobilize activity as dance. If the resistances to learning dance are also what assemble the dancer, mastery will always be inadequate to account for what it commands. Rather, I want to focus on those differences in technique which assume different coordinations of the body that are, nonetheless, negotiated in the same body.

One way to think about these coordinations abstractly is in terms of the orientation of the interior space of the body to its exterior. The notion of a fundamental resistance or tension between the two spaces constitutes what Hillel Schwartz has referred to as "torque," which for him is a kinesthetic trope foregrounded in modern dance that displays something of the physiognomic logic of an industrializing society.[36] A quintessential movement that indicates this trope is the muscular contraction of the torso foundational to the technique of Martha Graham and evident in the first of the two teachers who share responsibilities for instruction in this particular university class.

Bearing in mind the perils of reductionism when describing the physiognomic characteristics of a given technique, much of the innovation in approaches to movement initially associated with Judson Church and then finding dissemination in a range of modern dance practices from contact improvisation to the work of Trisha Brown could be summarized under the term "release technique."[37] In contrast to the defiance of gravity through muscular exertion associated with earlier modern techniques, release technique purports to assimilate gravitational flows in the body's interior space to its exteriority. Rather than accumulating muscular resistance in the service of a coherent shaping of the body, release technique yields an emphasis on motional qualities as such. In practice, what appear as polar oppositionalities of these two technical platforms are more a matter of emphasis within a relation of interdependence between what holds the body up from gravity and what the mass of the body marshals in its own movement. While torque is a foundational principle of modern dance, release technique is still part of the heritage of modernism insofar as it emphasizes transcendence of the deformities that culture has wrought and is willing to entertain a pure bodily logic unencumbered by mindful speculation. The question, however, is what these differences are meant to emphasize.

It could certainly be tempting to associate torque and release as the dominant social kinesthetics that correspond to a periodizing schema of capitalist development, from industrialism to postindustrialism. The forward march of such prevalent modes for organizing the bodily sensibility of an age perpetuate the universalizing oppositions of primitive and modern, Oriental and Western, through other means. The clearly defined shapes and vectors of force are evocative of the Newtonian mechanics that inform the movement of an industrial economy. The more indeterminate flows of energy suggest popular images of quantum physics that have been applied to identify an info-atomic age.

But such simple and all-embracing contrasts, reliant as they are on discrete chronological identifications, can confuse more than they clarify. The term "postindustrial" is itself symptomatic of such confusion. That industrial capital has intensified its investments in machines over people within this country and has also left the United States to shift productive capacity to places where labor and other costs are cheaper does not lessen society's dependence on such production but, rather, indicates the global and technological dimensions of the division of labor. Further, that the bulk of workers in this country are employed in what is called the service sector (which aggregates together low- and high-wage jobs from food servers to software designers) indicates the extension of commodification and industrialization to new activities or spheres where it had been absent.

Rather than this global socialization of labor and development of productive techniques freeing the body in any absolute sense, the body stands as a terminus within the vast integration of inputs and outputs of the fully commodified economy. Hence for all its references to more natural ways of moving, release technique—to the extent that it emerges within and displays the broader social kinesthetic animated by the ongoing reformation of capitalist society—attends to a more profound socialization of the body (and not simply with regards to labor but in relation to gender, sexuality, and race as well) than could those methods based on notions such as torque. On the other hand, because dance movement, like the capitalization of society itself, develops unevenly, we can only expect those technical influences associated with certain historical formations to persist as residues within culture as a whole, as well as the body in particular.

Some information about how to jump, leap, or fall, generated within certain technical domains, will retain its resonance in others. It might appear that the differences between the two teachers of the university dance class, operating as torque and release, respectively, are generational, but this would overstate the progressivism in dance technique at the expense of what gets repeated within it. Yet, torque and release actually are of some heuristic value in identifying what are at times necessarily contrary principles of motion operative in any body, including that of the dancer. The traces of the state that instantiate relations of authority in the dance technique class override what may be irreconcilable differences within a given body. This subordination of otherwise contrary orientations to movement is accomplished within the always continuous demands to abide by whatever immediate commands are disseminated in the class. Indeed, it is the effort to reconcile contradictory movements in society under a consistently nameable authority which identifies the state function wherever it appears and whose problematic character is particularly recognizable in the dance class.

It is equally important, however, to maintain that the effort at reconciliation presupposes other efforts that sustain what is contradictory in body and society, and this is what the students in their practical accomplishment of relegated multiple techniques to a given body provide (albeit always within the limits of a given range of plurality). Where these contradictions are most visible is in bodily details through which the residues of one technique may collect even in the midst of another. The hands are often a place in the body where the tension between moving and thinking about moving is displayed, for the hands, especially when learning technique is foregrounded, serve to hold onto the information that directs the body in movement. This tension is not neutral with respect to what resides in the body about techniques, and therefore it is not at all uncommon to see hands held in a shape stylistically associated with jazz or ballet (which are the other technically defined sequences of dance class in the curriculum) in the modern class.

In another example, the persistence of the vertically held, torqued body evidently provided resistance to the apprehension of a fall forward onto the hands that was called for in the more release-affiliated class. One of the more accomplished students had difficulty executing this particular movement because she was holding her body in muscular tension which would be perfectly correct for a different type of fall but which made this one impossible to execute. Hence it is not a matter of being trained or untrained as some generic condition of the body but how one form of training may come to interfere with another. This interference is not dysfunctional to dancing but what makes the movement toward the accomplishment of movement palpable for the student in the class. In this instance, the mistake emerges where the seam in the intertextuality of techniques asserts itself.

Counterexamples exist as well in what could be called the torque class, such as when a student is asked to hold a contraction in the pelvis while maintaining weight on one leg with the other extended in front of her. Although it is supposedly the strength of the torso that is holding up the body and defying the gravitational pull, sustaining the position while the teacher discusses how to accomplish it, a quiver is produced in the dancer's thigh. This quiver could be taken as what is archaic in the dancer's body to the technique in question (recall Graham's notion of the primitive as emergent), in the sense that it displays something left behind in the dancer's body — not as some primordial recidivism but as a present resistance to technical subordination. But it could also be seen as the already released body of the other technical influence asserting itself in the midst of a torquing command.

The prospect that contending principles of movement reside within the same body suggests that part of the effort entailed in learning a technique has to do with the dancer's ability to generate terms of mediation among different demands on the body. In this process of self-governance, a technique for regulating techniques, the dancer must generate her own authority. The dancer's ultimate training as the amalgamation of all these technical presences in her body is what emerges as this broadening field of mediations. Susan Foster has indicated that this heterogeneity of technique marks a certain moment in the history of dance technique when, particularly among professionals, commodification itself usurps a given technical affiliation.[38] If that is so, this present situation of technical intertextuality, illustrated in the university curriculum discussed here, may more closely approximate the situation of bodies generally in a fully commodified physical culture, both within dance and without, that, as we saw in the last chapter, brought together the weak links of mediation and affiliation within the composite body.

Intertextuality itself needs to be viewed as more than a random collection of difference that adheres to what is other to it by virtue of mere contiguity. The principle of authority is, always at the very least, a mediation of the state beyond its formal institutional apparatus, given that it incorporates some of the power to which it is ultimately answerable. Hence, it is important to grasp how this principle recurs in each instance of difference and thereby provides what may be continuous in the movement within both subject and object. In this I refer not only to the range of identities through which a given subject is positioned but also to that subject's implication in a range of relations of dominance through which it is always at least partially constituted.

Put in terms of the dance technique class, we see that it is always against the continuity of authority (maintained across different teachers) that the multiplicity of physical capacities (even when these are in kinesthetic conflict) is available to the dancer. This range of available capacities circulates between what authority denies in the way of corporal self-government and what its demands on bodies afford as an occasion for dance practice. The intrinsic oppositionality between state (mediated through authority) and body (negotiated through technique) rarely gets mobilized as an explicitly counterhegemonic expression even in the politics of the classroom. But as an oppositionality, it renders the movement toward the participation that generates consent also a move against the coercive hold on the body whose necessity appeared absolute in the process of learning how to dance. This was evidenced symptomatically in the example of the mistake and in the displacement of authority in modeling the ideal from teacher to student.

Dancing against the State

The logic of the state as the authority that is present in every site of activity —even those seemingly farthest removed from its command—presents a negation of that logic as well. At least, that is, insofar as what is continuous as an authorizing object permits each of those sites to appear as if they were themselves discrete domains of authority. It was precisely this apparent autonomy of the object in a context that provided for that object's obligatory interchangeability (or exchange for the sake of exchange) that Karl Marx analyzed so cogently in his account of the fetishism of the commodity.[39] In the terms of this analysis, however, the state is the ultimate object subject to fetishization, insofar as it objectivizes a form of authority which serves circulation in a manner that is indifferent to the value of what circulates. What appears as the state's own imperative to maintain order turns out to obscure what is systemic in this imperative.

And yet what was thought to circulate merely as a world of objects turns out to be constitutive of a certain type of subjectivity as well, one that can be grasped only as embodied. The commands to which a state subjects its citizens go way beyond repression in the face of the transgression of law but get instantiated in the very incorporation of what spans the productive citizen from the regimentation of labor to the identification of desire. In one of his final reflections on the capitalist state, Nicos Poulantzas remarks:

> To be sure, the body is not simply a biological entity, but a political institution: the relations of the State to the body are thus considerably more complex and extensive than those of repression. Nevertheless, the State is always rooted in its physical constraint, manipulation and consumption of bodies. In every State, this takes place in two ways: through institutions which actualize bodily constraint and the permanent threat of mutilation (prison, army, police, and so on); and through a *bodily order* which both institutes and manages bodies by bending and moulding them into shape and inserting them in the various institutions and apparatuses.[40]

It is to the "bodily order" that technique contributes, but what is here an important addendum to Poulantzas's understanding of the state is that once inserted in the institutions and apparatuses, bodies engage the technical through their very "bending and moulding." When the regimen that is contained within the dance technique class gets applied to what is beyond it, the practical contours of this order begin to emerge.

It is not simply the ability to hover precariously on the edge of the curb waiting for the traffic light to change, the ability to negotiate one's shopping cart through the crowded aisles of a supermarket, or the incessant pushing on the surfaces of machinery, characteristic of so much contemporary wage labor, that draws affinities with the dance technique class. The misrecognition of the accomplishment of each of these activities with the authority putatively given out by the state makes it possible for people to identify periodically with a capitalist project even as the latter abandons them to their corporal capacities without reward. For while it is unremarkable how little the state does for the bulk of its citizenry, it is more surprising to consider that the same bulk would see a place for the state (beyond any given governmental administration) in what it does for itself. For Lauren Berlant,

this contradiction is fundamental in the maintenance of the social contract
of state and civil society in the United States:

> Nevertheless, we can see a real attraction of abstract citizenship in the
> way the citizen conventionally acquires a new body by participation in
> the political public sphere. The American subject is privileged to sup-
> press the fact of his historical situation in the abstract "person": but
> then, in return, the nation provides a kind of prophylaxis for the per-
> son, as it promises to protect his privileges and his local body in return
> for loyalty to the state.[41]

Dance technique is a situation in which the process of production and
its product—the body dancing and the dancing body—are tightly joined in
local bodies and in which an ascribed affiliation far short of the kinds of
participation in the political public sphere promised by substantive citizenship may, nonetheless, be keenly felt as a depoliticizing form of prophylaxis.
Hence, the form of bodily exchange Berlant describes for the abstract citizen
operates in those institutional spheres such as the dance class that provide
the grounds for consent without the political content promised by the full
privileges of citizenship. It is the coercive aspect of this consent, the mastery
of technique as such, that acts to limit the scope of bodily demands to the
immediate instance of institutional competency. The abstract citizen finds
its corollary in the universal body conceived (but not put into practice)
by the modern dance technique class. The promise of gain, of progress, if
the particularized and primitive body is abandoned in favor of the modern
marks the class as the scene of an origin for the body, rather than as a site of
the body's appropriated labor.

Yet, exactly in the midst of such a domain, where an idealization of citizenship could readily be constructed, we find so much capacity for difference and differentiation generated by the very efforts to meet the demands
of measurable competency that appears as a kind of technical imperative.
Thus, there may be more space than was previously imagined by political
theory for the state-initiated social contract on behalf of capital to generate something other than an assimilation to its authority. Here, but also in
the aerobics class, at BAM, and at Judson, what is kinesthetically exceptional
in dancers not only proves the rule but displays something of what, beyond adherence to such authority, is self-constituting across a whole array

of technically accomplished subjectivities. If in a domain as strictly regimented as dance there is more than domination, it may be easier to embrace what authority gives rise to but cannot contain. The acceptance of the authority of the technique class suppresses the local histories that the dancer bears. Exercising this same authority suppresses its own dependence on what it commands. Because these two dependencies are of different orders, one that identifies activity with command and the other that misrecognizes a command for activity, the social contract is destabilized as it is made.

Modern dance also produces a primitive body whose colonization proceeds through the application of technique. If the forces in colonization and modern dance aspired to make the world one, to be a secular universal, the progress they prescribe does not recognize the diversity of creativity unleashed in their wake. Dance technique claims to command every conceivable movement, to devise abstract conceptions of time and space freed from their location in history and society. As with other officiating techniques, it seeks to pass off to its adherents the hold it has on the body as a kind of enhanced participation in a project to free the self to become fully aesthetic—that is, to appear as an autonomous originality. Yet in the particular city of women studied here, the male gaze that observes, instructs, and accompanies their movement becomes, in the course of the class and throughout their training, marginal to their activity.

The authority that was supposedly indifferent to gender here gives rise to it as that social category that can act against what denies it. The universalizing claims of modernity, in dance and other spheres where activity is governed, organize nations of peoples whose allegiances lie elsewhere. For despite and because of all the formative subjugations that dancers endure, their trained bodies generate a commitment to the activity of dance that will allow for their most free association. In the end, technique is more than a system of administration that states the self in terms of authority. Technique also marks a spot where diverse capacities and practical differences that compose a self are assembled. What remains unstated is an activity, at once self-critical and self-forgiving, torqued and released, that dance makes legible wherever bodies move.

Fire in the streets. Fire on the screens. Deficits char universities. Tuitions go up like smoke. Broken borders. Saturated identities. Defensive knowledges. Departments freeze. Strange times, these, to be speaking of new disciplinary formations. In the name of urgency, it is tempting to return to basics, if only their bases were transparent. Under the sign of sacrifice, a call can be heard to pare down to essentials, if only those essences would stay put. And what of discipline itself? Could anyone survive asking for more? Certainly not more of the same. Conversely, if something has recently been set loose, can calls for discipline be far behind? The discipline wittingly or unwittingly records the oddity of the newly unfamiliar. So don't new formations necessarily draw on what is strange in their times?

Any arguments for new disciplinary formations, therefore, would want to take account of the social and epistemological movement afoot in the broadest possible terms. A comprehensive understanding of a whole way of thinking, or episteme, would promote the most radical appreciation of the relation between the context for the production of a specific form of knowledge and the form and content that knowledge assumes. The prospect for a critical dance studies to emerge out of the variegated intellectual attentions that have already been given to dance depends on developments in both disciplined knowledges and cultural practices. Dance studies, properly reconstituted, promises to help materialize in thought a whole series of problems that have run homeless through the academy as well as through the world.[1] In what follows, I would like to treat dance studies not simply as the empirical collection of all that has been written about dance but also more speculatively as a project that relates to various modes of thought and from which it is possible to imagine a whole range of applications, both to dance and to other practices. Whatever turns that project eventually takes, its theorization as something that could be not only allows the various potentialities of critical dance studies to be marshaled but also helps establish the discursive terrain in which it would take its place.

Hence, I will not claim here that the present moment originates dance studies as such. Rather, like the creation of all dance, which starts in the midst of those capacities for movement that dancers already embody, so too dance studies must begin in the middle of what has been produced under its sign. To start in the middle entails the recognition of the debt to other initiatives and findings so that the project of dance studies as I imagine it might best be positioned to reflect on the domains of practical knowledge into which it intervenes. When compared with what most bodies do most of the time, dance would typically be considered a minor movement. In relation to the quotidian practices of the body, dance is a marginal endeavor, both in terms of its degree of incorporation into total daily activity and in terms of how it is inscribed with meaning and value in the pantheon of those activities.

Because dance is but a minority of the movement most people engage in, the claims that can be made for its formal political impact or direct social significance are limited. Yet, from the perspective of the minority, what often conventionally appears as informal and indirect takes on its strongest explanatory resonance. The seemingly minor mobilizations in life may reveal more about the weak linkages or mediations that allow our sensibilities to relate to one another within the body politic than may the ways in which we are accustomed to perceiving and evaluating politics. If we are used to seeing politics as a stable inscription on the social terrain, as something written into the social contract, then what actually moves the political may be missed altogether. Yet, no doubt, such established writing is everywhere. I have argued that what in dance evades representation can extend our grasp of mobilization, which is itself so crucial to an understanding of politics. But in certain respects, the study of dance has paid a theoretical price for its difference. The very resourceful and suggestive ways in which dance eludes the grasp of inscription can isolate dance from everything else that has engaged the critical attention of writers and therefore threatens dance studies with a kind of conceptual ghettoization.

What I attempt to show here is the way that dance studies could mobilize in writing the conceptual challenges that dance offers to conventional ways of understanding politics and the world, in turn arguing that dance can be specified as that cultural practice which most forcefully displays how the body gets mobilized. The emphasis on dance as bodily mobilization, rather than as any determinant movement form, may ultimately help to efface the distinction between incorporation and inscription that has divided dance and writing and allow us to imagine that middle to what is otherwise ceded in the binary relation between the linguistic and the bodily. It is this middle ground, this terrain of mediations, that I would like to see dance studies occupy and articulate.

Undisciplined Formations

An argument for dance studies, not as the topic it has always been but as an emergent field of knowledge that is its most radical promise, must understand the underlying relation between the terms "dance" and "studies." The question is a projective one. Rather than a review of all that has been accomplished by dance scholars, the obligation of the present writing is to understand how a disciplinary field is constructed. Different meanings of "dance" and "studies" could be combined to create very divergent conceptions of the field, but it is important first to imagine how the two terms could be problematized such that the epistemological and political significance of their union would be made explicit. The space of this union constitutes a certain epistemological present, a realm of imagination from which we wonder how we come to know what we claim to know. From the epistemological present, we can ask the following questions: What is discipline now? And, what is dance now? The concern with what is to become of their being suggests that something else can be announced as having just passed. In other words, to claim that dance studies could emerge under certain conditions is to assert that it comes into being after becoming something other than what it has just been. It could be said that, until recently, the specifying point of reference for dance had been body movement. Now, however, the departure from this definitional base must be conceptualized. The status of dance as a focus of inquiry, then, has to be reevaluated in light of two changes in theory and practice. The first is the loss, in recent dance practice, of pure movement for its own sake as a fundamental defining feature. The second shift has been the ubiquity of the body as an object of study by disciplines across the humanities. These disturbances to the epistemological status of dance raise the question of what its privileged object of analysis is and therefore address the issue of its specificity.

For studies, the second term in the formulation, it is equally important to ask what the status of disciplinary formations is, particularly after such movements of interdisciplinarity as cultural studies and the politics of multiculturalism have introduced the grounds for an extensive critique of knowledge in a globally constituted capitalist society. This critique opens up the problem of context. By summoning cultural studies to challenge the prevailing epistemological field, I am clearly granting it more ideological coherence and institutional effect than it has, up to now, been able to muster.[2] Similarly, as I suggested in Chapter 3, many disparate and, at times, antagonistic politics have been marshaled under the banner of multiculturalism. My aim in granting, at least for the moment, dance studies, cultural studies, and multiculturalism more stability and apparent conceptual unity as I imagine them here than they may have achieved in their practical formations is to envision the significance of each of them as a *project* that is never exhausted or fully realized in any of its myriad concrete instances. Surely the work of envisioning what we want these projects to be is crucial if we are to establish the criteria to evaluate what we take to be the limitations of existing forms of multiculturalism, dance, and cultural studies. Let me examine the definitional questions of the founding terms of my inquiry — namely, the conceptual status of dance and the epistemological standing of disciplinary studies — to see how they delimit a field for dance studies.

Such philosophers as Suzanne Langer have striven to make of dance itself a subject, or what she terms "dynamic image," an "expressive form" that objectifies the "nature of human feeling" (in opposition to the materiality of body and space out of which it is composed). What specifies dance with respect to other arts is that it "creates a world of powers, made visible by the unbroken fabric of gesture."[3] For Langer, these powers are virtual, not actual, a distinction that might allow dance and politics to appear in separate domains. The autonomy of dance from actual or quotidian uses of the body is fundamental to the conception of dance as pure movement, or movement for movement's sake.

The foundation for a conception of dance as pure movement can be located in John Martin's definitional statement in 1939 that "all dance is essentially one in so far as it is the externalization of the inner, emotional force of some kind in terms of bodily movement."[4] Movement is granted its autonomy from other social relations as an object of aesthetic reflection (this is what is intended here by modernism) because of what it displays as a feature of its own internality, namely, emotion.[5] While Martin's conception of dance is modernist, it is not confined to a particular dance idiom but rather is presumed to apply to the "essential unity" of dance as a human universal that he terms "basic dance," "the common impulse to resort to movement to externalize states which we cannot externalize by rational means."[6] The universality of dance as a human expression grounds the autonomy of the irrationally constituted aesthetic from the rationality of the social and the political, which in turn generalizes the split between mind and body transhistorically and cross-culturally. The cultural and historical specificity of these conceptual divides, which dance negotiates in practice and criticism accomplishes through theorization, leaves the critic's own positionality unspecifiable.

These modernist foundations for criticism — the unreflexive self-assignment of a universalizing authority that separates dance and politics — continue to exert their influence on contemporary discussions of the philosophical status of dance.[7] Graham McFee's recent study of dance aesthetics, *Understanding Dance,* departs from Langer's and Martin's cultural and historical generalizations to confine the appellation of dance to Western practices of ballet and modern dance. Ballet and modern dance can be joined through modernist evaluative criteria (as opposed to stylistic uniformities) to the degree that they conform to standards of aesthetic judgment. At first glance, McFee deviates significantly from conceptions of dance as pure movement; rather, he focuses on the evaluative criteria that would identify a context within which human activity could be considered dance. In the interests of specificity, which he scarcely specifies, institutional criteria are advanced that grant the "tradition" of dance an authority to arbitrate what may join this tradition which he refers to as the "Republic of Dance": "In the specific case of dance, the 'Republic' will be composed of choreographers, producers, dance theatre owners and so on, and, in particular (other) dance critics and theorists. Any movement sequence put forward as dance (self-election) and accepted by others (other-acclamation by the Republic) is indeed a dance."[8] Interestingly, McFee insists that this institutional definition of dance is separable from sociologies of dance, "which offer insight into society, but not into dance."[9]

McFee appears to employ an extreme form of nominalism to avoid movement sequences from other societies or from popular culture which could be "mistaken" for dance but which are not art. He asserts "that whether or not movement sequence X is indeed dance depends, roughly, on whether or not it is called dance by the society which gives rise to it."[10] The translation problem, namely, that English is established as a linguistic standard that other languages must be converted into and compared on the basis of, applies to the very logic of argumentation, not simply to the word itself. For the Republic of Dance rests on a self-constituted authority that is being denied responsibility for or access to the context that makes of it a context. McFee's book, then, is ultimately an argument for the autonomy of artistic judgment from the "general condition of society." Hence, with his culturally exclusionary definition of dance, he appears to proceed from the opposite point of departure from that of Langer and Martin, with their universalist aspirations for dance-as-human-essence.[11] Yet he winds up reaffirming what is essential to their common conception of dance studies, namely, the separation of the dance object from the rest of what transpires within society, or the autonomy of the aesthetic from the political, which I take to be the underlying assumption of modernist criticism.

The complication of these modernist assumptions for the study of dance, the very project that concerns me, is itself no simple matter. For example, to suggest that dance has lost its definitional foundation as pure movement seems doubly dubious. Such a claim first assumes that we know what dance is and have already consolidated all the practices that could be called "dance" under the definition. Second, it assumes that these practices had not only sustained this loss of definition but survived it. Another possibility, however, is that, while dance retains its diversity, the epistemological foundations for the claim to be able to isolate pure movement from other forms of art and of life have been shaken by a shift in how we think about the relation between theory and practice. For the corollary of movement purity in dance practice is a presumed autonomy for the aesthetic in the realm of theory, which is, in the above examples, what grounds, without needing to name or situate, the authority of the theorist or critic.

When the ideal of aesthetic autonomy within ballet and modern dance is problematized, so too the whole modernist theory of criticism is challenged as well (as I suggested in Chapter 2 regarding the critical reception of Bill T. Jones in its efforts to contain the choreography's political effects). Even when the concert forms of ballet and modern dance retain their institutional modes of production—from the administratively driven economies of fund-raising, subscription, and touring to the fixed investments of scenographic shops and proscenium stages—their aesthetic materials and syntax incorporate cultural sources in a way that undermines the conceptual stability of the autonomy of pure movement. This is not to suggest that Balanchine's work is at risk of suddenly disappearing from the repertory at the New York City Ballet or that Merce Cunningham now sees himself as telling stories through his work. Consider the constant slippage between ironical references to dance made through dancing and parodies of the holiness of consumption drawn through a nonmovable feast on stage in Mark Morris's *Hard Nut* (1992), or the connective function of dance to suture the enactment of social vignettes in David Rousseve's evening-length *Urban Scenes/Creole Dreams* (1992), or the use of frenzied passages of the corps de ballet to offset the rise and fall of Michael Milken in Karole Armitage's *Predator's Ball* (1996). These deployments of dance and narrative figure a relation of mutual disruption and integration between movement as an absolute horizon of the body and a panoply of contexts in which the kinesthesia of daily life becomes discernible, from the suburban living room to the street corner to the stock exchange.

The point is not that these urban and suburban vistas are novel settings for concert dances to depict but that the movement content of these contexts is now put into circulation through the development of technical vocabularies so as to reassign the production of aesthetic value from the stage back into culture at large. With the conceptual reassignment of where value is produced, the criteria for what dance makes cultural reference to become more inclusive and ambitious than the forms of cultural example that were allowable within the older framework. More inclusive because a site of dancing (club, house, school, square, television) can no longer be assumed to specify the dancerly. More ambitious because the fundaments of dance would have to be located in the field of cultural production (and hence society) as a whole rather than resting securely in the tautologically contained definition of art (art is what artists do). Pure movement, then, however it is defined, is not lost to dancing in its myriad sites and forms but to evaluative criteria. On the contrary, because of the very proliferation of movement materials both within dancing and without, the condition by which these materials mix must now be theorized in a way that situates, as the modernist critic does not, the very politics of theory and criticism.

But while the multiplicity of movement provides new resources for dance studies by substantially widening its scope, the preponderance — across the humanities — of the body as an object of study could just as readily eclipse as it could fortify the emerging field. The burgeoning interest in the body as an object of study needs to be taken as the context within which critical studies in dance could emerge, rather than a jealous competitor in a zero-sum academic marketplace, where there is only so much intellectual resource to go around. To the extent that critical dance studies frames its problematic as one that focuses beyond an understanding of dance per se, it also addresses a larger audience that can be drawn into the specificities of dance practices.

The visibility of the body in recent academic studies could be attributed to the general textualization of cultural practices that widened the field of what could be read or taken as an intellectually legitimate object of study. But the gain of a textualized body could not always provide an adequate perspective from which to theorize what bodily practices reference beyond their textual representation. This referential, nontextual dimension of the bodily slides back into the text in discussions of literature, medical manuals, fashion, or penal codes so as readily to overlook the utility of studying practices that foreground bodily mobilization as opposed to representation, as dance can.[12] When this happens and to the extent that they do not notice what they are missing, then the openness of the various disciplines to dance studies is cast into doubt. To put the matter this way indicates that the future of dance studies is not wholly self-determined on the quality or merits of the work produced but rests on the larger epistemological context that generates the conditions of reception for any given field of study. For there is no appellate court to which a case could be made that would allow disciplines to rise or fall on their own merits. It becomes necessary to grasp the transformation of the means of knowledge production in its entirety, what could be called the epistemic domain, to assess the potential for new spaces of knowledge. The strongest claims for dance studies would lie in this new situation for knowing and not in some absolute status for what can be known.

Institutionally speaking, it is clear that the rhetoric of zero-sum economies of cultural capital often subverts the substantiveness of intellectual discourse. Without doubt, problems of allocating funds, of assessing needs, and of identifying demands are inescapable. At the same time, when these issues are couched in narrowly institutional terms, they can do more to conceal their political stakes than to make those stakes available for discussion and decision. This is why it makes more sense to begin with the broad sociointellectual transformations that have affected the disciplines and then begin the war of position over what institutional ramifications may ensue. Thus while interdisciplinarity, which I am taking as the underlying condition of possibility for the emergence of dance studies, always has concrete institutional effects, these effects are so fully mediated that their politics can be determined only locally (whether, for example, to form departments or interdepartmental affiliations). But the epistemic shifts signaled by interdisciplinarity can be addressed in a more general fashion.[13]

To avoid the feigned innocence of claiming grounds for dance studies as an absolute or original discovery, it would be worth pursuing the hypothesis asserted by Michael E. Brown that disciplines always have interdisciplinary foundations.[14] The way we think about disciplined knowledge today in the United States owes a great deal to the professionalization of what could most broadly be termed intellectual labor that occurred toward the end of the nineteenth century. Professions may, for a time, have succeeded in creating the impression of self-generated grounds for their expertise, but this did not free them from other contradictions. The development of such occupations as medicine and architecture reveals the tensions between the specialist's disciplinary claims to the monopolization of knowledge on the basis of a more generalized process of rationalization within capitalist society, on the one hand, and the ethical questions of how this newly constituted particular interest might serve the universal good, on the other.[15]

According to the logic of rationalization, the universal good is best served when the development of knowledge proceeds according to the functional requisites of its object. Hence doctors have both the commitments and the resources required to further medical practice, the gains of which are then disbursed to the population at large. Yet the resources that must be expended to assure that other practices do not occupy the privileged space of the medical profession potentially limit innovation and dissemination of knowledge. This last conflict between the particular and the general displays the traces of interdisciplinarity within the disciplinary rhetoric of the professions, for they are always constituted against what they resemble but must exclude if their practice is to remain the privileged site for the object of knowledge over which it claims to have authority. That these contradictions play themselves out in very different ways is evident in comparing the medical profession, which succeeded in placing itself at the center of the whole constellation of sickness and health (its privileged object), with architecture, which historically has been marginal to its object (only a fraction of construction is actually driven by architectural practice).

The creation of specific institutional sites for academic practices (university departments) around the same time as professionalization partially masks and partially resolves some of these questions of privilege but submerges the presence of interdisciplinary foundations in a rather similar manner. It is precisely this submergence that generates the ideology of foundations as something intrinsic to a discipline that is then incapable of specifying what the conjuncture for that discipline was. The object of knowledge is thereby presented as something both eternal, in the sense of being without origin or end, and absolute, insofar as it is seen as being constitutionally stable within the discipline.

The formation of academic literary studies rested on a dual movement. On the one hand, classical languages were displaced by modern language as the privileged repositories of culture. On the other hand, a universalizing humanism, which literary culture was seen as transmitting, after Matthew Arnold, was amalgamated with a particularizing scientificity associated with historical and philological studies. While the tensions between these sources continued to produce different ideologies of literary study, they were nonetheless the elements that had granted the new field its autonomy.[16] Even more specific, if American sociology were to have a foundational text (one written nearly a half century after the departmental formation of the field in the United States), it would have to be Talcott Parsons, *The Structure of Social Action,* a reading of the logic of social theory out of disciplines adjacent to sociology.[17] In both these examples, what subsequently appears as an indifference to origins, in the sense of their unspeakable ontological status, marks the point at which the authority to occupy a certain space of knowledge production is transferred from the disciplinary practice (with its attendant history and politics) to the more abstract object of knowledge itself within disciplined discourse.[18]

Once knowledge appears as a property of a certain specialized speech without history or politics, debates can be confined to disagreements over what should properly be represented within the literary canon, as opposed to addressing the institutional and epistemological supports of the canonical apparatus.[19] When the basis of authority for who claims truth never itself comes up for review, it is possible to argue over the nature of society without reference to what the stakes of those arguments are for the intellectuals who make them. It follows, then, that the disciplinary suppression of interdisciplinarity renders inaccessible to discussion an account of the means and ends of the work that disciplines perform and concedes the situatedness and interests of the intellectuals who perform those tasks within society. Hence, not only are disciplined objects of knowledge absolute, but disciplined intellectuals are also, in Karl Mannheim's terms, "free-floating," that is, unencumbered by their actual relations to societal institutions for the production of knowledge.[20]

Because the suppression of what is taken to be interdisciplinary within disciplines (the context, not the origin of their foundation) amounts to an aporia over the ties of knowledge and power, the stakes of the emergent interdisciplinarity of the last decades that places dance studies on the agenda can now be appreciated. The new interdisciplines, most broadly grouped under the rubric of cultural studies, constitute a critique of the absolute object of knowledge and the self-positioning of the intellectual. This critique can also be applied to the whole formation of specialization and professionalization that underpins the modernist ideology of a rational society. While each of these formations (from women's, queer, black, Latino, and Asian American studies to cultural studies itself) has an expression within the academy, each is also explicitly linked to something that extends beyond the academy. This linkage was certainly one consequence of the sixties movements that joined the insistent recognition of difference with the institutional materialization of this recognition, as evidenced in a range of phenomena from civil rights legislation to budgetary allocations for new academic departments. The critique of disinterested knowledge, associated with Jürgen Habermas and indebted to the student movements of the late sixties, was one way of grounding intellectuals in terms of their own context for knowledge production.[21]

But the assertion that the object of knowledge became fundamentally destabilized when its own sources were constituted across a complex societal field where gender, race, and class cultures lie, introduced an indeterminacy about where knowledge was constituted in relation to its object.[22] All this is to say that the double of interdisciplinarity of the last decades was not the specializing demands of universal reason, as had been asserted a century before, but the reflexivity of difference in the process of identification, the terrain of this process being what I want to refer to as the social base for multiculturalism. The previous disciplines had insisted on a climate of certainty, a positivism with respect to the relation between the professional knower and the disciplined known. Interdisciplinarity after the likes of cultural studies now rests on problematizing the status of hitherto existing conditions of knowledge production and therefore raises the level of uncertainty about what objectivities and which subjectivities get produced. We can, for example, revisit the debate that emerged over the epistemological status of the subject during the past decade, in which a tension was expressed between the critique of the transcendental ego and the assertion of the authenticity of the hitherto unrepresented to speak for themselves. If these divergent perspectives are taken in their totality as a sociological phenomenon, then the antagonism itself can be seen as a critical resource for the elaboration of the cultural politics of difference, not simply a point of division for that politics.[23] The return of the repressed in cultural studies is what here joins interdisciplinary content with multicultural context in a way, as Bruce Robbins notes, that foregrounds the institutionality of knowledge work and hence extends the politicality of the new formations.[24]

That so many attacks on cultural studies emanate from beyond the university's hallowed halls indicates how grounded in the ways of the world discussions over the possibility and commitment of knowledge have become, rather than being seen as governed by the sui generis demands of disciplinary objects.[25] It is for this reason as well that the sixties remain the obsession of the Right into the nineties (as discussed in Chapter 2), as if by obliterating both the memory and the efficacy of those earlier times we could return to a still prior originary moment of truth claims, indifferent to their politics of production. In this light, it seems less surprising that the unreconstructed antagonism toward any variant of multiculturalism could be powered by a nontheological religiosity perhaps misleadingly labeled as fundamentalist. These religious fundamentalisms can be understood as nontheological in the sense that they are disinterested in critically investigating the kinds of ontological questions that typically occupy religious institutions.

One of the key tropes in this religiosity is a form of corporal exchange where the body of the born (actually the woman who bears) is substituted for the unborn (an entity that bears no traces of this necessary labor).[26] Whatever the demographics of the adherence to this trope as a phenomenon of belief, it is its ability to circulate and structure the discourse of discourses that strikes me as most significant. This putatively seamless exchange of bodies (present for absent, different for same) underpins the negative response to the gains made in the field of multiculturalist mobilizations from which the reflexive interdisciplinarity of cultural studies springs. For the substitution of the (rights of the) unborn for the (rights and capacities of the) living has the effect of naturalizing the very process of exchanging living labor for its abstract product such that the former disappears in the service of the latter.

A formulation as general as this for the imbrication of a capital logic in society would be of little use in a historicized account of the emergence of interdisciplinarity if it could not be translated more specifically into certain prevalent features of the negative response to multiculturalism to have surfaced during the 1980s and 1990s. What becomes legible through this particular trope of bodily exchange is a relation between two figures of control that are much more extensive forces in the reproduction of capitalist hegemony than those that apply strictly along the lines of gender. The first figure is exposed when the implicit demand for consent to a ubiquitous surveillance of every space of social life assumed by the outing of women's reproduction choices is made plain. For the call to end those choices assumes an agreement to police not simply labor but also desire, wherever it may emerge, as that which is fundamental to the general social contract. Here women double as metaphors for unrestricted production through their fecundity and as metonyms for producers through their very concrete possession of actual means of production whose juridical virtuality as ownership is being denied them. Hence submission to the generalized surveillance over what can be produced replaces the uncertainty of (knowledge) production associated with the most self-critical forms of multiculturalism with a certifiable allegiance to the (here patriarchal) demands of production without concern for use.

The consent to generalized surveillance signaled in the trope of bodily exchange under the New Right that was asserted in the eighties is closely bound to a second figure of this economy of social control that is part of a more general reaction to the sixties that I seek to sketch. Surveillance over bodies and bodily production assumes an agreement with respect both to being watched and to watching for practical transgressions. A regime of surveillance operates not merely as an attitudinal adjustment but also as an entire structure of participation. It therefore assumes that every occasion for surveillance presents itself as a transgression in need of punitive containment. In the most strident and revealing formulations of antiabortionists, it is not enough for women to be told they are without reproductive choices; they must be stopped and punished should they make the wrong choice. To uphold the law of life's production in the abstract, the concrete producers must be sacrificed.

In turn, their sacrifice requires an apparatus of coercion—to force their absentable product from its presentable absence—the crux of choice in the production of reproduction that is women's special collective capacity. Surely, the language of production itself risks reducing what women are or could be to specific effects of their labor. Further, the double meanings of labor as it is used here overstates the Right's ability to treat reproduction as subject to a fully commodified economy. But the point in showing where women's actual historical self-articulation joins a generalized climate aimed at repressing multicultural articulations is to indicate the specifications that are necessary if any more comprehensive conception of a historical moment (here, one where the body becomes a privileged object) is to be possible. The forces that bear on emergent formations and tensions within the university setting do not emanate from within that particular site.

At the same time, part of the challenge of radical variants of multiculturalist politics is to see what travels and what doesn't as other manifestations of difference are included in the account. The trope of presence and absence is a figure for the more general denial of the conditions for the social reproduction of labor on which any appropriation of surplus rests. As such, the rhetoric of visibility needs to be combined with an analysis of what is considered public and private and how the institutional arenas of paid economic activity and domesticity are treated by the state as it seeks to manage the population by means of the divisions from which the likes of racism, sexism, and homophobia flow.

Patricia Williams masterfully weaves these issues together, as she plucks examples from the daily fare of media representation and legal casework. She notes that when the interconnection between woman and fetus is lost to the substitution of the former for the latter, "the fetus becomes an incorporation of the woman, a business fiction, an uncomfortable tapestry woven from rights-assertion-given personhood. It is an odd, semiprivate, semipublic undertaking, in which an adversarial relationship is assumed between the public and the private."[27] When the business of reproductive technology meets the economics of race, damage is likely to be reported. Williams cites the example of a white couple in which the husband made a deposit at a sperm bank; the wife returned for artificial insemination, gave birth to a child "she describes as black," and, after enduring the "racial taunting" of her child, filed a wrongful birth suit.[28] Williams herself ponders the implications of systematized reparations for blackness, including the "intellectual castration" from the black community as a price of her own professionalism and, concomitant to this, her status as a childless and single woman, when "black babies have become worthless currency to adoption agents — 'surplus' in the salvage heaps of Harlem hospitals."[29]

As race becomes articulated with socioeconomic status, gender, and sexuality, the body remains in focus as a contested site, but the opposition to this realm of difference can no longer be summarized so neatly as rightist or fundamentalist. What returns to minimize the now raced and gendered body's labors are the more abstract and impersonal forces of the market assigning its hierarchies of devaluation and dispossession. If the labor of the woman is disavowed and made absent, the "surplus" of black bodies seems to be represented excessively, as unadoptable children, as unemployable teenagers, as incorrigible and incarceratable youth, but also as bodies with star quality that brings in the gold.

The current traffic in black bodies is, of course, the legacy of slavery, on which, as Cheryl Harris has argued, race and property become fused, so that whiteness is attributed with the legal rights and ontological status of an inalienable self, with protections to use and enjoy its privileges through exclusion and appropriation of what belongs to it. Black bodies, in contrast, are alienable, not in possession of themselves, yet their value derives from their very presence, which, once purchased, signifies unpaid labor for others. While the juridical framework to exercise white privilege has eroded with emancipation, civil rights, and affirmative action, the expectation to dominate has continued. Harris notes: "In protecting the property interest in whiteness, property is assumed to be no more than the right to prohibit infringement on settled expectations, ignoring countervailing equitable claims predicated on a right to inclusion."[30]

It is important to reaffirm that the entitlements associated with those expectations have also diminished. Here, I refer not only to government-provided benefits but also to lowered wages and restricted access to consumer credit, mortgages, higher education, and health care—in short, the whole material infrastructure of social reproduction. So too have the very terms of exclusion and inclusion changed from the days of slavery, as I suggested in my overreading of Bill T. Jones's choreography in Chapter 2. For while under slavery the exclusion of blacks from the use and enjoyment of the bodies of others as property was what included them within a productive economy, the present exclusions figure blackness as the source of a surplus population—as those displaced from the labor market when means of production are reorganized—rather than as producing surplus labor. However exploited, the accumulation of black bodies was intrinsic to an economy that now seeks, in certain sectors and instances, to live without them. Increasingly in public representations of crime, welfare, single motherhood, and workfare, black bodies come to stand for the more general figure of expendability and exclusion against an earlier promise of emancipation to a universalizing development of modern society. Perhaps another dimension of the demonizing attacks on black cultural output is to destroy the idea that exlusion from the coercive forces of labor markets themselves might be a source of freedom. Again, it is important to emphasize that this figuration elides the vast majority of African Americans who are actively part of the workforce—for them, actual relations of exploitation do not make the news or have their day in court. Yet, in the current wisdom of investment, the display of newly expendable domestic bodies is linked to images of equally superfluous bodies in certain zones of the former second and third worlds, in the nightly rites of this nation's news, where it appears that homicide, genocide, and ethnic cleansing are the moral attributes of surplus populations, rather than factors in their production.

For the present formulation of white supremacy, it is the combination of retaining privilege against others who could share in claims to equity with the specter of becoming a surplus population, extraneous to the circuits of appropriated labor, that blackness is now intended to figure for some putative, white common sense. Between surplus labor and surplus population, bodies overused and rendered useless, lies the divide between culture and nature, abundance and scarcity, civilized and savaged, the binaries that recur to sever the no longer necessary from those who can still board the train to progress. Even for those on the train, many will be diverted from the promised land of imagined inclusion. So many of the newly minted jobs pay less than the ones they have replaced, and the standard measures of economic expansion and political stability deliver less confidence in the future than had similar reports of prosperity in decades past. Where progress based on forced inclusion in a capitalist world order once promised universal inclusion, new wealth seems less contingent on holding all populations within its mastery. Surplus population depends on labor cycling in and out of productive activity as requirements of accumulation change. The refurbished racism, sexism, and homophobia of the present are oriented toward this ability suddenly to exclude what was once (and may once again) be economically necessary.

The emphasis placed on the body in this macabre vision of humanity against itself allows the selection process to appear as a feature of the immanent characteristics of individual bodies before the judgment of the market. While anyone can make it, collectivities can be addressed only in the negative, as figures of failure. Animated by this renewed logic of scarcity and exclusion, life chances are determined by free will without the organization or intervention by the state. This should remind us of the double meaning of privatization—a denial of the role of the state as it acts to secure the conditions for the accumulation of wealth, and a disavowal of the claims of those who historically were excluded from the public arenas that recognize needs and demands as political, that is, that the needs of such persons are merely private matters.[31] But privatization as a state-mediated project entails the administration of bodies in the domestic sphere, with respect to the legislation of sexuality, domestic violence, and the civic conduct on which decolonized settings become desirable and penetrable, as M. Jacqui Alexander has observed in her study of the Bahamas.[32]

The connection between decolonization and deprivatization should not be lost for a critical multiculturalism's bodily politic. The refusal to be contained by the boundaries of the colonial or the private and the ability to self-recognize the unruliness of the various differences I have been discussing fits with the two dimensions of multiculturalism that I identified in Chapter 3. The body that is at once mediated and performative is also an instance of the principle of composition, which points to a surplus of the social beyond the instrumentalities of appropriation. For what is a surplus population from the perspective of the market may nonetheless be constitutive of a whole dimension of human association that generates an excess or surplus of social activity and cultural production beyond what the market can absorb. The economies of consumption oriented around differentiated market niches depend on but cannot exhaust the appeal of expansive sexuality, of exotic personality, of excessive fecundity, and of extravagant bodily achievement. The task of expanded accumulation for global capitalism is to sunder the labors of these various productivities (that now include attributes of culture and identity) from the populations that generate them. The problem for administering an amplified field of use values is that the social accomplishment that created the value in the first place constitutes a collectivity that enters, as it deepens and diversifies, the world of the political. As I suggested in Chapter 1, the mobilization that gives momentary form to these collectivities (there, that unstable presence called "audience") does not leave a trace of itself. Rather, the mark of mobilization is left in the policies, commodities, and configurations of space that are assimilated to the body by means of various techniques (Chapter 4).

Much in the policies and rhetoric of governments inspired by rightist ideas during the eighties and nineties did represent a highly repressive realignment of consent and coercion in its domestic and foreign extensions of surveillance and sacrifice. It would not be difficult to trace through some of these manifestations with respect to, for example, a highly destabilizing credit economy that joined first world consumers and third world nations in a computerized frenzy of increasingly supervised subsistence expenditure. Nor would it be hard to see parallels in the militarization and penalization of society at home and abroad incumbent in a war on drugs that took as prisoners small (marijuana) farmers and a (Panamanian) president. The rightist inspiration for the government appears to at times be voted in and out of office. Yet the more general oscillations between coercion (applied to and constitutive of surplus bodies) and consent (individualized participation in the market that appropriates and addresses bodily surplus) remain perhaps the most vivid idea in U.S. politics. Communications superhighways are hardly at odds with escalating surveillance. Riot control without riot and new taxes without social programs are still taken as political common sense.

It is in this broader context that the prospects for interdisciplinarity promised by a multiculturalism from the base must be considered, not only in terms of institutional resources but with respect to its general appeal. In the light of these constraints, multiculturalism needs to be seen above all as a social process that, as long as the imperium is intact, remains incompletable. By reasserting interdisciplinarity here, after discussing how a rhetoric of bodily exchange has been marshaled in the service of the repression of a critical multiculturalism, I very much want to suggest where dance studies could align itself within an epistemological conjuncture. The Right sees the body as everywhere, and everywhere the Right sees it, the body is presently ungovernable and in need of further repression. This surplus can be grasped only in relation to some other economy of bodily exchange whose effects the surplus seeks to mask and oppose.

Dance studies could take the opposition of this opposition as its outer horizon where epistemology and politics meet. Even if in its particular instances it left this context implicit, dance studies could serve to articulate the condition of the bodily in a manner that would dramatically enlarge the stakes and interest in what is frequently associated with dance.[33] Again, it is toward the articulation of that aspiration for dance studies, rather than the delimitation of its practical possibilities, that I direct the present comments. I have just sketched something of the field within which dance studies might intervene. It remains to outline what some of the claims of that intervention might be.

Mobilizing Dance

That dance studies could be poised for an intervention into a larger cultural and political field already assumes that it has broken free of a certain condition of its (pre)production for a way of knowing that could only have been internal to it. It is now placed in a position to act projectively, to imagine itself critically and to influence other fields. This point at which a project can articulate itself out of its own internal history, the moment at which it raises its intellectual stakes as a field in its own right, I refer to as an "epistemological break," after Althusser's use of Gaston Bachelard.[34] What Althusser intended for a reading of marxism through Marx's own work was the point where Marx can be differentiated from the very critical climate out of which he emerged. This does not mean that a specifiable schism exists in Marx's personality or a set of texts can render the history of reading Marx suddenly unrecognizable. Rather, this break represents a departure for reading in which what is different in Marx as a foundation for theorizing can now be mobilized.

It seems to me that such a moment could be located for dance studies in the mid-1980s and signaled in the distance between the collection of essays edited by Roger Copeland and Marshall Cohen titled *What Is Dance?* and Susan L. Foster's monograph *Reading Dancing.*[35] Under a single question of content, Copeland and Cohen assemble several centuries of critical writing on Western concert dance by such authors as Jean-Georges Noverre, Selma Jeanne Cohen, Francis Sparshott, Yvonne Rainer, Roland Barthes, and Joann Kealinohomoku. It can be distinguished from other volumes by its conceptual comprehensiveness in the editorial organization of the field of dance studies. The essays in the collection are grouped under the following headings: "What Is Dance?"; "The Dance Medium"; "Dance and Other Arts"; "Genre and Style"; "Language, Notation, and Identity"; "Dance Criticism"; and "Dance and Society." This classificatory scheme permits a logical movement from specifying the dance object as such to seeing how dances "reflect and illuminate the cultural mores of the societies in which they are created."[36] No doubt the same authors could be grouped in ways that supported different conceptions of classification. In this instance, the underlying idea that is sustained is that of the modernist separation between dance and society, as implied by the metaphor of reflection as a process between two mutually external and fixed entities.

The editors begin their introduction to the book by asking, "Can we formulate a definition comprehensive enough to cover the wide variety of activities routinely referred to as dance? Unfortunately, the theoretical literature of dance provides only limited help in answering this question. . . . If we are to arrive at a satisfactory conception of dance we have much to gain by appealing to the most influential traditional theories of art and the dance literature that is informed by them."[37] Here the appeal to tradition is meant to overcome the "resistance" to theorize dance rather than to mobi-lize that resistance.[38] Consequently, dance theory has an object, but it lacks the means to think its own practice until, like a vessel, it is filled from the outside. Paradoxically, then, their comprehensive treatment of the problem of definition of dance results in an idea of dance that remains pretheoretical.

By organizing these very different studies, with their different disciplinary inflections, under the same investigating authority, the editors of *What Is Dance?* seek to stabilize the object, dance. They do so not only by ordering contrasting definitions into a dialogue but also by exploring "the inherent limits of the dance medium," which entails asking the question, "At what point does dance begin to exceed its competence and encroach on the do-main of other arts?"[39] One might include among these arts the various disciplinary fields themselves, especially philosophy. This volume's appro-priation of interdisciplinarity is very much that of the founding moment of academic disciplines a century before. It is not, however, sufficient to articu-late a disciplinary project in the present given the multicultural revision. The assembled disciplines in question — philosophy, history, anthropology, sociology, literary criticism, and so forth — are what remain foregrounded in these studies and offer a point of return from which dance is a specialized foray. This is not in any way to question the value of these studies of dance but merely to suggest that the return home to their respective disciplines did not bring with it a registerably disruptive effect on their own intellectual foundations. Studying dance did not necessarily interfere with disciplinary business as usual. While these studies are dispersed across disciplines and hence appear well poised to articulate this interdisciplinarity, they have not been able to identify what their own founding interdisciplinarity entails and can therefore more easily fall back into their particular sites. In this vein, very useful studies of dance from a variety of perspectives could (and do) continue to get written without staking a claim for dance studies as a speci-fiable epistemological domain.[40]

In contrast to Copeland and Cohen's definitional project to specify the object of dance, Susan Foster's theory of dance representation produces dif-ferent modes of reading autonomous dance practices. Hence, each particu-lar instance is normalized and made familiar through an explicit theoretical procedure that accepts four tropes or figures of speech: metaphor, me-tonymy, synecdoche, and irony, derived from literary theory as embodying the fundamental relations between all things in the world (including dance). Hence the elusiveness of the ways in which dances produce meaning is rendered into a set of structural categories that are evident in any set of human practices. This procedure is stated apart from her main text in extensive footnotes, which can be read in their entirety as methodological appendixes.

Foster is not aiming to identify the essence of dance history so much as to present "outlines of paradigmatic approaches to making and viewing dances."[41] In this she is concerned with emphasizing those apparatuses by which dance is appropriated in writing rather than in reading, in order to feature the self-constitution of the production and reception of dance in dance commentary. This entails providing categories for distinguishing between dance work that yields "a sustained, humorous, critical and communal practice," as with improvisationally based dance experimentalists of the 1970s Grand Union or Meredith Monk, on the one hand, and reflexive dance practice "that reinforces conservative values even as it leads to a profound sense of alienation," as evident in Twyla Tharp's choreography.[42]

At the same time, Foster retains a sensitivity to the historical. Her embrace of Foucauldian taxonomy for the representation of historically constituted forms of discursive practice suggests a solution to essentialist historiography that is not without its own complications. "Instead of advocating a single aesthetic project by showing its resilience over time or its development through various stages, the arrangement of historical dance forms side by side supports and encourages a diversity of choreographic pursuits." Yet while she appears to have avoided a periodization that relies on finality, teleology, she presents the autonomous periods of "distinct cultures or strata" where these distinctions depend on an absolute chronology ("1400 to 1650, 1650 to 1800, and 1800 to some time in the early twentieth century").[43] What she is able to avoid in denying finality, she yields to in subjecting periods to an abstract and historicizing standard.

Her effort to project an isomorphism between the tropes of choreography and those of historiography relies on Hayden White's discussion of tropes in *Metahistory*. "Following White, I assume that the mode of representation—the tropological equation that allows art to represent life—offers the primary entry point into each period's epistemological organization."[44] White's study of major historiographers of the nineteenth century, however, was intended to identify the relationship of their selection of tropes to their politics. Foster avoids political assessments in all but the reflexive episteme of the sixties and seventies to discriminate between the "conservative" choreography of Tharp and the "critical" work of Monk and Grand Union.

Within each discursive episteme of metaphor, metonymy, synecdoche, and irony, the primary mode of representation identifies both the signifying chain of a dance form (from conception through performance to interpretation) and its relation to history. "The nature of that relationship may be more precisely expressed as follows: [Deborah] Hay maintains a metaphorical relation with the Renaissance dances by *resembling* them. [George] Balanchine's relation to the eighteenth century is metonymic, or *imitative*. [Martha] Graham, as emblematic of expressionist dance [1890–1950,] stands in synecdochic relationship to it. And [Merce] Cunningham retains an ironic distance from his objectivist descendants." [45]

The isomorphism that Foster attributes to literary trope, choreographic mode of representation, and contemporary and historical choreographic examples begs the question of politics in favor of an idealization of epistemes. In the environment of difference that makes up the aesthetic Foster wants to champion, the principle of communal practices she sees as responsible for a resistive form of dance making and viewing cannot be accounted for historically. The tension between the aesthetic autonomy among the different tropes and the engagement of difference necessary to produce community is lost in Foster's framework. There is no sense of historical contexts or problems that choreographers, dancers, and publics might respond to and emerge within as a condition for their work. Rather, the structural characteristic of a period marks the structure of a given dance work. The very analytic procedure that frees her to theorize the construction of meaning in a particular work occludes access to the interference between conflicting choreographic or social principles that could give dance its historical quality.

Such a procedure does distance itself from the judgmentalist attitude toward works that Foster justifiably seeks to avoid and allows her to refrain from the essentialism of asserting boundaries among works. But it does so at the expense of historical context and the social principles with which works are animated. In effect, by beginning with the autonomy of a given artist's discursive practice, the emergent character of the work — and thus its historical character — is left unaccounted for. She evades the relationship of the work to the broader interdiscursive field within which all choreographic projects collide. As Foster acknowledges in her discussion of Tharp, on the one hand, and Monk and Grand Union, on the other, not all the play of difference yields collectivity. Foster wisely avoids any reference to the reflection by dance of "its" time. Instead, she imputes a structural identity to dance and history that does not specify conditions of production. The autonomy of epistemes achieved through a radical refamiliarization of a given aesthetic project appears to segregate accounts of the arts from accounts of society, agency, and history.

Foster's work, *Reading Dancing,* could be considered a text of the break, as Althusser calls it, because it makes it necessary to think of dance not as a particular site but as a condition for the production of a certain knowledge. It is with her work that the project of thinking through dance—rather than identifying dance—receives its seminal articulation. That knowledge is more, but not less than, what the various hyphenations of dance (history, anthropology, aesthetics, notation, kinesiology) provide, namely, a foregrounding of how a given form of knowledge gets produced. In the supplementation of the question of what dance is with how dancing can be read, a double movement is implied. The first takes us from the stable object of knowing to the contingencies of its production through a reading. This allows a shift from site to condition of knowledge. The gaze that could fix dance within a given disciplined space now becomes a certain way of grazing across an entire terrain. The conventional way of defining dance and the focus on definition as dance studies' principal charge provoke anxiety over whether a given site that contains a specifiable content is adequate to the appellation "dance" and can therefore sustain the demands of an autonomous aesthetic. Critical studies, however, emphasizes a more ambitious indeterminacy over what to make of the proliferous activity of dancing that is not confined to privileged sites of performance.

Once dancing is established as a condition and not merely a location (or, in the case of dance, a given content), the issue of its production and its product is thereby raised. While dance lends itself to infinite readings, it presents itself as a discrete thing in need of interpretation; it remains an object of knowledge. Instead, the emphasis on dancing demands attention to an activity that must be produced through an incessant process where the product of that process is itself a cultural practice. This shift from object to practice, manifest in the conceptual priority of dancing over dance, is precisely what cultural studies has offered interdisciplinarity that makes those foundations explicit and available for epistemological reflection and political commitment. What precisely are the gains of such a maneuver?

For cultural studies, "practice" is a key term that joins epistemology and politics. Practice is what emerges at the juncture between what is given or structured of a particular historical moment and what is generated through forms of agency. Structure concerns the organizational principles for social relations and agency, the means for acting on the world it inhabits in a way that generates social materiality. Hence, a practice is not simply an effect of agency, because agency itself emerges already conditioned by structural effects. Yet, as discussed in Chapter 1, insofar as structure and agency retain the discrete separation of object and subject, practice emerges instead as the already amalgamated process of these last two terms. From the perspective of practice, it is no longer possible to insert human activity into a fixed landscape of social structure; both moments are formed in perpetual motion.

Where this insight has its immediate political application is to the series of practices articulated through race, class, gender, and sexuality. Each of these words points to a systemic structuration that appropriates different forms of surplus through racism, exploitation, sexism, and homophobia. By extending a productionist model to domains not generally associated with an economy oriented toward exchange, I want to take seriously Marx's understanding of capitalism. He treats it as forcibly constituting, by the very organizing boundaries it erects and then transgresses, in pursuit of increasing magnitudes of surplus, the global collectivity, the "combination, due to association," that he understood as the socialization of labor. The extension of Marx's concept of socialization to a widening range of practices deepens rather than detracts from the power and aims of his analysis. To take the production of surplus seriously in these other domains should not reduce practices to mere instruments of the ends of domination where race, gender, or sexuality are in turn nothing more than products in a profit-taking market. Rather, the emphasis on surplus identifies what is productive in race, gender, and sexuality such that the proprietary claims of the dominant position in each system are exposed as emerging only through what dominance subordinates through appropriation. The unacknowledged dependence recurs along different dimensions of dominance on what it subordinates through appropriation. This dependency of the dominant is one reason that white-ness is both the hatred of and the desire for blackness, that misogyny aspires to the rape and reverence of the feminine, and that homophobia is the rejection of sameness and the need for it. In short, the appropriation not only produces the divide between dominance and subalternity but also the demand for further appropriation as a very condition of social reproduction. That race, class, gender, and sexuality, as the very materiality of social identity, are also produced in the process indicates the practical generativity — the ongoing social capacity to render life as history — necessary for any cultural product. Therefore, it is not that a productionist approach assigns race, class, gender, and sexuality the same history, political effects, or practical means. Instead, this approach is intended to imagine the context for critical analysis that would grant these four articulating structures historicity, politics, and practice in relation to one another, that is, in a manner that is mutually recognizable.

To speak of practices, rather than objects of knowledge, as what disciplines serve privileges the capacity for production over the already given product-object as a founding epistemological premise. The focus on practices also allows production to be named historically so as to situate it with respect to existing political mobilizations. If the older set of disciplinary formations constantly had to ask, "Knowledge for what?"[46] it was because the autonomy of knowledge from other social relations was assumed. The practices of cultural studies imply commitments that are constitutional to knowledge as such and can therefore be used to ask how one set of practices could be articulated with another.

The problem that these critical insights pose for the existing institutionality of disciplines is that the language of practices must find a way of circulating in a disciplinary world that (still) finds its conditions of existence through objects, in this case, objects of knowledge. Although English and sociology can be practiced, they take their epistemological occasion to be a specifiable object: language and society, respectively. What is signaled in the movement between dance and dancing (a movement that flows in both directions) is how an object becomes practical. If dance studies can be instituted on these terms, then it marks the conditions under which the disciplining of knowledge production can emerge as practice.

Dance studies would be helpful in the articulation of cultural studies more broadly, which has not been free of the object insofar as the joining of the popular to what was once reserved for the canonized elite is taken as the addition of so many cultural texts or artifacts, each one now equivalent to the other.[47] If a comic book is just as valid and intrinsically complex an object as a prized literary work, then the gain of access to existing institutionalized formations can be attained without much guarantee of transforming the disciplinary structure of institutions.[48] On the other hand, the question arises of what is practical about the comic book. This would entail its readerliness, the way it circulates, its relation to social fantasy, its relation of interruption with other media (intertextuality), and so on. If these issues are now taken to structure how literature must be taught and not simply what objects are included on lists of required assignments, then the result is altogether more radical.

What can be claimed for dance in this regard is that its proper analysis demands that it be viewed as a practice. When the practical is absent from representations of dance, dancing becomes almost impossible to specify. This claim rests on an argument that the relation of dance to its own means of textuality is very different from that for other arts, including other performing arts. In art history and criticism, the language of the photographic slide seems well established as a means to talk about what is represented in a given artistic object and of what is absent from that representation in terms of authenticity. Reading certain musical texts can be taken as logically prior to musical practice when that practice results from an already written score. Similar relations hold between a dramatic performance and a play script. While the lexicon of dance is no more originary than other aesthetic expressions—movement, like literature, has always already happened before it is temporalized in performance or reading—the fullness of its absence in the traces left by dancing, whether as notation, video, or kinesthetic memory, enacts the very shifting from object to practice where the latter asserts its necessity over the former.

This is not to say that no modes of representation exist that expose dance, that no writing can address it, that no textuality binds it. Dance, like any other practice, is suffused with all these possibilities. Rather, representations of dancing map the performance of detextualization, the moment at which any practice, including logophilic ones, displays that it is more than language and thereby opens the door to the "prison house."[49] Detextualization, it must be emphasized, is not atextuality. Dance is not without text, it is not free of objectification as if it were some pure instance of spirit, nor is the bodily lost in the absolute divide of some binary that makes it inaccessible to intellection or mind.

Detextualization is precisely the movement from object to practice (recalling that practice is not pure subjectivity but the labor process that amalgamates subject and object, agency and structure). That movement is what occasions dance studies. But because the shift from object to practice that occasions dance studies is in turn transformed by the internal production of the new interdiscipline, movement is rendered into something else by its identification as a practice. That something else I have termed "mobilization," the means through which bodies gather and are assembled and the materialization of identity that is accomplished in the process. It is as a consequence of mobilization that the grid is generated in which sociohistorical space and time are plotted.

If different dance practices embody different principles of mobilization, then what dance studies as a whole produces is a theory of the contingency of chronotopic, or space-time, environments.[50] Space and time are no longer the abstract raw materials out of which practice is made; rather, the mutual transfusion of spatiality and temporality is what practice produces. Dance studies tracks how units of temporality circulate within a given performance to the point at which they occupy space (the way in which a slow traversal across a stage marks its dimensionality and metaphorizes its scale) and how in turn spatializations of bodily form give temporal units their apparent boundary (as when a repeated step generates the perception of tempo). Hence, dance studies adopts mobilization as the tracking of traces in an accumulation of materialized identity effects (those social productivities of race, class, gender, and sexuality).

The foundational epistemological transformation from object to practice that dance studies effects in its internal dialectic of movement and mobilization is far from innocent with respect to its interdisciplinary context of cultural studies and its political context of multiculturalism. Just as cultural studies could benefit from the way in which dancing refuses to be just another cultural object, text, or artifact, a critically reconstructed multiculturalism and, as I argued in the introduction, politics more generally inform and can be informed by the shift in inflection from movement to mobilization. For example, even in the rhetoric of the New Left, oppositional politics were characterized as "the movement."

As is now well rehearsed in the multicultural critique of the Left in the United States, this well-bounded entity credited with articulating the distinct and nonreducible effectivities (that is, the capacity for influence) of race, class, gender, and sexuality could also produce an elision of any of the remaining three terms in the assertion of the one. The boys of antiwar were accused of having others do their legwork, and the women, of looking a certain way. Labor, of loathing the politics of others. Gays, of being free of labor. African Americans, of having a single sexuality. Yet what all these caricatures betray, beyond the homophobia, racism, sexism, and classism of their formulations, is something of why the critique of these appropriative practices can be generated only within a properly multicultural terrain.

As with the more abstract terms of time and space, the issues generated over the meaning of multiculturalism have provided (like dance studies may provide) the means through which the critique of each of the appropriations could circulate through a given mobilizing process. As such, it is not "the movement" that has produced these critical insights and the practical language through which they circulate. Rather, the very proliferation and mobilization of the terms of societal differentiation around which relations of domination and appropriation crystallize generate materialized identity effects through a whole conditioning of sites where politics is today staged. Although it is not the case, for example, that sexuality becomes race, it is evident that sexual practices are racialized, not in the sense of having a given (or essential) racial content but insofar as practical effectivities of sexuality are always mobilized in a racial formation.[51] The insistence on mobilization is what makes the particular accumulated effect of a given practical moment both contingent on the mobilizing principle at play and specifiable not as absolutely original but as immanently contextual.

If mobilization allows the body to be detextualized in the way that multiculturalism articulates the internal circulation of practical politicalities, what then does dance studies do to this mobilized body? Here it becomes possible to suggest how dance studies could offer a methodology for an economy of the body different from that of the exchange of absent for present (unborn for the labor of those already born), the divide of surplus labor and surplus population (in the reconstitutions of racism that dispossess the body as a spectacle of expendability from its own laboring capacities), or the initiatives of a doubled privatization (to recolonize newly constituted socialities for the market and to depoliticize the needs they generate). This entails treating the body, like historical agency more generally, as a complex circulation of identity effects and a concrete site for the composition of multiple and mutual association, where one practice articulates rather than cancels another. The body is viewed, then, not as a unity but as an economy with its own internal and nonreducible effectivities. Time and space condition and are produced by bodies, but they do not account for a circulating body's composition. Terms that can more fully articulate the body's materiality may prove more helpful in identifying this economy.[52]

The language of the senses provides a vocabulary different from that of space and time for imagining bodily interiority. Clearly, any adoption of the senses for critical analysis is not philosophically innocent. Since Aristotle, senses have been seen to carry the burden of an essentialized, putatively universal human body. Adopted uncritically, such a view of senses and bodies risks treating political questions in purely formal terms and subsequently aestheticizing knowledge as the search for the truth of those forms. Dance studies could offer a shift toward a view of the senses as subject to persistent negotiations over their significance and the place they occupy within the bodily economy. In this economy, the senses are not properties or faculties of the body but a strategy that is constitutive of body. If the association of movement with the body as a tightly bounded entity could not permit the internal circulation attributed to mobilization, then perhaps the body itself should not be assumed as an outline or, worse still, a self-policing fortress. Even solo dancing implicates other bodies and assumes that the expressivity of what circulates as interiority is not confined or contained to that edge or boundary we attribute to the skin. That such a belief could move within a culture attests not to the truth of physiology (which tells us of hair follicles and permeable membranes, of electric fields, and of incessant exchanges, not of some vacuum-packed slab of meat) but to the truth of vision, whose failure has been typically understood as a bout of false consciousness. Dancing constantly enters into a space that is not yet visible out of which it will subsequently disappear as it makes that space disappear. Yet it is worth entertaining the possibility that these entrances and exits are not simply from the visible but into other registers of sensation as well.

One would want to inquire, for example, into an acoustic approach to dancing to see how different spatial and temporal figures distributed among a group of dancing bodies could generate kinesthetic effects. Or, one could study how spatiotemporal affiliations generate an absence in the collective interiority of those bodies present. Certainly in multicultural mobilizations one would want to attend to effects generated in the negative spaces and polyphonic temporalities of the range of practices set in motion. This is a more productive approach to the appreciation of political effects that elude the visible than is captured by the term "unintended consequences." It should also be plain that the importation of acoustic models to dance or other practices does not mean that sound can be essentialized as a stable sense-presence. If the senses are treated as socioperceptual systems, then we must inquire into how they operate as activities, and not what processes of seeing or listening possess as a given content. To listen to dance, to hear dancing, must be more than the percussive encounter of bodily surfaces against their own built environment; these sensitivities must inform the whole way we attend to a practice. While the visual and the acoustic interact with dance in potentially productive ways, dance is most frequently associated with the art of the kinesthetic, which would render its most familiar sense system that of touch. Yet, as with the other senses, this touching or feeling is not necessarily that of physical contact but that of a sensed contact organized through some circulation of the physical. In certain respects, then, the dance-generated notion goes beyond the use of structure of feeling in the work of Raymond Williams, in which it designates a historical sensibility that is itself nascent in a range of practices. The ability to be implicated in a mobilized physical presence makes a body attend to the prospect of mobilization. That this ability could be applied to dancers and their audience suggests a way beyond the chasm sometimes found in cultural theory between production- and reception-centered accounts. By locating dancing among bodies that are differentiated into performers and audience, we can sustain and distribute what is productive and the necessary receptivity implicit in communication across those seemingly binary positionalities of producer and receiver.[53]

Between and Beyond: Choreography and Dance Technique

That dancing takes surfaces as depth, fleshy contacts as the confusion of means and ends, is yet another form of bodily circulation, now of interiority with its own exteriority. To say this, however, is already to imply a term other than dancing that is constitutive of it, one that has animated but has also been long absent in this chapter, namely, choreography. What is specific to dance are its own constituting practices, dancing and choreography. I want to conclude with a discussion of the resonance of these terms for cultural studies and a political economy for multicultural bodies.

By multicultural bodies, I mean to gather the conceptual momentum built up in these pages and speak of the mobilization of difference materialized momentarily in various social kinesthetic practices or techniques. Multicultural bodies are composite, instanced by immediate and mediated associations, and not amalgamations of fixed identities within stable group memberships. Although what these bodies produce is subject to appropriation and commodification, bodies' specific forms of mutual interdependence generate a social surplus that leaves its mark in the configurations of space and time in which we live. It is toward the elaboration of society itself and against the subordination of social life to domination and exploitation that these differences make a difference or create a politics. No doubt, this articulation of multicultural bodies is complicated by the acts of state and economy that seek to deny difference its context and convert, by means of what is recognized in rights or what circulates as commodity, an irreducible multiplicity into so many units of discrete, monocultural identities. I would not want to suggest that such reductive and subsumptive recognitions are without utility to the critical multiculturalism being invoked here. Although meant for control and profit, relations of state and economy (not, in the last instance, readily separable) are also themselves transformed by what they seek to co-opt and assimilate. Official multiculturalism would have difference be a property of individual bodies. The efforts at this line of administration constantly run into resistance, however, because difference is what relates and composes bodies as collectivities. One of the predicaments of a radical multicultural politics is how to evaluate the efficacy of its own capacities for mobilization, when it is invited to recognize itself in the arrested motion of resources targeted for a fixed position. This problem alludes to the crisis of theory and politics with which I opened the book and is one that I hope dance can address with its own special resources.

At first glance, choreography and dancing would appear to be the local variants for dance of the now familiar opposition between structure and agency that the shift from object to practice was intended to complicate.[54]

In actuality, the two constitutive features of dance offer their own ultimately helpful complications to the conjoined mobilization of subject and object attempted by cultural studies and required to realize the politics of multiculturalism. One reason dance can contribute to the larger political discussion is that both choreography and dancing remain practices that present their own amalgamation of structure and agency. The choreographer is situated between the dead body of her existing work and the living bodies who make the continuation of that work possible. The work of those living bodies presents itself as a problem that is at once organizational and aesthetic.

Organizationally, the choreographer must institute a process that ultimately rids itself of her if it is to come to fruition. It must trespass on her founding linguistic authority if it is to come into being as the embodied activity she desires for what a dance, at its creative inception, not yet is.[55] These organizational resources of the choreographer are joined with the aesthetic ones by means of a ligation of the usually implicit rules generative of rehearsal processes, which are aimed at mobilizing bodies, together with the syntax for those rules designed to organize movement. Clearly, the choreographer draws from more than her own history of choreography. Instead, she appeals to the broadest historical horizon in a stream of kinesthetic mediations — that is, the place at which choreography is drawn out of a given physical culture. Hence, especially and most commonly when the choreographic function is not personified, as in the case of myriad popular dance forms, the enunciation of dance from a more generalized cultural disposition toward movement is crucial.

But it is exactly here, at its founding sources, that choreography reveals its own internal relation to its apparent opposite, for the process through which movement is articulated as dance depends on something generally attributed to dancing itself, namely, technique. This means (techne) for generating movement, for practical mobilization of the body, assumes some capacity for the internalization of syntactic structures that might be associated with choreography. In the dialectic of technique and virtuosity, it is the moment of detextualization, in which mobilization momentarily eclipses what has mobilized it, on which the West has pinned its desire for dance through the figure of the star.[56] No doubt, we would not have to reach for such heights to notice detextualized bodies, which, as already suggested, are constitutive of all mobilizations.

Dancers, whatever the cultural status of their dancing, exist in relation to some technical foundation for movement whether it is explicit or implicit, whether its pedagogy is self-referential or unnamed as such. While choreographer and dancer (even if these are the same person) depend on each other for their particular agency, that agency is already made possible by the structural interpenetration of choreography and technique. In this regard, choreography is a metatechnique. It is a method for generating means of movement and offers a basis for differentiating movement values out of a given cultural context that provides the orienting principles for a body of techniques.

It follows that technique is itself metachoreographic. For a choreographer cannot initiate a particular dance by originating, in any absolute sense, the movement of which it is composed. As I said at the opening of this chapter, the creation of all dances must begin in the middle—that is, in the midst of those capacities for movement which the dancers embody. Dance technique, as is apparent as soon as one changes teachers, classrooms, or cultural locations, is highly situational. What each site for dance technique displays is a certain aspiration for an entire condition of the body, a body that technique valorizes. Thus, techniques are not neutral with respect to a given culture. They are also choreographically inflected or, to be more precise, they are the materialized possibility of a given choreographic trajectory.

The premise that wherever there is dance, choreography and technique are mobilized through dancing, is an open and ongoing hypothesis that dance studies must continually pose. For to answer or prove this hypothesis definitively would conclude the final dance study. But what is an immediate undecidability for dance studies can turn out to be an enormous resource for multiculturalism. The epistemological break for dance came when it was realized that dancing could be treated as a language like other forms, removing the shackles of a prelinguistic autonomy from the world of cultural discourse. That dance can now enter discourse means that it must be able to show its own differentiation from the discourse and how it can, in turn, further epistemic transformation as a whole. This is important because cultural studies assumes that real political gains can be had in the struggle over the conditions of knowledge production not simply as a means of official validation but as a means of valuation for the myriad mobilizations in which people are already engaged.

It is from language, from dance studies' newly found comfort with dance as text, that a break within language itself is now possible. For if dance were to assume the mantle of what language has accomplished for cultural studies — the circulating mobilization of structure and agency in practice — it would have to show the gains of inserting the dialectic of choreography (with its metarelations to technique) and dancing (with its bodies of circulating senses) into the epistemological spaces that have now been opened. By this I am referring to the basic distinction found in Saussure between langue, or the structural capacity for language, and parole, or the specifiable speech act or utterance.[57] Cultural studies, at least as imagined here as a critical project that encompasses emergent dance studies, represents the most powerful use and critique of this linguistic model. It promotes an extensive democratization of identity at the same time as it has examined where the cultural theorization of language has failed that democratic project.

Without rehearsing either of these aspects of cultural democracy, I want to turn to the problem that langue and parole have posed for radical multicultural politics: a theory of structure and agency that polarizes the two terms to the point where the prospect of their mutual historical transformation becomes difficult to conceptualize. The polarization of structure and agency is especially problematic for multicultural politics given that it represents precisely the field where such transformations occur. Indeed, much of the politics of representation, to say nothing of representational politics, has stumbled on this point, for it is difficult to have one's voice heard when an utterance is lost to its structural occasion because the universalizing langue cannot be recognized in the particular parole. Similarly for representational democracy, the call to "throw the bums out" does little to assure that the very distance between formal structures and needs could be ameliorated only by different principles of representation.

By introducing choreography and dancing at the crossroads of the crisis of representation that has shaken the epistemological foundations of the West, I do not want to succumb to the temptation of posing interpersonal proximity as a solution to the woes of a globally constituted society.[58] On this last construction of a multicultural world system, there seems to be no conceivable (or, I would argue in a different context, desirable) alternative. Any notion of a return to the past is unavailable both logically and politically as a model or ideal. Invoking a nostalgic return as a figure for the future has invariably meant excluding the bulk of those in the present. The beauty of the small assumes the universalization of both the small and the beautiful, a rather large idea and one that confuses size of social units and societal scale (after all, what could be smaller, historically speaking, than imagining a society composed of five billion nuclear families of one?).

All this is to say that what dance offers cultural studies and politics is not a new theory of small groups that provides a template for social engineering. Instead, critical dance studies can develop an account of the interpenetration of structure and agency that makes palpable the radical contingency (the possibility of mutual influence and therefore difference) of these two analytic terms, without losing sight of the appropriation of surplus that necessitates a critique of domination. Radical contingency assumes that appropriation is neither unidirectional nor unidimensional, not that all outcomes are equally likely or desirable. It is thus possible to recognize the histories of cultural appropriation that have undermined the basis for human association while acknowledging that the multiple borrowings of practices from diverse sources is constitutive of multicultural bodies. This capacity to incorporate difference establishes affiliations that can be drawn on to undermine the imaginaries of partition and division. It is not simply the ability to identify with the other but to depend for one's own movement on what one has learned as productive in an other that can serve to enlist participation in various multicultural mobilizations. These steps taken may enhance the very avenues of exchange, even if they operate in the shadows of those who traffic in stolen goods, for ownership tends to steal the limelight, but not the stage, from those who dance to further their own devices.

The circulation of the body through the various fields of the senses (a sort of simulacra for multiculturalism itself) sustains a heterogenous range of cultural and historical difference in its incessant exchange of absence for presence, public for private, and a social surplus for surplus labor and population. And with each circuit of this exchange, the socialized labor so vivid in the close encounter of choreography and dancing multiplies the capacities, the effectivities, and the desire of this new political economy of the body. Its novelty resides in no small measure with what gets valued, namely, the very capacity for mobilizing difference, which choreography treats as its most fundamental resource and leaves intact as the social surplus that makes further dancing possible. It is not that choreography can exist without a momentary objectification of dancing labor or commodification of choreographic time in performance. Rather, this labor becomes the means of choreographic agency in its encounter with the public reception that realizes the value of this productive process as the association of bodies mobilized in performance. In this, dance performance makes legible a principle of society in which labor itself is the ends of human association and not merely its means. What is radically close in the encounter of choreography and dancing is not necessarily apparent at the level of the interpersonal but rather emerges when the interpersonal already reflects what makes it possible politically and epistemologically. As such, an analysis cannot begin with proximity but must view what is close in time and space as the consequence of the way in which those terms get constituted globally.

Because struggle issues both out of and through oppositional terms, dance is not simply a product but a labor process of what struggle could be. This last possibility is that of a socialized economy of the body radically different from that proposed by the rightist call for sacrifice and surveillance under the sign of exchange of the unborn for those who bear, the spectacle of racialized surplus bodies, or the privatization of need on behalf of an ever expanding circulation of commodified want. If interdisciplinarity is to be more than just another better idea waiting for its successor, it will be a production of ideas in the service of realizing what this socialized economy demands if it is to come to prominence but cannot yet know. The desire for this knowledge animates the project of dance studies I have imagined here.

Beyond the concrete works that emanate from it, this project has three inflections. The first is the challenge to the conventional ways of understanding politics. The place of the theoretical gaze with respect to what it looks at has too often taken this separation for granted. The result is not simply a divide between who can speak and what is spoken for but also a sense that the latter is fixed and immobile, an interest awaiting activation. The mutually constitutive relations of agency and critical presence concretely yet unstably mobilized in performance allow the basis for politics to be recognized as already in motion and not suffering the crisis of arrested development. Second, critical dance studies holds the promise of developing this language of mobilization beyond its present state of affairs that too often renders political movements as insufficient to the demands of their times and, in effect, minimizes recognition of the efficacy of future mobilizations. For these theoretical resources to be developed, dance must be taken as a kinesthetic practice that puts on display the very conditions through which the body itself is mobilized, rather than as simply a privileged aesthetic object.

Finally, dance studies can take up the critique of representation developed in cultural studies to find an analytic ground between incorporation and inscription, the bodily and the linguistic, historical subject and agency. The body of the text can be used as a metaphor for the materiality of language and its practical enactment. But this specification of text can come at the expense of rendering the body, the attributes of materiality, and the conditions of enactment as generic. So too, overidentifying body and word as a kind of architectural skeleton can entomb a process that is not yet dead.[59] The elaboration of the critique of representation, a charge of radical multicultural intellectuals, cannot avoid representation's own internal difference, as, for example, between ideas that speak *for* social formations (proxy) and those that portray or speak *of* collectivity.[60] Yet this critique, even when it acknowledges the differences between subject and agency, cannot be confined to speech about speech. So much of human practice cannot be spoken for, and even a portrait needs to be composed through applications of bodily techniques. What is left out of language, what animates speech, can also be subjected to a historical and materialist analysis that can allow us to sense what continues to develop even when ideas, invariably tied to the mast of events, appear to fail. The political undertaking of supporting an expansive body of the social (against its appropriative reduction), just when the idea of community seems so much at risk, can renew the significance of socialism. It is toward this project that dance studies may lend a certain vocabulary.

Notes

Introduction: Iterations of Dance and Politics

1   One might say that any analysis that rests on a scheme of periodization is susceptible to these strict terms of comparison between past and present to the extent that these two concepts rely on a conception of a clear and irretrievable break between two qualitatively different moments in time. Symptomatic here are the divergent invocations of marxism with respect to the contemporary present, sometimes referred to as the postmodern condition. Following in the tradition of Ernest Mandel's historical schema in *Late Capitalism* (London: Verso, 1975), Fredric Jameson in *Postmodernism, or, The Cultural Logic of Late Capitalism* (Durham: Duke University Press, 1991) and David Harvey in *The Condition of Postmodernity: An Enquiry into the Origins of Cultural Change* (Oxford: Basil Blackwell, 1989) have directed a marxist inquiry into social and cultural movements that set up not altogether healthy comparisons with those of the past.

   On the other hand, in their *Hegemony and Socialist Strategy: Towards a Radical Democratic Politics* (London: Verso, 1985), Ernesto Laclau and Chantal Mouffe have treated the same rupture as the basis for a postmarxism. Laclau and Mouffe begin with a similar observation to the one that informs this book: "The very wealth and plurality of social struggles has given rise to a theoretical crisis" (2). But they treat this situation as the basis for making general statements about the end of "normative epistemology" and "the era of universal discourses" (3) that are still more sweeping than those they reject on precisely these grounds of being "totalizing."

   Two recent studies cast doubt on the very utility of the distinction between new and old social movements that frequently divides the literature. See Alan Scott, *Ideology and the New Social Movements* (London: Unwin Hyman, 1990), and Klaus Eder, *The New Politics of Class: Social Movements and Cultural Dynamics in Advanced Societies* (London: Sage, 1993).

2   Along these lines, many texts have been influential, including Mikhail Bakhtin's development of multiple voicedness in *The Dialogic Imagination: Four Essays,* ed. Michael Holquist, trans. Caryl Emerson and Martin Heidegger (Austin: University of Texas Press, 1981); Martin Heidegger's treatment of disclosure to interface theory and practice in *Being and Time,* trans. John Macquarrie and Edward Robinson (Oxford: Basil Blackwell, 1962); Maurice Merleau-Ponty's phenomenology of the body in *The Phenomenology of Percep-*

tion (London: Routledge and Kegan Paul, 1962); Michel Foucault's biophysics of power in *Discipline and Punish: The Birth of the Prison*, trans. Alan Sheridan (New York: Vintage, 1979); Gilles Deleuze and Felix Guattari in their mutually disrupting productive and antiproductive forces of capitalism in *Anti-Oedipus: Capitalism and Schizophrenia* (Minneapolis: University of Minnesota Press, 1983); Jacqueline Rose's feminist elaboration of Lacanian psychoanalysis in *Sexuality in the Field of Vision* (London: Verso, 1986); Gayatri Chakravorty Spivak's articulation of nonreducible and coterminous politics in *In Other Worlds* (London: Routledge, 1988); and certainly all these in the service of a certain reading of production and circulation in Marx's *Capital*, ed. Friedrich Engels, trans. Samuel Moore and Edward Aveling (New York: International Publishers, 1967). I have attempted to come to terms with the literature on the body and the problem of the subject-object relation in my *Performance as Political Act: The Embodied Self* (New York: Bergin and Garvey, 1990), especially chapters 1–4.

3   This work has had very different intellectual influences and political dispositions. See, for example, Murray Edelman, *The Symbolic Uses of Politics* (Urbana: University of Illinois Press, 1964), which draws on the dramaturgical perspective of social interaction found in George Herbert Mead and in Kenneth Burke, and the French situationist Guy Debord's *Society of the Spectacle* (1967) (Detroit: Black and Red, 1983), which anticipates much of Jean Baudrillard's writing.

4   Speech act theory, based on the work of J. L. Austin, makes a distinction between constative utterances, which assert, and performatives, such as saying "I'm sorry," which enact an apology. See Austin, *How to Do Things with Words* (Cambridge: Harvard University Press, 1955).

In his fascinating analysis of the appeal of nationalism through its ability to sustain a "nondiscursive kernel of enjoyment" that grants an "ethnic community" its "ontological consistency" (202), Slavoj Žižek endows the operation of performative speech acts with enormous subversive capacity (237) that assumes a strict regulation of the self and the social within a linguistic economy. See his "Enjoy Your Nation as Yourself," in *Tarrying with the Negative: Kant, Hegel, and the Critique of Ideology* (Durham: Duke University Press, 1993), 200–37. Judith Butler critically elaborates Žižek's account of the centrality and limits of "political signifiers" in mobilization, while acknowledging that "it is, of course never quite right to say that language or discourse 'performs,' since it is unclear that language is primarily constituted as a set of 'acts'" (281). See *Bodies That Matter: On the Discursive Limits of "Sex"* (New York: Routledge, 1993), also "Arguing with the Real," 187–222.

The power of such analyses is in their tendency to associate performance with a linguistically based practice, eclipsing in no small degree attention to more literally enacted forms. Hence, in a recent attempt to ground politics in a certain embodied productivity, Michael Hardt and Antonio Negri want to distinguish their approach "from the many contemporary attempts to employ 'performance' or 'performativity' as a paradigm for social analysis and social practice: although performance highlights the social importance of *signifying or discursive practices*, we use labor instead to focus on *value-creating practices*." For the present writing, the latter, while never free from the former, is substantially consistent with the notion of performance. See their "Communism as Critique," in *Labor of Dionysus: Critique of the State Form* (Minneapolis: University of Minnesota, 1994), 2–21; quotation from 7–8. For a critique of performativity on behalf of bodily practices of live performance, see Sue-Ellen Case, *The Domain-Matrix: Performing Lesbian at the End of Print Culture* (Bloomington: Indiana University Press, 1996).

5   Alain Touraine, whose work has been curiously peripheral to that done in the United States, has sought to found a sociology on the idea that "social life is produced by cultural achievements and social conflicts, and at the heart of society burns the fire of social movements"; see *The Voice and the Eye: An Analysis of Social Movements*, trans. Alan Duff (Cambridge: Cambridge University Press, 1981), 1.

6   Gustave Le Bon, *The Crowd: A Study of the Popular Mind* (New York: Macmillan, n.d.). See also Michael E. Brown and Amy Goldin, *Collective Behavior* (Pacific Palisades, Calif.: Goodyear, 1973), for a critical review of this literature.

7   Mancur Olson, *The Logic of Collective Action* (Cambridge: Harvard University Press, 1965).

8   See Carol McClurg Mueller, "Building Social Movement Theory," in Aldon Morris and Carol McClurg Mueller, eds., *Frontiers in Social Movement Theory* (New Haven: Yale University Press, 1992), 3–25, esp. p. 3.

9   Marxist state theory in the seventies and eighties was indebted to the work of Nicos Poulantzas. See his *Political Power and Social Classes* (London: New Left Books, 1973) and *State, Power, Socialism* (London: New Left Books, 1978).

10 A good sense of the field and the critique that it had incorporated at the end of the seventies can be found in Mayer N. Zald and John D. McCarthy, *The Dynamics of Social Movements: Resource Mobilization, Social Control, and Tactics* (New York: Little, Brown, 1979). The confluence of urban and grassroots approaches can be found in Michael Peter Smith, ed., *Breaking the Chains: Social Movements and Collective Action* (New Brunswick, N.J.: Transaction, 1991). Daniel A. Foss and Ralph Larkin offer a contemporary critique from outside the resource mobilization framework in *Beyond Revolution: A New Theory of Social Movements* (South Hadley, Mass.: Bergin and Garvey, 1986).

11 Illustrative here is Anthony Giddens, *The Constitution of Society: Outline of a Theory of Structuration* (Berkeley: University of California Press, 1984), and Piotr Sztompka, *The Sociology of Social Change* (Oxford: Basil Blackwell, 1993).

12 A recent review that asks whether the entire enterprise has run its course is Steven M. Buechler, "Beyond Resource Mobilization? Emerging Trends in Social Movement Theory," *Sociological Quarterly* 34 (May 1993): 217–35.

13 See, for example, Ron Eyerman, *Social Movements: A Cognitive Approach* (University Park: Pennsylvania State University Press, 1991).

14 In *Power in Movement: Social Movements, Collective Action, and Politics* (Cambridge: Cambridge University Press, 1994), Sidney Tarrow notes the separation of power and movement in the literature but insists that the "common denominator" that triggers mobilization is "interest" (5).

15 Jacques Derrida makes this point as he contributes to the focus on Francis Fukuyama's *The End of History and the Last Man* (New York: Free Press, 1992) in *Spectres of Marx: The State of the Debt, the Work of Mourning, and the New International* (London: Routledge, 1994).

16 The literature on "collapse" is now legion. A good sampling of perspectives can be found

in Robin Blackburn, ed., *After the Fall: The Failure of Communism and the Future of Social-ism* (London: Verso, 1991), and, more recent, Bernd Magnus and Stephen Cullenberg, eds., *Whither Marxism: Global Crises in International Perspective* (New York: Routledge, 1995). One of the more spirited theoretical orientations that takes this position is that of radical democracy; for recent articulations that may unwittingly contribute to the frag-mentation they seek to overcome, see Carl Boggs, *The Socialist Tradition: From Crisis to Decline* (New York: Routledge, 1995), and Stanley Aronowitz, "The Situation of the Left in the United States," *Socialist Review* 23, 3 (1994): 5–79. In our work, Michael E. Brown and I have attempted to come to terms with the underlying assumptions of these literatures. See, for example, "Rethinking the Crisis of Socialism," *Socialism and Democracy*, no. 14 (1991): 9–56, and "Left Futures," *Socialism and Democracy*, no. 18 (1995): 59–90.

17 Raymond Williams, *Marxism and Literature* (Oxford: Oxford University Press, 1977).

18 For a seminal development, see John Clarke, Stuart Hall, Tony Jefferson, and Brian Roberts, "Subcultures, Culture, and Class," in Stuart Hall and Tony Jefferson, eds., *Resis-tance through Rituals: Youth Subculture in Post-War Britain* (London: Hutchinson, 1976), 9–74.

19 James C. Scott's *Weapons of the Weak: Everyday Forms of Peasant Resistance* (New Haven: Yale University Press, 1985) is a key text here.

20 For an illuminating discussion, see Mark Franko, *Dancing Modernism/Performing Politics* (Bloomington: Indiana University Press, 1995).

21 I discuss these issues of gender and dance more fully in "Is the Body of Dance Sexed?" *Journal of Dramatic Theory and Criticism* 1 (Fall 1990): 7–24.

22 See, in particular, Patricia Clough, *The End(s) of Ethnography: From Realism to Social Criticism* (Newbury Park, Calif.: Sage, 1992), and, from within the position of fieldwork, Nancy Scheper-Hughes, *Death without Weeping: The Violence of Everyday Life in Brazil* (Berkeley: University of California Press, 1992). I have discussed the question of ethno-graphic authority and performance more broadly in *Socialist Ensembles: Theater and State in Cuba and Nicaragua* (Minneapolis: University of Minnesota Press, 1994), 1–24.

1   Dancing the Dialectic of Agency and History

1 The performance took place Monday, November 11, 1991. Peggy Peloquin was the chore-ographer.

2 While various systems of dance notation exist, they do not enjoy the generalized appli-cation of a standardized reference that characterizes the status of the musical score or dramatic script. Writing is decentered with respect to the institutions of dance produc-tion. The subfield of dance restoration or reconstruction already indicates a break between what can be taken as evidence that a dance once was and what is required of representation if the dance is to come again into being. The "graphy," or writing, in "choreography" is an inscription of moving bodies in space and not on paper or video screen, where movement activity is a precondition for inscription. It is not that signals for movement patterns can never be transmitted to dancers except through movement (which is therefore, somehow,

unmediatable). The more important point is that the choreographic idea is dependent on its ultimate expressive activity (dancing) for its inscription in a manner qualitatively different from any other performance idiom. This fundamental difference in the materiality of the object and its representation displayed in dance may also reveal the limits on the metaphor of writing as it is applied to other media.

Classical ballet, hip hop, and Balinese or Ghanaian dance routinely treat movement or steps as items of a vocabulary that was established prior to a given work. Unlike video or dance notation that would claim to document the dance object, such vocabularies are systems for naming movement that bear all the ambiguities of the relation between a sign and the referent that lies outside it. Especially for the latter three forms, the question of how to situate the choreographic function is particularly complex in terms of the way dance making is instantiated in other cultural processes. For in these cases, dance is already a mediation of a social kinesthetic that may first be viewed in terms of gender, technology, politics, or community. In contrast, the lexicon for modern and experimental dance is more diffuse, whereas the choreographic role tends to be attributed indexically—that is, as a function of generating the particular dance rather than as a precondition for choreography. Consequently, the specificity of the rehearsal process to create a work of dance is privileged (as was the case for the piece performed at Judson Church). While, analytically speaking, such forms of contemporary Western concert dance are just as replete with the broader social kinesthetic as their so-called popular counterparts, the localized vocabulary of modern dance movement supports an ideology of the autonomy of the aesthetic for its social context, which suffuses the choreographic process.

In this ideology of the creative process, modern dance forms treat their own choreographic practice as an originary expression whose value lies in sheer difference from any other instance of dance. This autonomy joins together the representations of dance production (the language of the rehearsal process) and reception (the conventional dance review). Consequently, the rehearsal process and the review serve not only as sites for dance creation but also as a means to imagine the bracketing of the creative process from both the history of dance and the larger physical culture, these two being subordinate during rehearsals to the immediate authority of the choreographer. This persistence of the auteur in dance, of the mythology of a creator who gives the name to movement and by so doing gives rise to creativity as such, has diluted the impact of certain features of postmodernism in other art forms that through eclectic historical references confront the failure of the ideology of originality and the modernist imperative to innovation. It could be argued, however, that the very weakness of dance to represent itself has meant that it has been relatively free of these myths of a burden of the past. Consequently, analysis of dance may provide the basis for writing about an object to reflect more profoundly on the meaning and workings of history. For a recent set of reflections raised by representing dances past so that they may be danced again or reconstructed, see Barbara Palfy, ed., with Claudia Gitelman and Patricia Mayer, *Dance Reconstructed: Modern Dance Art Past, Present, and Future* (New Brunswick: Rutgers University Press, 1993).

3   Jacques Attali, *Noise: The Political Economy of Music* (Minneapolis: University of Minnesota Press, 1985), 25.

4   See Ferdinand de Saussure, *Course in General Linguistics,* trans. Wade Baskin (New York: McGraw-Hill, 1966), 111–22.

5   For a similar concern about the limits of the semiotic model for dance, see Philip Auslander, "Embodiment: The Politics of Postmodern Dance," *Drama Review* T120 (Winter 1988): 21 n. 5, in which he cites the work of Wilfried Passow.

6   Roger Copeland and Marshall Cohen make the point in the preface to their extensive edited volume *What Is Dance?: Readings in Theory and Criticism* (Oxford: Oxford University Press, 1983) that "the dance community pays a considerable price for this bias against theory. It rarely enjoys the sort of vigorous intellectual debate that enlivens discussions of the other arts" (viii).

7   See Claude Lévi-Strauss, *The Savage Mind* (Chicago: University of Chicago Press, 1966).

8   Herbert Blau develops this concept at length in *The Audience* (Baltimore: Johns Hopkins University Press, 1990). This volume can be seen as contributing to an ethnographic procedure that highlights the disruptive effects of the exotic other it "captures and chronicles" through representation. The audience figures in his account precisely, and paradoxically, as the indeterminacy of a specific representation internal to performance and therefore to its reception, as if the audience were both a simulation and a protective membrane of the autonomous theater, history being something that is added after the fact. Hence, Blau states, "the audience will serve as a heuristic principle for what is not altogether a secondary purpose of this book: a reflection upon recent cultural history in relation to performance as an activity of cognition" (28). Beyond the specificity of theater, Blau sees the relation of history and performance as featuring what may be missed at a time when global circuits of cultural commodities approach a hegemonic culture that eclipses not only theater per se but also the forms of immediate community suggested by relations of live performance.

9   This phrase appears in the opening of Deborah Jowitt's dance history, in which she relates the critic's task of viewing dances to ethnographic activity. See *Time and the Dancing Image* (Berkeley: University of California Press, 1988), 7.

10   See Friedrich Nietzsche, *The Use and Abuse of History* (1873), trans. Adrian Craft (Indianapolis: Bobbs-Merrill, 1949), 12–22.

11   For a succinct discussion of the term "modern" and its relation to modernity, see Jürgen Habermas, "Modernity—an Incomplete Project," in Hal Foster, ed., *The Anti-Aesthetic* (Seattle: Bay Press, 1983), 3–15.

12   Karl Marx, *The Eighteenth Brumaire of Louis Bonaparte* (1852), in Karl Marx and Friedrich Engels, *Collected Works,* vol. 11 (New York: International Publishers, 1979), 103.

13   See, for example, Eric Hobsbawm, *Primitive Rebels* (New York: W. W. Norton, 1959), and *Bandits* (New York: Delacourt, 1969); George Rudé, *The Crowd in the French Revolution* (Oxford: Oxford University Press, 1959); and Raphael Samuel, ed., *East End Underworld: Chapters in the Life of Arthur Harding* (London: Routledge and Kegan Paul, 1981).

14   Edward Palmer Thompson, *The Making of the English Working Class* (New York: Knopf, 1963).

15   Quote from the preface to Richard Johnson, Gregor McLennan, Bill Schwarz, and David Sutton, eds., *Making Histories: Studies in History, Writing, and Politics* (Minneapolis: Uni-

versity of Minnesota Press, 1982), 11; this volume raises questions over the development of people's history and its elaboration in Britain through cultural studies.

16 Edward Palmer Thompson, *The Poverty of Theory* (London: New Left Books, 1978).

17 See Louis Althusser and Etienne Balibar, *Reading Capital,* trans. Ben Brewster (London: New Left Books, 1970).

18 Bill Schwarz, " 'The People' in History: The Communist Party Historians' Group, 1946–56," in Johnson et al., *Making Histories,* 69.

19 Michael E. Brown, "History and History's Problem," *Social Text* 16 (Winter 1986/87): 158–59.

20 For recent examples of work in this vein, see Michael E. Brown et al., eds., *New Studies in the Politics and Culture of U.S. Communism* (New York: Monthly Review, 1993).

21 Michael E. Brown, "Issues in the Historiography of Communism," part 2, "Some Principles of Critical Analysis," *Socialism and Democracy* 5 (Fall/Winter 1987): 9.

22 See, for example, Lynn Hunt, ed., *New Cultural History* (Berkeley: University of California Press, 1989), and the collection of essays by Roger Chartier, *Cultural History: Between Practices and Representations* (Ithaca: Cornell University Press, 1988), both of which have introductory chapters that discuss the trajectory of the social to the cultural that characterizes developments after *Annales.* Fernand Braudel's own methodological reflections can be found in *On History* (Chicago: University of Chicago Press, 1980).

23 Alain Touraine, *Return of the Actor: Social Theory in Postindustrial Society* (Minneapolis: University of Minnesota Press, 1988), 11. Writing in a different vein, Agnes Heller has stated, "We are historicity; we are time and space," in *A Theory of History* (London: Routledge and Kegan Paul, 1982), 3.

24 For a more complex formulation of micro and macro that is not free of the problems that accompany these terms, see Anthony Giddens, *The Constitution of Society: Outline of a Theory of Structuration* (Berkeley: University of California Press, 1984).

25 For a critique of the consumer model of audience in mass media, see Fred Inglis, *Media Theory* (Cambridge, Mass.: Basil Blackwell, 1990), 134–55. For an elaboration that emphasizes the "work" of consumption, see Daniel Miller, *Material Culture and Mass Consumption* (Cambridge, Mass.: Basil Blackwell, 1987).

26 I would suggest that ethnography is most appropriate for exploring the relation of agency and history simulated in performance. Ethnography is an appropriate method for appreciating the disruptive presence that divides representation and its object. It conveys through language that the ethnographic procedure is radically different from what it looks at. An activity of textual appropriation of difference, ethnography rests on a prior cultural appropriation through colonial contact. Hence, while ethnography results in representation, with sufficient methodological reflection, it points to what is lost to representation, just as does the performer-audience relation in dance.

In terms of the preceding discussion of people's history, this turn from history to ethnography was one of the methodological foundations for the development of cultural studies in Britain at the Birmingham Centre for Contemporary Cultural Studies. The search for the people's voice had led to oral history and, from there, to the traces of the popular in contemporary culture, an investigation well suited to ethnography, whose seminal bridge text in this regard is Paul Willis's *Learning to Labor: How Working Class Kids Get Working Class Jobs* (New York: Columbia University Press, 1981). Willis effectively showed that the very efforts to colonize the minds of working-class youth generated an autodidactic culture of resistance in the classroom that was supportive of decolonization. In this manner, ethnography transferred the object of people's history into the present, but again, not without introducing certain problems of its own.

These problems must be addressed with the understanding that although ethnography and historiography refer to different disciplines, they can share a commitment to a given conception of history defined by the mobilization of critical publics. My account of the performance at Judson Church was ethnographic in that it wrote the observation of my own lost traces of participation. In pursuing traces of the critical public manifest as audience, my dance ethnography turned its agency toward history. While oriented toward history, this form of representing the difference generated by an encounter is also critically disposed toward other ethnographic practices.

For a programmatic statement on oral history, see Paul Thompson, *The Voice of the Past: Oral History* (Oxford: Oxford University Press, 1978). For a critical but sympathetic reflection, see Ronald J. Grele, "Movement without Aim: Methodological and Theoretical Problems in Oral History," in Grele, ed., *Envelopes of Sound: The Art of Oral History,* 2d ed. (Chicago: Precedent Publishing, 1985). My own reflections on ethnography can be found in Randy Martin, "Dance Ethnography and the Limits of Representation," *Social Text* 33 (Winter 1992): 103–23; Randy Martin, *Socialist Ensembles: Theater and State in Cuba and Nicaragua* (Minneapolis: University of Minnesota Press, 1994), 1–24; and Randy Martin, "Agency and History: The Demands of Dance Ethnography," in Susan Foster, ed., *Choreographing History* (Bloomington: Indiana University Press, 1995).

27   I have discussed the insertion of these theaters into their social context in my *Performance as Political Act: The Embodied Self* (New York: Bergin and Garvey, 1990).

28   It is no small irony, however, that experimental work — once conceived of as autonomous from the instrumentalities of the social — would be drawn into the sanctuary of a church to escape the wrath of an assault cloaked in the mantle of religion. Some of the documentation of that dance history bears repeating, and Sally Banes, *Democracy's Body: Judson Dance Theater, 1962–1964* (Ann Arbor: UMI Research Press, 1983), serves as a key reference.

Judson, Banes informs us, was founded on a goal of community service and a principle of not "proselytizing in a community that was primarily Italian Catholic" (36). Its mandate for theater under Minister Al Carmines was "one, not to do religious drama. Two, no censorship after acceptance" (37). Its refusal to stamp its religious "content" on the poetry, visual art, theater, and dance presented there permitted a range of artistic possibilities. The Judson dancers took their name from an activity of writing or inscription in a virtual space. That space was actualized, although only briefly, by bringing dance to a place already defined as oppositional by other, nonartistic activities. The possibility for democracy came by situating a generative principle for dance activity within the particular framing provided by the church that had as its project the constitution of a public aesthetic sphere presumably freed from certain instrumentalities of the market.

While not theorized as such, Banes's study of Judson indicates what may be some of the more familiar aspects of postmodern art, though in unfamiliar manifestations (for discussion, see Sally Banes, *Terpsichore in Sneakers,* 2d ed. [Middletown, Conn.: Wesleyan University Press, 1987], and Susan Manning, "Modernist Dogma and Post-Modern-Rhetoric: A Response to Sally Banes' *Terpsichore in Sneakers,*" *Drama Review* 32, 4 [1988]). Pastiche is evident in the parody of styles and genres of dance presented in the course of an evening's concert. The leveling of high and popular culture is apparent in the framing of pedestrian movement as dance; it is complicated, however, by Judson's maintenance of an avant-gardism and its dancers' links with the canons of modern dance and ballet through their technical training and professional work. Finally, the fragmenting of authorial integrity, identified with the 1960s attack on bourgeois individualism and the myth of the self, is displayed in Judson's collaborative process, only to reveal something of the fragility of that critique.

The premise of the 1962–64 dance initiatives at Judson was to couple a nonhierarchical and participatory principle, a body politic, with a nonauthoritative compositional process. Judson's breakup represents a contradiction of participatory process and participation. If the democracy produced by Judson yielded to "an influx of younger participants," or the presence of Robert Rauschenberg in some of the later concerts introduced hierarchy, or accessibility of Judson's work to those outside the New York community produced conflicts over where and when to perform, it was at the very least a highly exclusive and troubled democracy. In her closing words, Banes seems to accept this account of the movement of innovation in art, which she terms "cyclical," with a kind of confidence one might attribute to some inexorable, evolutionary process: "And the expansion of dance as an art, so much of which had taken place at the Judson Dance Theater workshops and concerts, proliferated" (*Democracy's Body,* 213). Proliferation, expansion, growth, but of something that no longer showed even the traces of the democracy that had been, according to Banes, its original project. This too is resonant of other experiences, but neither the contextualization of the split in democracy's body nor the internal contradiction between expansion and participation is registered in Banes's account. It would be unwise not to exercise caution in drawing conclusions about historical movements such as Judson, so as to avoid confusing an analytic frame that may make democratic impulses and processes available with an expected autonomy of art from its social context. Otherwise, democracy appears altogether unsustainable, in life as in art.

29   The phrase is from Roland Barthes, "From Work to Text," in Josué V. Harari, ed., *Textual Strategies: Perspectives in Post-Structuralist Criticism* (Ithaca: Cornell University Press, 1979), 76.

2 *Overreading* The Promised Land: *Toward a Narrative of Context in Dance*

1   I have never seen an actual performance of *Last Supper at Uncle Tom's Cabin/The Promised Land* but have relied on multiple viewings of a video of the November 9 performance screened at Lincoln Center's Dance Library. The video was viewed several times before I

wrote my own narrative of it and several times after I produced an initial account. Hence, my representation of the dance video in what follows is a reading of a reading that treats an effect of dance performance that is already inscribed in the context of reception — in this case, a center of research. A step removed from the dance, I will not attempt to locate the authenticity of performance, but of context.

2   Curt Sachs, *World History of the Dance* (1937) (New York: Norton, 1965), 18.

3   John Martin, *Introduction to the Dance* (1939) (Brooklyn: Dance Horizons 1965), 13–14.

4   This critique is developed most programmatically by Lévi-Strauss in *The Savage Mind*.

5   See Catherine Clement, *Opera, or the Undoing of Women* (Minneapolis: University of Minnesota Press, 1988).

6   Roland Barthes, *S/Z: An Essay* (New York: Hill and Wang, 1974), 4.

7   Ibid., 6.

8   Fredric Jameson, *The Political Unconscious: Narrative as a Socially Symbolic Act* (Ithaca: Cornell University Press, 1981), 82.

9   For Paul Ricoeur, history and fiction are both "rooted in reading" (3:180) at the same time that they are situated in and situate the world, the "whole set of references opened by every text" (1:82). In his view, narrative is a human disposition that renders coherent the ceaseless temporality of that world, interweaving history and fiction and dialectically linking time and narrative, which they reference. While it is difficult to imagine how his universal claims could be sustained, the anxiety over the decidability of representation's relation to the real is a problem of no small contemporary resonance. By refusing any pure phenomenology of time, Ricoeur attaches order-giving (narrative) form to the (non-narrative) experiential indeterminacy of movement in history. See his *Time and Narrative*, 3 vols. (Chicago: University of Chicago Press, 1985).

10   Edwin Denby, *Dance Writings* (New York: Knopf, 1986), 534, 538.

11   See Michel Foucault, *The Archaeology of Knowledge*, trans. A. M. Sheridan Smith (New York: Pantheon, 1972), 7.

12   Denby, *Dance Writings*, 539.

13   This trajectory is pursued by Terry Eagleton in *The Ideology of the Aesthetic* (London: Blackwell, 1990).

14   Jameson, *The Political Unconscious*, 82. Althusser puts the matter this way in a section of his essay on capital (in *Reading Capital*) titled "The Errors of Classical Economics: An Outline for a Concept of Historical Time": "It is not enough to say, as modern historians do, that *there are* different periodizations for different times, that each time has its own rhythms, some short, some long; we must also think these differences in rhythm and punctuation in their foundation, in the type of articulation, displacement and torsion which harmonizes these different times with one another. To go even further, I should say that we cannot restrict ourselves to reflecting the existence of *visible* and measurable times in this way; we must, of absolute necessity, pose the question of the mode of existence of *invisible* times, of the invisible rhythms and punctuations concealed beneath the surface of each visible time. . . . It shows, for example, that the time of economic production is a specific time, it is a complex and non-linear time — a time of times, a complex time that

cannot be *read* in the continuity of the time of life or clocks, but has to be *constructed* out of the peculiar structures of production" (100–101).

15   The inaugural address was originally delivered March 4, 1865. From *The Collected Works of Abraham Lincoln,* ed. Roy P. Basler (New Brunswick: Rutgers University Press, 1953), 8:332.

16   For a rich discussion of the minstrelization of *Uncle Tom's Cabin* in the 1850s as placing on display the entire social unconscious of the antebellum United States, see Eric Lott, *Love and Theft: Black Face Minstrelsy and the American Working Class* (New York: Oxford University Press, 1993), esp. chap. 8, "Uncle Tomitudes: Racial Melodrama and Modes of Production," 211–33.

17   The range of stylistic demands on the dancers' bodies suggests a certain affinity between choreography and slavery in terms of a particular mutual indifference to the origins of what they appropriate. As Gilles Deleuze recognized in his study of Nietzsche, an indifference to origins always generates an account of origins that fixes conjunctural relations as ontological categories that can then be scaled in value. See Deleuze, *Nietzsche and Philosophy* (New York: Columbia University Press, 1983).

18   This moment in the dance is also one of the literalizations of the Stowe text where the whole series of disruptions that generate the flight and return are initiated when the slave trader Haley sees Eliza's son, Harry, dancing through myriad characterizations of the times. See Harriet Beecher Stowe, *Uncle Tom's Cabin* (1852) (New York: Viking, 1981), 44.

19   These connections are established quite effectively with respect to two of the key points of reference for contemporary race relations in the United States: Anita Hill's testimony at the Clarence Thomas confirmation hearings, and events keyed to the Rodney King trial. See Toni Morrison, ed., *Race-ing Justice, En-gendering Power: Essays on Anita Hill, Clarence Thomas, and the Construction of Social Reality* (New York: Pantheon, 1992); and Robert Gooding-Williams, ed., *Reading Rodney King/Reading Urban Uprising* (New York: Routledge, 1993).

20   This, of course, is Gage's own account, quoted in Mari Jo Buhle and Paul Buhle, eds., *The Concise History of Woman Suffrage: Selections from the Classic Work of Stanton, Anthony, Gage, and Harper* (Urbana: University of Illinois Press, 1978), 103.

21   See Maya Wallace, "In Search of the Promised Land," *Dance Magazine,* October 1991, 58.

22   See the interview with Jones by R. M. Campbell, "A Test of Faith," *Los Angeles Times,* March 10, 1991, sec. C, pp. 5 and 62.

23   Bruce M. Metzger and Roland E. Murphy, eds., *The New Oxford Annotated Bible* (New York: Oxford University Press, 1991), 625.

24   See Cornel West, *Prophesy Deliverance! An Afro-American Revolutionary Christianity* (Philadelphia: Westminster Press, 1982), and *Prophetic Fragments* (Trenton: World Africa Press, 1988).

25   For accounts of the tour and the casting, see Allison Sarnoff, "Getting into the Promised Land" and "The Presenter's Challenge," and Elizabeth Zimmer, "Ten Hours at Uncle Tom's Cabin," all in *Dance/USA,* May/June 1991, 24–26.

26   Elizabeth Zimmer, "Moving Truths," *Elle,* November 1990, 221.

27   See Umberto Eco, *A Theory of Semiotics* (Bloomington: Indiana University Press, 1976), 7.

28   Both quotes from *A Testament of Hope: The Essential Writings of Martin Luther King, Jr.*, ed. James Melvin Washington (San Francisco: Harper and Row, 1986), 218.

29   See James Snead, "Repetition as a Figure of Black Culture," in Russell Ferguson et al., eds., *Out There: Marginalization and Contemporary Cultures* (Cambridge: MIT Press, 1990).

30   Quoted in "Nudity in Promised Land Causes a Stir," *Dance Magazine,* November 1990, 13.

31   In Amiri Baraka, *Dutchman* (New York: William Morrow, 1964), 36.

32   Bill Bissell, "Faith in the Larger Sense," *High Performance* (Fall 1991): 36–39.

33   Sarnoff, "The Presenter's Challenge," 26.

34   Quoted in Steven C. Dubin, *Arresting Images: Impolitic Art and Uncivil Actions* (New York: Routledge, 1992), 180.

35   Jones, quoted in Campbell, "Test of Faith," 62.

36   Jack Anderson, *New York Times,* October 4, 1992, Arts and Leisure section, p. 8.

37   Jennifer Dunning, *New York Times,* September 6, 1992, sec. H, p. 17.

38   Hal Foster, "Postmodernism: A Preface," in Foster, ed., *The Anti-Aesthetic: Essays on Postmodern Culture* (Port Townsend, Wash.: Bay Press, 1983), xii; ibid.,; and Anderson, *New York Times,* 8.

39   Sid Smith, *Chicago Tribune,* March 12, 1992, 30, 32.

40   Deborah Jowitt, "Take on the World," *Village Voice,* November 27, 1990, 119.

41   All quotes from Lewis Segal, "An Unfulfilling 'Last Supper,'" *Los Angeles Times,* March 16, 1991, sec. F, p. 12.

42   Michel Foucault, "What Is an Author?" in Josué V. Harari, ed., *Textual Strategies: Perspectives in Post-Structuralist Criticism* (Ithaca: Cornell University Press, 1979), 159.

43   Regarding the 1994 choreography by Bill T. Jones *Still/Here,* the reviewer for *The New Yorker,* Arlene Croce, explained that she refused to view the dance because she felt "excluded by reason of its express intentions," which she termed "victim art." Her accusation was that the piece transgressed the codes of representation by incorporating the really dying. Ironically, she missed a work that exuberantly danced against death. She traces the "mass delusion" of victim art to the 1960s, which led to art of the 1980s being held hostage to "community." By addressing the critical reception of his work choreographically, Croce hears Jones silencing her, "Jones' message was clear. . . . No back talk!" The loss of monopoly over who speaks and who is spoken for "[has] effectively disarmed criticism." See Croce, "Discussing the Undiscussable," *The New Yorker,* December 26, 1994–January 2, 1995, 54–60. For a fuller discussion, see Carol Martin, "High Critics/Low Arts," in Gay Morris, ed., *Moving Words: Re-writing Dance* (London: Routledge, 1996), 320–33.

44   George Dondero, "Modern Art Shackled to Communism," in Charles Harrison and Paul Wood, eds., *Art in Theory, 1900–1990: An Anthology of Changing Ideas* (London: Blackwell, 1992), 657.

45   See Ronald Schliefer, *Rhetoric and Death: The Language of Modernism and Postmodern Discourse Theory* (Urbana: University of Illinois Press, 1990), esp. "Historicizing Modernist Rhetoric: Modernism, Materialism, and the End of Europe," 27–51, which traces the anxiety over death (here, of the gentry) that Schliefer argues is constitutive of modernism

and hence points to a refusal to narrate an end and could thereby serve to counter the very centrist project that gives rise to the narrative of eternal renewal.

46   *Fortune,* December 1945, 187.

47   The article, dated February 17, 1982, was in a clippings file entitled "Business and Dance" in the New York Public Library Dance Collection at Lincoln Center. Leila Sussman has written a sociology of the dance boom, "Anatomy of the Dance Company Boom, 1958–1980," *Dance Research Journal* 16, 2 (1984): 23–38.

48   Roger Copeland, "A Curmudgeonly View of the American Dance Boom." *Dance Theatre Journal* 4, 1 (1986): 10–13.

49   William Baumol and William Bowen, *Performing Arts: The Economic Dilemma* (1966; reprint, Cambridge: MIT Press, 1968).

50   Judith Blau, *The Shape of Culture: A Study of Contemporary Cultural Patterns in the United States* (Cambridge: Cambridge University Press, 1989).

51   See, for example, Baumol and Bowen, *Performing Arts;* Douglas C. Dillon, "The Economic Crisis in the Arts," in Gideon Chagy, ed., *Business and the Arts* (New York: Paul Ericksson, 1970); and Dick Netzer, *The Subsidized Muse* (Cambridge: Cambridge University Press, 1978). Note that these studies were all published before the putative "bust."

52   Quoted in Jan Van Dyke, *Modern Dance in a Postmodern World: An Analysis of Federal Arts Funding and Its Impact on the Field of Modern Dance* (Reston, Va.: National Dance Association, 1992), 25.

53   Both references from ibid., 45, quoting Michael Useem's 1976 study.

54   Alice Goldfarb Marquis, *Art Lessons: Learning from the Rise and Fall of Public Arts Funding* (New York: Basic, 1995), 64.

55   Van Dyke, *Modern Dance in a Postmodern World,* 28–34.

56   See Robert E. Elder, *The Information Machine: The United States Information Agency and American Foreign Policy* (Syracuse: Syracuse University Press, 1968).

57   Charles A. Thomson and Walter H. C. Laves, *Cultural Relations and U.S. Foreign Policy* (Bloomington: Indiana University Press, 1963), 125.

58   W. McNeil Lowry and Gertrude S. Hooker, "The Role of the Arts and the Humanities," in Paul J. Braisted, ed., *Cultural Affairs and Foreign Relations* (Washington, D.C.: Columbia Books, 1968), 59.

59   Both quotes, from Kennedy speeches in 1961 and 1963, respectively, in Marquis, *Art Lessons,* 55–56.

60   Ibid., 26.

61   See the introduction to *National Endowment for the Arts Annual Report* (Washington, D.C.: NEA, 1986).

62   See Robert Pear, "A Hostile House Trains Its Sights on Funds for the Arts," *New York Times,* January 9, 1995, sec. A, p. 1 and sec. B, p. 9.

63   Reported in "An Interview with Frank Hodsoll," with William Keens, *American Arts,* January 1982, 8.

64   See *National Endowment for the Arts Annual Report* (Washington, D.C.: NEA, 1981) and *National Endowment for the Arts Annual Report* (Washington, D.C.: NEA, 1991).

65   See, Dubin, *Arresting Images*, for a careful tracking of these controversies. He notes that it "technically lapsed at the end of the 1990 fiscal year on October 1 1990" (266). This was before the premiere of *Last Supper* but after it was commissioned and choreographed.

66   See ibid., 261.

67   See his essay of that title in Houston Baker Jr., *Long Black Song: Essays in Black American Literature and Culture* (Charlottesville: University Press of Virginia, 1972), 42–57.

68   See, for example, Janet Siltanen and Michele Stanworth, eds., *Women and the Public Sphere: A Critique of Sociology and Politics* (London: Hutchinson, 1984); Joan B. Landes, *Women and the Public Sphere in the Age of the French Revolution* (Ithaca: Cornell University Press, 1988); and Frances Bonner et al., *Imagining Women: Cultural Representations and Gender* (London: Polity, 1992). For a critique of these categories in a postcolonial frame, see M. Jacqui Alexander and Chandra Talpade Mohanty, eds., *Feminist Genealogies, Colonial Legacies, Democratic Futures* (New York: Routledge, 1997), in particular the essay by Anannya Bhattacharjee, "The Public/Private Mirage: Mapping Homes and Undomesticating Violence Work in the South Asian Immigrant Community," 308–29.

69   For a useful discussion, see Bennett Harrison, *Lean and Mean: The Changing Landscape of Corporate Power in the Age of Flexibility* (New York: Basic, 1994), and David M. Gordon, *Fat and Mean: The Corporate Squeeze of Working Americans and the Myth of Managerial "Downsizing"* (New York: Free Press, 1996).

70   For formulations on the current conjuncture of the capitalist political economy, see Michel Aglietta, *A Theory of Capitalist Regulation: The U.S. Experience* (London: Verso, 1979); Harvey, *The Condition of Postmodernity;* and Stuart Hall and Martin Jacques, eds., *New Times* (London: Verso, 1990). None of these discussions, to the extent that they assume a periodizing break and despite their own debts to structuralism, are free of the assumptions of historicism. They are perhaps most fruitfully read to indicate how the introduction of new temporalities to ongoing "regimes of accumulation" deepens the unevenness in the structures of capital.

71   See Adolph L. Reed Jr., *The Jesse Jackson Phenomenon: The Crisis of Purpose in Afro-American Politics* (New Haven: Yale University Press, 1986).

72   See Manning Marable, *Race, Reform, and Rebellion: The Second Reconstruction in Black America, 1945–1990*, rev. 2d ed. (Jackson: University Press of Mississippi, 1991).

73   Manning Marable, *Beyond Black and White: Rethinking Race in American Politics and Society* (London: Verso, 1995), 204–5.

74   For a breakdown of crime statistics by race, see Steven R. Donziger, ed., *The Real War on Crime: The Report of the National Criminal Justice Commission* (New York: Harper Collins, 1996). Ratios stated here are taken from Stephen Small, *Racialised Barriers: The Black Experience in the United States and England in the 1980s* (London: Routledge, 1994), 56.

75   In their *Racial Formation in the United States: From the 1960s to the 1990s*, 2d ed. (New York: Routledge, 1994), 152–59, Michael Omi and Howard Winant seem to suggest that the persistence of bipolar racial models reflects more the deficiencies of analysis (which it surely may) than the ideological powers of racial formation itself.

76   Ronald Takaki makes this point in "A Tale of Two Decades: Race and Class in the 1880s

and 1980s," in Herbert Hill and James E. Jones Jr., eds., *Race in America: The Struggle for Equality* (Madison: University of Wisconsin Press, 1993), 402–16.

77 Herbert Hill speaks to the sustained resistance on the part of labor unions in the United States to comply with Title VII equal opportunity statutes. See his "Black Workers, Organized Labor, and Title VII of the 1964 Civil Rights Act: Legislative History and Litigation Record," in Hill and Jones, eds., *Race in America*, 305.

78 Marx, *Capital*, 1:632.

79 For a useful discussion, see Juan Flores and George Yúdice, "Living Borders/Buscando América: Languages of Latino Self-Formation," *Social Text* 24 (1990): 57–84.

80 For a consideration of the significance of migration in the context of globalization, see Saskia Sassen, *Losing Control: Sovereignty in an Age of Globalization* (New York: Columbia University Press, 1996). Her estimate of 120 million migrants excludes undocumented workers (63).

81 All this is not to suggest that what Stuart Hall identified in the late eighties as "the exhaustion of consent" assumes some heyday free of coercion. See his *Hard Road to Renewal* (London: Verso, 1988). Stanley Aronowitz, in an early revisionist impulse, *False Promises* (New York: McGraw-Hill, 1973), reminded us of the "unsilent fifties" marked by repression of dissent and labor tumult.

82 For fuller contextualization, see Donald Lowe, *The Body in Late-Capitalist USA* (Durham: Duke University Press, 1996).

83 A quote from a full-page ad circulated in major dailies should serve as a reminder of this: "The REAL CAUSE of the sex, violence, filth and profanity is with the writers, directors, producers, singers, actors, etc. But THEY can be controlled. All it takes is for the Boards of Directors of their companies to order them to stop! Remember when movies were wholesome family entertainment? That's when people at the top SET STANDARDS AND ENFORCED them. We're going to insist that happen again." This advertisement with petition and financial solicitation (IRS-approved tax-exempt) was paid for by A Project of American Family Association, Dr. Donald E. Wildmon, president, and appeared in the *Los Angeles Times*, Tuesday, March 2, 1993, sec. H, p. 6.

84 This deprofanation itself constitutes a countermovement to that of Stowe's own text. In her introduction to Stowe's *Uncle Tom's Cabin*, Ann Douglas remarks, "There is the gradually varied narrative turn from the profane to the sacred, from the common to the uncanny" (29).

85 Karl Marx, *Grundrisse* (New York: Vintage, 1973), 101.

86 See, for example, Ernesto Laclau and Chantal Mouffe, *Hegemony and Socialist Strategy: Towards a Radical Democratic Politics* (London: Verso, 1985), and, more recent, Ernesto Laclau, *New Reflections on the Revolution of Our Time* (London: Verso, 1990).

3   *The Composite Body of Dance: Re(w)rapping the Multicultural Nation*

1 Jeffrey Louis Decker contextualizes the debate in "The State of Rap: Time and Place in Hip Hop Nationalism," *Social Text* 34 (1993): 53–84. For indications of rap's diverse reception,

see "'Fight the Power': Rap Music Pounds Out a New Anthem for Many Black Students," *Chronicle of Higher Education,* February 14, 1990, 1 and 29–30; "Rap Music, Positive or Negative? Passing Fad or Cultural Force? Censored or Uncensored?" *Black Collegian,* November/December 1990, 181–83; "The Political Proclamations of Hip Hop Music," *Black Collegian,* March/April 1990, 21, 195–97; "Yo! Rap Gets on the Map: Led by Groups like Public Enemy, It Socks a Black Message to the Mainstream," *Time,* February 5, 1990, 60–62; and "The Rap Gap: Class Divisions Divide the Black Community," *Utne Reader,* January/February 1990, 52. For critical interrogations of the form, see Michael Eric Dyson, *Reflecting Black* (Minneapolis: University of Minnesota Press, 1993), and Dyson, *Between God and Gangsta' Rap: Bearing Witness to Black Culture* (New York: Oxford University Press, 1996); and Houston Baker Jr., *Black Studies, Rap, and the Academy* (Chicago: University of Chicago Press, 1993). Tricia Rose, *Black Noise: Rap Music and Black Culture in Contemporary America* (Hanover, N.H.: University Press of New England, 1994), provides the most complete discussion of the cultural context, production, and politics of hip hop.

2   The term is developed by Raymond Williams to discuss the historically emergent or "pre-emergent," "inalienably physical" "changes of presence" in a given social formation. See *Marxism and Literature,* 128–35.

3   Wahneema Lubiano, "Like Being Mugged by a Metaphor," in Avery F. Gordon and Christopher Newfield, eds., *Mapping Multiculturalism* (Minneapolis: University of Minnesota Press, 1996), 69. The essays in this volume speak powerfully to the problematic uses of multiculturalism and its relation to race. Ann DuCille also speaks to the omission of race in Newt Gingrich's formulations of American culture and to the twinned problems of over- and underspecifying the location of race. See *Skin Trade* (Cambridge: Harvard University Press, 1996).

4   See Donna J. Haraway, "A Cyborg Manifesto: Science, Technology, and Socialist-Feminism in the Late Twentieth Century," in *Simians, Cyborgs, and Women: The Reinvention of Nature* (New York: Routledge, 1991), 149–82.

5   In contrast to this invocation of the postracial, David Hollinger has proposed a "post-ethnic" politics, which he takes to be a more inclusive term of "affiliation by revokable consent" that draws on the "civic character of the American nation-state" to straddle pluralist particularism and cosmopolitan universalism. His privileging of the "voluntarism" in U.S. diversity management comes at the expense of recognizing its role as a "proto-world-state." This latter emphasis would suggest a greater role for coercion in U.S. history and point to the state's affiliation with capital accumulation. Such linkages disrupt the consensual basis of participation and argue for the greater specificity of the racial in relation to the national than the notion of "ethnic" is able to provide. See Hollinger, *Postethnic America: Beyond Multiculturalism* (New York: Basic, 1995), 13–15.

6   See Randy Martin, "Resurfacing Socialism: Resisting the Appeals of Tribalism and Localism," *Social Text* 44 (Fall 1995): 97–118.

7   Judith Butler argues persuasively that precisely this type of substitution of coercion for violence (by freeze-framing and decontextualizing the video) constituted the visual basis for the successful defense of the police officers in the first trial for the Rodney King beat-

ing. See "Endangered/Endangering: Schematic Racism and White Paranoia," in Gooding-Williams, *Reading Rodney King,* 15–22. Many of the essays in the Gooding-Williams volume provide an important elaboration of what is being suggested here. See also the discussion of "policing the black body" in John Fiske, *Power Plays/Power Works* (London: Verso, 1993), 227–312, and Ellis Cashmore and Eugene McLaughlin, eds., *Out of Order? Policing Black People* (London: Routledge, 1991).

8   For a discussion of how these gendered categories are constructed in the legal system, see Dorothy Roberts, "Motherhood and Crime," *Social Text* 42 (Spring 1995): 99–123.

9   For an analysis of the political use to which this overrepresentation is put, see Joy James, *Resisting State Violence: Radicalism, Gender, and Race in U.S. Culture* (Minneapolis: University of Minnesota Press, 1996).

10   This is the anxiety expressed by Arthur M. Schlesinger Jr. in *The Disuniting of America* (New York: W. W. Norton, 1992).

11   In no small measure the temptation to mirror what one opposes suffuses all politics. But with multiculturalism, the discursive structure — the framework of representation — is itself fundamental to what is being contested, thus the demands to critique the form and terms of the debate as it is taking shape are all the more pressing. Hence even in critically minded collections such as the *Graywolf Annual 5: Multicultural Literacy,* ed. Rick Simonson and Scott Walker (St. Paul, Minn.: (Graywolf Press, 1988), one sees the acceptance of the syntax of a canonical list of terms (which appears at the end of the book) that can be supplemented without transforming the way materials are taught, what gets valued about them, or what they are assumed to represent. Similarly, an otherwise effective collection of writings titled *Multiculturalism in the United States: A Comparative Guide to Acculturation and Ethnicity,* ed. John D. Buenker and Lorman A. Ratner (New York: Greenwood, 1992), sorts and separates communities into discrete chapters that serve an unselfreflective universal of comparison.

12   Kobena Mercer makes this point with respect to what he terms "struggles over the sign" in "'1968': Periodizing Politics and Identity," in Lawrence Grossberg et al., eds., *Cultural Studies* (New York: Routledge, 1992), 424–49.

13   George Yúdice is particularly sensitive to these limitations of the discourse of multiculturalism; see his forthcoming book *We Are Not the World* (Durham: Duke University Press). Henry Giroux gives an incisive account of the corporate appropriation of multicultural representation in "Consuming Social Change: The United Colors of Benetton," in *Disturbing Pleasures* (New York: Routledge, 1994), 3–24. Avery Gordon discusses business multiculturalism in "Diversity Management: The Work of Corporate Culture," *Social Text* 44 (Fall 1995): 3–30.

14   Maps of that field can be found in Gerald Graff, *Beyond the Culture Wars: How Teaching the Conflicts Can Revitalize American Education* (New York: W. W. Norton, 1992); Henry Louis Gates Jr., *Loose Canons: Notes on the Culture Wars* (New York: Oxford University Press, 1992); Christopher Newfield, "What Was Political Correctness? Race, the Right, and Managerial Democracy in the Humanities," *Critical Inquiry* 19, 2 (Winter 1993): 308–36; Michael Geyer, "Multiculturalism and the Politics of General Education," *Critical Inquiry*

19, 3 (Spring 1993): 499–543; the symposium "Popular Culture and Political Correctness," ed. Andrew Ross, in *Social Text* 36 (Fall 1993): 1–39; and Ellen Messer-Davidow, "Manufacturing the Attack on Liberalized Higher Education," *Social Text* 36 (Fall 1993): 40–80.

15   I am here caricaturing much more complex renderings of a split between cultural and other social structures offered by Daniel Bell in *The End of Ideology: On the Exhaustion of Political Ideas in the Fifties* (1960; reprint, Cambridge: Harvard University Press, 1988); Jürgen Habermas in *The Theory of Communicative Action,* vols. 1 and 2 (Boston: Beacon, 1984, 1987); and more nuanced radical critiques of multiculturalism such as one published by *Critical Inquiry* 19, 3 (Summer 1993). In his article in this issue, "A Borderless World? From Colonialism to Transnationalism and the Decline of the Nation State," 726–51, Masao Miyoshi warns quite rightly that "we should not be satisfied with recognizing the different subject positions from different regions and diverse backgrounds. We need to find reasons for such differences — at least in the political and economic aspects — and to propose ways to erase such 'differences,' by which I mean political and economic inequalities" (751). Henry Louis Gates Jr. has recently expressed concern that "the vocabulary of multiculturalism occlude[s] race," in "Beyond the Culture Wars: Identities in Dialogue," in the MLA's *Profession 93* (1993): 6–11.

16   For a philosophical explication of this position, see Charles Taylor, *Multiculturalism and "The Politics of Recognition": An Essay,* with commentary by Amy Gutmann, Steven C. Rockefellar, Michael Walzer, and Susan Wolf (Princeton: Princeton University Press, 1992).

17   Benedict Anderson, *Imagined Communities,* 2d ed. (London: Verso, 1991), 36.

18   Paul Gilroy, *There Ain't No Black in the Union Jack: The Cultural Politics of Race and Nation* (London: Hutchinson, 1987), 45.

19   Ibid., 69.

20   Max Weber, "Politics as Vocation," in H. H. Gerth and C. Wright Mills, trans. and eds., *From Max Weber: Essays in Sociology* (New York: Oxford University Press, 1958), 78.

21   Anderson, "The Origins of National Consciousness," in *Imagined Communities,* 41–49, esp. page 43.

22   See John Rowe and Vivian Schelling, *Memory and Modernity* (London: Verso, 1991), and also Doris Sommer, "Irresistible Romance: The Foundational Fictions of Latin America," in Homi K. Bhabha, ed., *Nation and Narration* (London: Routledge, 1990).

23   Roger Bartra, *The Cage of Melancholy: Identity and Metamorphosis in the Mexican Character* (New Brunswick: Rutgers University Press, 1992), 1.

24   Ibid.

25   J. A. Armstrong, *Nations before Nationalism* (Chapel Hill: University of North Carolina Press, 1982), sees religion and politics rather than language as the primary sources of differentiation in the premodern nation (279). Anthony D. Smith, *The Ethnic Origins of Nations* (London: Blackwell, 1986), emphasizes a "myth-symbol complex" routed in a particular landscape as the slow-changing basis of ethnicity (15).

26   Aijaz Ahmad, *In Theory: Classes, Nations, Literature* (London: Verso, 1992), 7.

27   Partha Chatterjee, *Nationalist Thought and the Colonial World: A Derivative Discourse* (London: Zed, 1986), 169.

28 Writers such as James Cone have added complexity to Malcolm X's nationalism by placing it in dialectical relation to the integrationism associated with Martin Luther King Jr., where the latter figures systemic transformation, and the former, systematic division (exploitation). He further accents the internationalism of both. See *Martin and Malcolm and America: A Dream or a Nightmare?* (Maryknoll, N.Y.: Orbis Books, 1991).

29 Joe Wood, ed., *Malcolm X: In Our Own Image* (New York: St. Martin's, 1992), 15.

30 This is one way of understanding what Gilles Deleuze and Felix Guattari have termed a "minor literature," the "intensive use" of the "polylingualism of one's own language" that "oppose[s] the oppressed quality of this language to its oppressive quality." They find its closest contemporary expressions in such forms as black popular music: "This can be compared in another context to what blacks in America today are able to do with the English language. Minor literature is different; its cramped space forces each individual intrigue to connect immediately to politics. The individual concern thus becomes all the more necessary, indispensable, magnified, because a whole other story is vibrating within it. In this way, the family triangle connects to other triangles — commercial, economic, bureaucratic, juridical — that determine its values." [Due to] 'scarcity of talent' . . . 'everything takes on a collective value.'" See Deleuze and Guattari, *Kafka: Toward a Minor Literature* (Minneapolis: University of Minnesota Press, 1986), 26–27 and 17.

31 Gianni Vattimo, *The Transparent Society* (Cambridge: Polity, 1992), 10.

32 Ibid., 11.

33 Even in Homi Bhabha's very rich evocation of nationalism's contradictory emergence between figurations of progress and nostalgia as "a split between the continuist, accumulative temporality of the pedagogical, and the repetitious, recursive strategy of the performative," narrative is presumed to be adequate to constitute the affiliation with nation. See "DissemiNation: Time, Narrative, and the Margins of the Modern Nation," in Bhabha, ed., *Nation and Narration* (London: Routledge, 1990), 297.

34 Ibid., 300.

35 Dance has been figured cross-culturally as the embodiment of community for a range of political situations. For example, the specific spatial and temporal placement of dance in Dogon (of the Sangha region of Mali) cosmology articulates the expenditure of surplus during festivities that asserts the principle of the social with status differentiating processes of age sets and gender. See Marcel Griale, *Masques Dogon* (Paris: Institut d'ethnologie, 1938), and Michel Huet, *The Dance, Art, and Ritual of Africa* (New York: Pantheon, 1978). That dance is a specialized activity assembled across class lines but at every level associated with the temple affords a certain consolidation of nation in Bali, while the dance plays themselves display a critical and parodic thrust. See Beryl de Zoete and Walter Spies, *Dance and Drama in Bali* (London: Faber and Faber, 1952). In western Europe, dance was essential in the formation of the constitutive materiality of the state, as evidenced in the court dances of Versailles. As Mark Franko says in his study of baroque dancing, "Court ballets magnified and, in the process, distorted the acceptable forms of contemporaneous noble sociability in accordance with conflicting, first- and second-estate visions of the dancer as subject, and of royal subjects in their specular totality: the nation." Hence dancing could serve both to align difference (in this case both the class struggle between

"nobiliary rights" and "royal power" and the attempt at harmonizing politique between Catholics and Protestants in "peaceful masquerades") within the containable scene of the court as a literal site of the state and to assure the proliferation of dance styles and sites which that initial appropriative royal gesture opened up. Franko, *Dance as Text: Ideologies of the Baroque Body* (Cambridge: Cambridge University Press, 1993), 1, 34, and 69.

36   This particular prosecution represents more than a single instance and more than a merely juridical strategy to counter rap's own effectiveness in inscribing itself in public discourse. Attacks on rap music from police associations to candidates attributing it with everything from inciting insurrection to generating racism became part of the narration of nation during the 1992 presidential campaign. But there is no reason to suspect they will abate, as Alan Light of *Rolling Stone* put it: "Politically motivated suppression of minority expression has been one true sad legacy of the riots" (December 10–24, 1992, 79). Some of the legal assaults, including that on 2 Live Crew, are detailed in "It's Bad, It's Def—Is It Obscene?: Rap Music Takes a Bad Rap from Prosecutors," *National Law Journal* 12, 39 (1990): 1, 27–28. On Clinton's divisive decontextualization of Sister Souljah as an embarrassment to Jesse Jackson, see "Hip-Hop Hub Hewn by Recent Racial Uproar," *Variety*, June 22, 1992, 48, 54; and on the special attention given the racial remarks of Public Enemy's Professor Griff, see *New Statesman and Society* 15 (September 1989): 41–42.

37   On the complexities of cultural appropriation, see Bruce Ziff and Pratima V. Rao, *Borrowed Power: Essays on Cultural Appropriation* (New Brunswick: Rutgers University Press, 1997).

38   Alan Light, "About Salary or Reality—Rap's Recurrent Conflict," *SAQ* 90, 4 (Fall 1991): 859.

39   Simon Jones, *Black Culture White Youth: The Reggae Tradition from JA to UK* (London: Macmillan, 1988), xxi.

40   David Toop, *Rap Attack 2* (London: Serpent's Tale, 1991), 22.

41   Sterling Stuckey, *Slave Culture: Nationalist Theory and the Foundations of Black America* (New York: Oxford University Press, 1987).

42   Comment made in discussion at the conference on youth culture held at Princeton University, November 1992. The proceedings of this conference have been published in Tricia Rose and Andrew Ross, eds., *Microphone Fiends* (New York: Routledge, 1994).

43   Joseph D. Eure and James G. Spady, eds., *Nation Conscious Rap* (Brooklyn: PC International Press, 1991). For other inventories of hip hop culture, see William Eric Perkins, ed., *Droppin' Science: Critical Essays on Rap Music and Hip Hop Culture* (Philadelphia: Temple University Press, 1996); Steven Hager, *Hip Hop: The Illustrated History of Break Dancing, Rap Music, and Graffiti* (New York: St. Martin's, 1984); and Nelson George, Sally Banes, Susan Flinker, and Patty Romanowski, *Fresh: Hip Hop Don't Stop* (New York: Random House, 1985). For a longer view, see Arnold Shaw, *Black Popular Music in America: From the Spirituals, Minstrels, and Ragtime to Soul, Disco, and Hip-Hop* (New York: Schirmer, 1986). For articulations with Caribbean music, see Dick Hebdige, *Cut n' Mix: Culture, Identity, and Caribbean Music* (London, Methuen, 1987), and for African affinities, see Gary Stewart, *Breakout: Profiles in African Rhythm* (Chicago: University of Chicago Press, 1992).

44 The role of the racialized savage as fundamental to the constitution of the West is articulated by Michel-Rolph Trouillot, "Anthropology and the Savage Slot: The Poetics and Politics of Otherness," in Richard G. Fox, ed., *Recapturing Anthropology: Working in the Present* (Santa Fe: School of American Research Press, 1991), 17–44.

45 Between 1991 and 1993 coverage of crime on the major networks tripled so that by the latter year, "crime was the leading story on the network news." Donziger, *The Real War on Crime*, 69.

46 Lisa Lewis, *Gender Politics and MTV* (Philadelphia: Temple University Press, 1990).

47 Ernest Mandel, *The Second Slump* (London: New Left Books, 1977).

48 Chuck D. cited in *Artforum*, September 1989, 20, by David Sternbach.

49 Video of Ice Cube, "Wicked," from the album *The Predator*, Priority Records; author's transcription.

50 Sean Cubitt, *Timeshift: On Video Culture* (London: Routledge, 1990), 35.

51 Ibid., 106–7.

52 Angela Davis refers to this interview with Ice Cube in Gina Dent, ed., *Black Popular Culture: A Project by Michele Wallace* (Seattle: Bay Press, 1992), 325; a number of essays in the volume deal with the issue of the representation of women in black popular forms, especially the question of blaming the female victim, including Davis's own contribution, "Black Nationalism, the Sixties, and the Nineties"; Tricia Rose, "Black Texts/Black Contexts"; Jacquie Jones, "The Accusatory Space"; and Michele Wallace; "Boyz in the Hood and Jungle Fever."

53 Tricia Rose affirms the centrality of location as a main feature of the genre; see *Black Noise*, 10.

54 *Yo! MTV Raps*, produced by Jac Benson II, broadcast January 23, 1993.

55 For an account of this urban transformation, see Manuel Castells, *The Informational City* (Cambridge, Mass.: Basil Blackwell, 1989), 218.

56 Neil Smith, "Contours of a Spatialized Politics: Homeless Vehicles and the Production of Geographical Scale," *Social Text* 33 (Winter 1992): 54–81.

57 See Toop, *Rap Attack*, 180.

58 Ice Cube quote from Robin D. G. Kelley, "Straight from Underground," *The Nation* 254, 22 (1992): 793.

59 Versions of *Thriller* and *Beat It* from *Making Michael Jackson's Thriller*, produced by Optimum Productions, 1983, distributed by Vestron Video, Stamford, Conn.; author's transcription.

60 For a more complete reading of Jackson's *Thriller* video, see Kobena Mercer, "Monster Metaphors: Notes on Michael Jackson's *Thriller*," in *Welcome to the Jungle: New Positions in Black Cultural Studies* (London: Routledge, 1994), 33–52.

61 Quoted in Serge Denisoff, *Inside MTV* (New Brunswick, N.J.: Transaction, 1988), 292.

62 Katrina Hazzard-Gordon, *Jookin': The Rise of Social Dance Formations in African American Culture* (Philadelphia: Temple University Press, 1990), 155.

63 The projection of an assimilationist myth that elides Asian identity has been effectively taken to task by such writers as E. San Juan Jr.; see, for example, his *Racial Forma-*

tions/Critical Transformations (Atlantic Highlands, N.J.: Humanities Press, 1992), which also contains an excellent overview of the political economy of racialization and its effects in the United States. I mention this here because a significant number of those who regularly attended the class were Asian Americans, a commitment that disturbs the presumptions of cultural antipathy.

64 For a critical articulation of some of these other dimensions of national affiliation, see the essays collected in Andrew Parker, Mary Russo, Doris Sommer, and Patricia Yaeger, eds., *Nationalisms and Sexualities* (New York: Routledge, 1992).

65 Eric Lott's finely complex study of minstrelsy in the antebellum United States is particularly instructive here in elaborating how a particular performance idiom mapped the contradictory relations of race, class, and gender on the eve of their dramatic reinscription. Yet I wonder if the present conjuncture doesn't offer some reconfiguration of these racialized relations of spectacle and performance. While white repugnance of blackness is still constructed through the spectacle of watching it (now on television, rather than in the theater), the desire for blackness is complicated by displacing what was an audience for certain spectacles into performative practices, from street basketball to the aerobics class discussed here. See Lott, *Love and Theft*.

66 Paul Gilroy has suggested that modernity itself is constituted by the double consciousness of a diasporic identity that circulates in what he terms the "black atlantic." By attending to this rewritten history, it becomes possible to imagine a "politics of the next century in which the central axis of conflict will no longer be the colour line but the challenge of just, sustainable development and the frontiers which will separate the overdeveloped parts of the world (at home and abroad) from the intractable poverty that already surrounds them." *The Black Atlantic: Modernity and Double Consciousness* (Cambridge: Harvard University Press, 1993), 223.

67 The term "heterotopia" is based on the work of Michel Foucault, "Of Other Spaces," *Diacritics* 16 (1986): 22–27, and developed by Edward Soja in *Postmodern Geographies: The Reassertion of Space in Critical Social Theory* (London: Verso, 1989). The spatial dimension of cultural practices is also usefully developed by Michel de Certeau in *The Practice of Everyday Life* (Berkeley: University of California Press, 1984), esp. 91–130.

4   Between Technique and the State: The Univers(ity) in Dance

1 I am identifying here a certain tendency that has been difficult to avoid in thinking about modern dance. For example, Selma Jeanne Cohen is sanguine about the difficulties of definition yet contributes as well to the mythos of the individual creator. In her introduction to a book that will allow choreographers to speak for themselves, she offers the following remarks: "The modern dance, on the other hand, externalized—projected, communicated—an emotion that was not only personal but 'authentic.' The choreographer felt the emotion deeply, but—further—was convinced that, by revealing his experience, he was also revealing a basic truth. For America, the story had started at the turn of the century, when Isadora Duncan and Ruth St. Denis each began groping toward a style of dance that

would allow a freedom of expression they could not find in contemporary ballet" (introduction to *The Modern Dance: Seven Statements of Belief* [Middletown, Conn.: Wesleyan University Press, 1965], 5).

2   In this vein, consider Walter Sorell's remarks about Isadora Duncan: "It was by mere chance that Isadora found herself dancing without sandals one day. It was different and seemed attractive to her, and the barefoot dancer was born. Her costumes and draperies were Greek in inspiration, but the movement, she correctly felt, was American in the freedom of its expression" (Sorell, *Dance in Its Time: The Emergence of an Art Form* [Garden City, N.Y.: Anchor Press, 1981], 318).

3   Hence, Don McDonagh remarks, "there has always lurked about modern dance something of newness and the feeling of revolutionary activity." He goes on to state quite succinctly the mythos I have been describing: "Modern dance does not look to European dance models for the primary sources of its movement techniques. Modern dance in its strongest impulses looks within the individual, whose expressive needs then determine the types of gesture that will emerge when the dancer starts to move" (McDonagh, *The Complete Guide to Modern Dance* [Garden City, N.Y.: Doubleday, 1976], 1).

4   The words are those of Marcia B. Siegel, who in the introduction to her *Shapes of Change: Images of American Dance* (Boston: Houghton Mifflin, 1979), 10, cogently states many of the claims made here.

5   The phrase "Our America" is that of the nineteenth-century Cuban revolutionary José Martí. See "Nuestra América," in *Tres Documentos* (Havana: Editorial José Martí, 1984). Roberto Fernández Retamar has written an important essay that contextualizes this issue, "Caliban: Notes toward a Discussion of Culture in Our America," in *Caliban and Other Essays* (Minneapolis: University of Minnesota Press, 1989), 3–45.

6   Duncan, in the 1927 essay "I See America Dancing," resists the influence of "jazz rhythm," fox-trot, or Charleston in her conception of dance-as-nation: "rather would it be the living leap of the child springing toward the heights, toward its future accomplishment, toward a new great vision of life that would express America." She goes on to spin her originary tale, denying the influence of the Greeks and insisting instead that "the origin, the root" of her dance had "probably some of the gestures of the Redskins themselves, and, again, a bit of Yankee Doodle." In Sheldon Cheney, ed., *Isadora Duncan: The Art of the Dance* (New York: Theatre Arts Books, 1969), 47–48.

7   Martha Graham, "Affirmations, 1926–37," in *Martha Graham* (1937), ed. and with a foreword by Merle Armitage (Brooklyn: Dance Horizons, 1966), 99–100.

8   By putting into play the terms "capitalism," "state," and "nation" in various combinations, I want to suggest that the relations between societal organization, social regulation, and population (as the sociological entities that these terms reference) are themselves expressed in various ways. For useful recent discussions, see E. J. Hobsbawm, *Nations and Nationalism since 1780: Programme, Myth, Reality* (Cambridge: Cambridge University Press, 1990); Bob Jessop, *State Theory: Putting Capitalist States in Their Place* (University Park: Pennsylvania State University Press, 1990); Etienne Balibar and Immanuel Wallerstein, *Race, Nation, Class: Ambiguous Identities* (London: Verso, 1991); and, with respect to

performance in particular, Loren Kruger, *The National Stage: Theatre and Cultural Legiti-mation in England, France, and America* (Chicago: University of Chicago Press, 1992).

9   For a discussion of Graham and other choreographers aligned with leftist social move-ments during the 1930s, see Franko, *Dancing Modernism*.

10   Bruno Latour, "Technology Is Society Made Durable," in John Law, ed., *A Sociology of Monsters: Essays on Power, Technology, and Domination* (London: Routledge, 1991), 129.

11   Foucault, *Discipline and Punish*, 220–21.

12   Peter Brinson has made a more affirmative argument for teaching dance in relation to national formation in Britain; see *Dance as Education: Towards a National Dance Culture* (London: Falmer Press, 1991).

13   Helen Thomas has conducted an ethnography of a dance class that grants greater focus to the conversational ties among women; see "An-other Voice: Young Women Dancing and Talking," in Thomas, ed., *Dance, Gender, and Culture* (New York: St. Martin's, 1993), 69–93.

14   The terms "coercion" and "consent," as dimensions of state rule, or hegemony, are de-veloped by Antonio Gramsci: "The 'normal' exercise of hegemony on the now classical terrain of the parliamentary regime is characterized by the combination of force and consent, which balance each other reciprocally without force predominating over con-sent. Indeed, the attempt is always made to ensure that force will appear to be based on the consent of the majority, expressed by the so-called organs of public-opinion — newspapers and associations—which, therefore, in certain situations, are artificially mul-tiplied." Quoted in *Selections from the Prison Notebooks of Antonio Gramsci*, ed. and trans. Quintin Hoare and Geoffrey Nowell Smith (New York: International Publishers, 1971), 80. The complete *Prison Notebooks* (New York: Columbia University Press, 1992) have now been retranslated by Joseph Buttigieg.

15   The question is not whether dance can summon armies but where its disciplining effects join in the more general incorporation that extends to what Gilles Deleuze and Felix Guattari call the war machine, the technical capacity to engage in struggle that is not only irreducible to the state apparatus but actively disperses or deterritorializes it as well. See their *A Thousand Plateaus: Capitalism and Schizophrenia* (Minneapolis: University of Minnesota Press, 1987), 355.

16   For a discussion of these resistances, particularly with respect to Vietnam, see Randy Martin, "Who Went to War?" in G. Boulanger and C. Kadushin, eds., *The Vietnam Veteran Redefined: Fact and Fiction* (Hillsdale, N.J.: Lawrence Erlbaum Associates, 1986), 13–24.

17   This substitution of the word for the deed, of symbol for object, marks what Jacques Lacan called the "name of the father"—but in reverse (*The Seminar of Jacques Lacan: Book II, The Ego in Freud's Theory and in the Technique of Psychoanalysis, 1954–1955*, ed. Jacques-Alain Miller, trans. Sylvana Tomaselli [New York: W. W. Norton, 1991], 259). For an instructive Lacanian analysis of the state, see Joan Copjec, "The *Unvermögender* Other: Hysteria and Democracy in America," *New Formations* 14 (Summer 1991): 27–41.

18   Saussure, *Course in General Linguistics*, 104.

19   The question as to how signs are encoded and decoded in a given setting so that activity

is constituted as "passing" is taken up by Erving Goffman in *Stigma: Notes on the Management of Spoiled Identity* (New York: Simon and Schuster, 1963). The bracketing of the disruptive effects of doubting the tacit authority that allows passable social interaction to retain its fluency is explored in Harold Garfinkel, *Studies in Ethnomethodology* (New York: Prentice-Hall, 1967).

20 Michael Taussig, *Mimesis and Alterity: A Particular History of the Senses* (New York: Routledge, 1993), 252.

21 Walter Benjamin, "Theses on the Philosophy of History," in Hannah Arendt, ed., *Illuminations: Essays and Reflections* (New York: Schocken, 1968), 257–58.

22 This notion of the continuous subject is developed in Peggy Phelan, *Unmarked: The Politics of Performance* (London: Routledge, 1993).

23 I have attempted one such map in my essay "Modern Dance and the American Century," in Townsend Ludington, ed., *Modernism in the United States* (Chapel Hill: University of North Carolina Press, 1998).

24 My understanding of these movements is indebted to Nancy Ruyter, "Antique Longings: Genevieve Stebbins and American Delsartean Performance," and Linda Tomko, "Fete Accompli: Gender, 'Folk-Dance,' and Progressive Era Political Ideals in the United States," both in Susan L. Foster, ed., *Corporealities: Dancing, Knowledge, Culture, and Power* (London: Routledge, 1995).

25 Quoted in Suzanne Shelton, *Divine Dancer: Ruth St. Denis* (Garden City, N.Y.: Doubleday, 1981), 98.

26 Ibid., 96.

27 Ibid., 98.

28 For an example of dance writing that both identifies Orientalist tropes such as the veil in Western concert dance while also taking on certain features of Orientalism as an analytic frame, see Jowitt, *Time and the Dancing Image*. I examine her work more closely in "Dance Ethnography and the Limits of Representation."

29 The phrase is Rosalind Krauss's from the essay in which she explores in regards the visual arts many of the claims made here with respect to dance; see "The Originality of the Avant-Garde," in *The Originality of the Avant-Garde* (Cambridge: MIT Press, 1985), 157.

30 Louis Horst, *Modern Dance Forms* (San Francisco: Impulse, 1961), 17.

31 Quoted in Marian Horosko, *Martha Graham: The Evolution of Her Dance Theory and Training, 1926–1991* (Chicago: a cappella books, 1991), 2, a compilation of statements by those who worked with Graham over the years.

32 Doris Humphrey, *The Art of Making Dances* (New York: Grove, 1959), 47.

33 This tension of self and society, the local and the global, identity and differentiation, and extentionality and intentionality is taken as constitutive of modernity. For a recent defense of such universalizing claims, see Anthony Giddens, *The Consequences of Modernity* (Stanford: Stanford University Press, 1990), and *Modernity and Self-Identity* (Stanford: Stanford University Press, 1991). Clearly the literature on modernity is vast, and its recent critical advocacy is most strongly voiced by Jürgen Habermas, *The Philosophical Discourse of Modernity* (Cambridge: MIT Press, 1987), and Raymond Williams, *The Politics of Mod-*

ernism: Against the New Conformists (London: Verso, 1989). In this chapter, I have allowed complications in the figure of modern dance to open up the claims of modernity without attempting to resolve these tensions here through some programmatic account of postmodernism.

34   Susan Manning, in her important revision of modern dance history (displacing its centeredness on America by focusing on the German dancer Mary Wigman), offers an account of dance as a site for the construction of gendered and national identities. The nationalization of dance offered by standard reckonings elides formations, such as those dancers associated with the Left and the Communist Party in the United States, that complicate the universalized expression of a dancing self as nation. See *Ecstasy and the Demon: Feminism and Nationalism in the Dances of Mary Wigman* (Berkeley: University of California Press, 1993), esp. 265–70.

35   What is textual in dance technique is generally inscribed in class. But for an example of how modern dance technique (rather than a notation system) constitutes a universal grammar for movement, see Ernestine Stodelle, *The Dance Technique of Doris Humphrey and Its Creative Potential* (Princeton: Princeton Book, 1978). Such abstract universal terms as "time," "space," and "motion" are common to the discourse of modern technique and allow the dancer to understand herself through these categories. A succinct document of this sort is Gay Cheney, *Basic Concepts in Modern Dance: A Creative Approach,* 3d ed. (Princeton: Dance Horizons, 1989).

36   Hillel Schwartz, "Torque: The New Kinesthetic of the Twentieth Century," in Jonathan Crary and Sanford Kwinter, eds., *Incorporations: Zone 6* (New York: Zone, 1992), 70–127.

37   For history and discussion, see Banes, *Democracy's Body* and *Terpsichore in Sneakers;* Susan L. Foster, *Reading Dancing: Bodies and Subjects in Contemporary American Dance* (Berkeley: University of California Press, 1986); and Cynthia Novack, *Sharing the Dance: Contact Improvisation and American Culture* (Madison: University of Wisconsin Press, 1990).

38   Susan L. Foster, "Dancing Bodies," in Crary and Kwinter, *Incorporations,* 480–95.

39   Marx, *Capital,* vol. 1, chap. 1.

40   Poulantzas, *State, Power, Socialism,* 29.

41   Lauren Berlant, "National Brands/National Body," in Hortense Spillers, ed., *Comparative American Identities* (New York: Routledge, 1991), 113.

5   *For Dance Studies*

1   A body of work is already gathering under the rubric of critical dance studies, a movement that makes this a propitious moment for the kinds of speculations that I venture here. See, for example, the interdisciplinary collections: Susan L. Foster, ed., *Choreographing History* (Bloomington: Indiana University Press, 1995); Foster, *Corporealities;* Ellen W. Goellner and Jacqueline Shea Murphy, eds., *Bodies of the Text: Dance as Theory/Literature as Dance* (New Brunswick: Rutgers University Press, 1995); Jane C. Desmond, *Meaning in Motion* (Durham: Duke University Press, 1997); Helen Thomas, ed., *Dance, Gender, and Culture*

(New York: St. Martin's, 1993); and Gay Morris, *Moving Words: Re-writing Dance* (London: Routledge, 1996). In addition, a number of notable monographs have recently been published, among them Sally Banes, *Greenwich Village, 1963: Avant-Garde Performance and the Effervescent Body* (Durham: Duke University Press, 1993); Jane Cowan, *Dance and the Body Politic in Northern Greece* (Princeton: Princeton University Press, 1990); Mark Franko, *Dance as Text: Ideologies of the Baroque Body* (Cambridge: Cambridge University Press, 1993); Manning, *Ecstasy and the Demon;* Sally Ann Ness, *Body, Movement, and Culture* (Philadelphia: University of Pennsylvania Press, 1992); Marta Savigliano, *Tango and the Political Economy of Passion* (Boulder: Westview, 1994); Susan L. Foster, *Choreography and Narrative* (Bloomington: Indiana University Press, 1996); Ann Daly, *Done into Dance: Isadora Duncan in America* (Bloomington: Indiana University Press, 1995); Helen Thomas, *Dance, Modernity, and Culture: Explorations in the Sociology of Dance* (London: Routledge, 1995); Ramsay Burt, *The Male Dancer: Bodies, Spectacle, Sexualities* (London: Routledge, 1995); Barbara Browning, *Samba* (Bloomington: Indiana University Press, 1995); Amy Koritz, *Gendering Bodies/Performing Art: Dance and Literature in Early-Twentieth-Century British Culture* (Ann Arbor: University of Michigan Press, 1995); and Franko, *Dancing Modernism.*

2   Indeed, cultural studies, after its initial institutionalization as a program at Birmingham, may be more recognizable in the United States in the form of journals such as *Social Text, boundary 2, Public Culture, Cultural Critique, Critical Inquiry, Semiotexte, Representations, Signs, Minnesota Review, October, Diacritics,* and so forth. Graeme Turner, *British Cultural Studies* (Boston: Unwin-Hyman, 1990), traces the Birmingham trajectory, and Lawrence Grossberg, Cary Nelson, and Paula Triechler, eds., *Cultural Studies* (New York: Routledge, 1992), survey recent output. The history of cultural strife that generated the field has been offered by Stanley Aronowitz in *Roll Over Beethoven* (Middletown, Conn.: Wesleyan University Press, 1993); something of an introductory text has been written by Fred Inglis, *Cultural Studies* (London: Blackwell, 1993); and some key writings have been collected in Simon During, ed., *The Cultural Studies Reader* (London: Routledge, 1993). Jane C. Desmond has explored linkages between dance and cultural studies in "Embodying Difference: Issues in Dance and Cultural Studies," *Cultural Critique* 26 (Winter 1993/94): 33–63.

3   Suzanne Langer, "The Dynamic Image: Some Philosophical Reflections on Dance," *Salmagundi* 33/34 (Spring/Summer 1976): 76–82. Originally published in her *Problems of Art* (New York: Charles Scribner's Sons, 1957), 1–12.

4   John Martin, *Introduction to the Dance,* 26.

5   Terry Eagleton frames the autonomy of the aesthetic in very broad strokes that I abbreviate with the term "modernism" as the still prevailing trope of critical authority: "The emergence of the aesthetic as a theoretical category is closely bound up with the material process by which cultural production, at an early stage of bourgeois society, becomes 'autonomous'—autonomous, that is, of the various social functions which it has traditionally served. Once artifacts become commodities in the market place, they exist for nothing and nobody in particular, and can consequently be rationalized, ideologically speaking,

as existing entirely and gloriously for themselves. It is this notion of autonomy or self-referentiality which the new discourse of aesthetics is centrally concerned to elaborate; and it is clear enough, from a radical political viewpoint, just how disabling any such idea of aesthetic autonomy must be. It is not only, as radical thought has familiarly insisted, that art is thereby conveniently sequestered from all other social practices, to become an isolated enclave within which the dominant social order can find an idealized refuge from its own actual values of competitiveness, exploitation and material possessiveness. It is also, rather more subtly, that the idea of autonomy—of a mode of being which is entirely self-regulating and self-determining—provides the middle class with just the ideological model of subjectivity it requires for its material operations" (*Ideology of the Aesthetic,* 8–9). It is neither Eagleton's intent nor my own to purge the aesthetic but rather to instantiate it within the political.

6   John Martin, *John Martin's Book of the Dance* (New York: Tudor Publishing, 1963), 8.

7   See Gordon Francher and Gerald Myers, eds., *Philosophical Essays on Dance* (Brooklyn: Dance Horizons, 1981), esp. Myers's essay and subsequent discussion, "Do You See What the Critic Sees?" 33–68. For a highly ambitious, if standard, treatment of the issues, see Francis Sparshott, *A Measured Pace: Toward a Philosophical Understanding of the Arts of Dance* (Toronto: University of Toronto Press, 1995).

8   See Graham McFee, *Understanding Dance* (London: Routledge, 1992), 72.

9   Ibid., 284.

10   Ibid., 287.

11   Judith Lynne Hanna has culled the cross-cultural material on dance in a more rigorous fashion to assert that "to dance is human" (*To Dance Is Human* [Chicago: University of Chicago Press, 1987]). Yet her methodology, the development of a "semantic grid" that can probe the meaning of dance cross-culturally, is not itself culturally located, thereby recapitulating the modernist universalizing of evaluation and judgment. See also her *Dance, Sex, and Gender* (Chicago: University of Chicago Press, 1988).

12   The emphasis on representation has certainly been the case with some of the most inspired and inspirational writing on the body. See, for example, Catherine Gallagher and Thomas Lacquer, eds., *The Making of the Modern Body* (Berkeley: University of California Press, 1987); Susan Rubin Suleiman, ed., *The Female Body in Western Culture* (Cambridge: Harvard University Press, 1986); and Michel Feher, ed., *Fragments for a History of the Human Body,* 3 vols. (New York: Zone, 1989). The volume by Jonathan Crary and Sanford Kwinter, eds., *Incorporations* (New York: Zone, 1992), contains several pieces on dance.

13   Michel Foucault's entire oeuvre can be considered a document of such epistemic shifts, from *Madness and Civilization: A History of Insanity in the Age of Reason,* trans. Richard Howard (New York: Vintage, 1973) to the three-volume *History of Sexuality,* trans. Robert Hurley (New York: Vintage, 1980–86). His most explicit methodological reflections are contained in *The Order of Things: An Archaeology of the Human Sciences* (New York: Vintage, 1970) and *The Archaeology of Knowledge.* Especially in this last book, he insists that epistemes themselves are never unitary or homogeneous, which contrasts with such notions of paradigmatic or normal scientific knowledge developed by Thomas Kuhn in *The Structure of Scientific Revolutions* (Chicago: University of Chicago Press, 1962).

14 This is a formulation that Michael E. Brown has developed to understand the conditions for interdisciplinarity in disciplined settings. See *The Production of Society: A Marxian Foundation for Social Theory* (Totowa, N.J.: Allen and Littlefield, 1986) and, more recent, "The Future of Marxism and the Future of Theory," in Chronis Polychroniou, ed., *Socialism, Crisis, Renewal* (New York: Praeger, 1993), esp. 230–32.

15 See, for example, Paul Starr, *The Social Transformation of Medicine: The Rise of a Sovereign Profession and the Making of a Vast Industry* (New York: Basic, 1982); John B. McKinlay, ed., *Issues in the Political Economy of Health Care* (New York: Tavistock, 1984); Diane Ghirardo, ed., *Out of Site: A Social Criticism of Architecture* (Seattle: Bay Press, 1991); and Magali Sarfatti Larson, *Behind the Postmodern Facade: Architectural Change in Late Twentieth-Century America* (Berkeley: University of California Press, 1993). On professionalization more generally, see Larson's *The Rise of Professionalism* (Berkeley: University of California Press, 1977).

16 For an account of these historical modulations, see Gerald Graff, *Professing Literature* (Chicago: University of Chicago Press, 1987).

17 Talcott Parsons, *The Structure of Social Action* (New York: McGraw-Hill, 1937). For a view of the emergence of the field in the United States, see Roscoe C. Hinkle, *Founding Theory of American Sociology: 1881–1915* (London: Routledge and Kegan Paul, 1980); and for a broader historical overview, see Dorothy Ross, *The Origins of American Social Science* (Cambridge: Cambridge University Press, 1991).

18 This, once again, is Gilles Deleuze's formulation of epistemological origins in *Nietzsche and Philosophy*. The so-called antifoundationalist move in philosophy associated with Richard Rorty argues against a universalist conception of foundations, although it leaves the claim uncertain of its own status with respect to universalism. See Cornel West and John Rajchman, *Post-Analytic Philosophy* (New York: Columbia University Press, 1985).

19 John Guillory observes, "It is just by suppressing culture in the ethnographic sense — or reserving that sense of culture for non-"Western" artifacts — that the traditional curriculum can appropriate the "great works" of Western civilization for the purpose of constituting an imaginary cultural unity." See his *Cultural Capital: The Problem of Literary Canon Formation* (Chicago: University of Chicago Press, 1993), 42.

20 Karl Mannheim, *Ideology and Utopia*, trans. Louis Wirth and Edward Shils (New York: Harcourt Brace Jovanovich, 1936).

21 See Jürgen Habermas, *Toward a Rational Society* (Boston: Beacon, 1970); Habermas's perspective is most systematically expressed in *The Theory of Communicative Action*.

22 Gayatri Chakravorty Spivak's work is exemplary here; see the essays in *In Other Worlds* and the interviews collected in *The Post-Colonial Critic*, ed. Sarah Harasym (New York: Routledge, 1990). For a useful mapping of positions, see Russell Ferguson, Martha Gever, Trinh T. Minh-ha, and Cornel West, eds., *Out There: Marginalization and Contemporary Cultures* (Cambridge: MIT Press, 1990).

23 For this reason, I am leery of overinvesting in the polarities of constructivism and essentialism, decentered subjectivity and identity, to describe or account for actual positions and politics, as much as I see the conceptual divide between new and old social movements to be intellectually and politically unhelpful to grasp current mobilizations. I take

support from Diana Fuss, *Essentially Speaking: Feminism, Nature, and Difference* (New York: Routledge, 1989); Paul Smith, *Discerning the Subject* (Minneapolis: University of Minnesota Press, 1988); Stuart Hall, "What Is This 'Black' in Black Popular Culture?" in David Morley and Kuan-Hsing Chen, eds., *Stuart Hall: Critical Dialogues in Cultural Studies* (London: Routledge, 1996), 464–75; and Gayatri Chakravorty Spivak's notion of strategic essentialism developed in "In a Word: Interview," in *Outside in the Teaching Machine* (New York: Routledge, 1993), 1–23.

24 See Bruce Robbins's introduction to his edited volume, *Intellectuals: Aesthetics, Politics, Academics* (Minneapolis: University of Minnesota Press, 1990), ix–xxvi, and the collection of his essays on intellectuals, *Secular Vocations* (London: Verso, 1994).

25 These issues are raised quite effectively by Michael Denning, "The Academic Left and the Rise of Cultural Studies," and Joan Wallach Scott "The Campaign against Political Correctness: What's Really at Stake," both in *Radical History* (Fall 1992): 20–47 and 58–79, respectively.

26 For a general discussion of the religious right and the attack against women and reproductive rights, see Susan Faludi, *Backlash: The Undeclared War against American Women* (New York: Crown Publishers, 1991).

27 Patricia Williams, *The Alchemy of Race and Rights* (Cambridge: Harvard University Press, 1991), 185.

28 Ibid., 186–87.

29 Ibid., 198 and 227.

30 Cheryl I. Harris, "Whiteness as Property," in Kimberlé Crenshaw, Neil Gotanda, Gary Peller, Kendall Thomas, eds., *Critical Race Theory* (New York: New Press, 1995), 276–91; quotation on 290.

31 See Nancy Fraser, *Unruly Practices: Power, Discourse, and Gender in Contemporary Social Theory* (Minneapolis: University of Minnesota Press, 1988).

32 See M. Jacqui Alexander, "Erotic Autonomy as a Politics of Decolonization: An Anatomy of Feminist and State Practice in the Bahamas Tourist Economy," in M. Jacqui Alexander and Chandra Talpade Mohanty, *Feminist Genealogies, Colonial Legacies, Democratic Futures* (New York: Routledge, 1997), 63–100.

33 This is the kind of framing that John Tagg provides for photography in his introductory essay to *The Burden of Representation* (Amherst: University of Massachusetts Press, 1988), 1–33.

34 See, for example, Louis Althusser, "From Capital to Marx's Philosophy," in Louis Althusser and Etienne Balibar, *Reading Capital*, trans. Ben Brewster (London: New Left Books, 1970), 11–69, esp. 43–46.

35 Copeland and Cohen, *What Is Dance?* and Susan L. Foster, *Reading Dancing.*

36 Copeland and Cohen, *What Is Dance?* x.

37 Ibid., 1.

38 This is the formulation in the preface. See ibid., viii. On the other hand, Paul de Man has conceived of the resistance to theory as the very condition of its practice, "the polemical opposition, the systematic non-understanding and misrepresentation, the unsubstantial

but eternally recurrent objections, are the displaced symptoms of a resistance inherent in the theoretical enterprise itself. . . . The resistance to theory is a resistance to the use of language about language. It is therefore a resistance to language itself or the possibility that language contains factors or functions that cannot be reduced to intuition" (*The Resistance to Theory* [Minneapolis: University of Minnesota Press, 1986], 12).

39 Copeland and Cohen, *What Is Dance?* ix.

40 Janet Adshead-Lansdale and June Layson, eds., *Dance History: An Introduction*, 2d ed. (London: Routledge, 1994), call for such a project to be launched from the quarters of dance history.

41 Susan L. Foster, *Reading Dancing*, 259.

42 Ibid., 260.

43 Ibid., 100, 248.

44 Hayden White, *Metahistory: The Historical Imagination in Nineteenth-Century Europe* (Baltimore: Johns Hopkins University Press, 1973); ibid., 248.

45 Susan L. Foster, *Reading Dancing*, 247.

46 After a book by Robert S. Lynd of the same title, *Knowledge for What? The Place of Social Science in American Culture* (Princeton: Princeton University Press, 1939).

47 This is a point made by Michael E. Brown with respect to the problem discussed in Chapter 1 of conceptualizing the popular in the literature on people's history. Recall that, for him, the radical otherness of "the people" to both the content and the methodology of what is conventionally represented as history must supplement standard accounts. See his "History and History's Problem"; "Issues in the Historiography of Communism"; "The History of the History of U.S. Communism," in Brown et al., eds., *New Studies;* and his unpublished manuscript, "Unaccountable History: Some Limits of Experience."

48 See John Frow, *Cultural Studies and Cultural Value* (Oxford: Oxford University Press, 1995).

49 The reference is to Fredric Jameson, *The Prison House of Language* (Princeton: Princeton University Press, 1972).

50 For a development of the concept of chronotope, see Mikhail Bakhtin, "Forms of Time and of the Chronotope in the Novel," in *The Dialogic Imagination*, 84–258.

51 For a historicizing account of racial formation, see Omi and Winant, *Racial Formation*.

52 For Marx, the materiality of anything, including the body, that has social utility, or use value, is both "limited by the physical properties" and yet "has no existence apart" from its social application. Hence, materiality emerges in the gap between the absoluteness of the physical and the social. A nature or a society that simply exists as a given is not subject to practice and therefore becomes a mere idealization. See Marx, *Capital*, 1:36.

53 Seminal statements of the problem of false consciousness can be found in Georg Lukács, *History and Class Consciousness: Studies in Marxist Dialectics*, trans. Rodney Livingstone (Cambridge: MIT Press, 1971); and Herbert Marcuse, *One-Dimensional Man* (Boston: Beacon, 1964). The political inflection of the visual is examined in Jacqueline Rose, *Sexuality in the Field of Vision*, and Martin Jay, *Downcast Eyes* (London: Verso, 1994). Critical views on visibility politics can be found in Stanley Aronowitz, *The Politics of Identity* (New York:

Routledge, 1992), and Yúdice, *We Are Not the World.* The essays collected in the volume edited by Susan L. Foster, *Corporealities,* can be read quite suggestively as constituting the basis for a historicized economy of the body through dance studies.

54   For an overview of the structure-agency (or process) opposition from the perspective of social theory, see Giddens, *The Constitution of Society.*

55   For an account of just such an organizational movement from the linguistic authority to the bodily, see Randy Martin, *Performance as Political Act,* chap. 6.

56   A historical account of the star system that emerges with the articulation of a globally oriented Western mind in the eighteenth century is provided by Attali, *Noise.*

57   See Saussure, *Course in General Linguistics.*

58   In the literature on globalization, this impulse often takes the form of a privileging of the local as the basis for agency. See, for example, Jeremy Brecher, John Brown Childs, and Jill Cutler, eds., *Global Visions: Beyond the New World Order* (Boston: South End Press, 1993); Richard J. Barnet and John Cavanagh, *Global Dreams: Imperial Corporations and the New World Order* (New York: Touchstone, 1994); and Robert Wilson and Wimal Dissanayake, eds., *Global/Local: Cultural Production and the Transnational Imaginary* (Durham: Duke University Press, 1996).

59   This affiliation of an architectural tie between word and body comes from Jacques Derrida, "Différance," in *Margins of Philosophy,* trans. Alan Bass (Chicago: University of Chicago Press, 1982), 1–27.

60   In these two meanings of representation, I am referring to what I take to be the most politically apposite critique, namely, Gayatri Chakravorty Spivak's reading of Marx (through the lens of Derrida, Foucault, and Deleuze and Guattari). See page 276 in her essay "Can the Subaltern Speak?" in Cary Nelson and Lawrence Grossberg, eds., *Marxism and the Interpretation of Culture* (Urbana: University of Illinois Press, 1988), 271–313.

Bibliography

Adshead-Lansdale, Janet, and June Layson, eds. *Dance History: An Introduction,* 2d ed. London: Routledge, 1994.

Aglietta, Michel. *A Theory of Capitalist Regulation: The U.S. Experience.* London: Verso, 1979.

Ahmad, Aijaz. *In Theory: Classes, Nations, Literature.* London: Verso, 1992.

Alexander, M. Jacqui. "Erotic Autonomy as a Politics of Decolonization: An Anatomy of Feminist and State Practice in the Bahamas Tourist Economy." In M. Jacqui Alexander and Chandra Talpade Mohanty, *Feminist Genealogies, Colonial Legacies, Democratic Futures,* 63–100. New York: Routledge, 1997.

Alexander, M. Jacqui, and Chandra Talpade Mohanty, eds. *Feminist Genealogies, Colonial Legacies, Democratic Futures.* New York: Routledge, 1997.

Althusser, Louis, and Etienne Balibar. *Reading Capital.* Trans. Ben Brewster. London: New Left Books, 1968.

Anderson, Benedict. *Imagined Communities* 2d ed. London: Verso, 1991.

Armstrong, J. A. *Nations before Nationalism.* Chapel Hill: University of North Carolina Press, 1982.

Aronowitz, Stanley. *False Promises.* New York: McGraw-Hill, 1973.

———. *The Politics of Identity.* New York: Routledge, 1992.

———. *Roll Over Beethoven.* Middletown, Conn.: Wesleyan University Press, 1993.

———. "The Situation of the Left in the United States." *Socialist Review* 23, 3 (1994): 5–79.

Attali, Jacques. *Noise: The Political Economy of Music.* Minneapolis: University of Minnesota Press, 1985.

Auslander, Philip. "Embodiment: The Politics of Postmodern Dance." *Drama Review* T120 (Winter 1988): 21.

Austin, J. L. *How to Do Things with Words.* Cambridge: Harvard University Press, 1955.

Baker, Houston, Jr. *Black Studies, Rap, and the Academy.* Chicago: University of Chicago Press, 1993.

———. *Long Black Song: Essays in Black American Literature and Culture.* Charlottesville: University Press of Virginia, 1972.

Bakhtin, Mikhail. *The Dialogic Imagination: Four Essays.* Ed. Michael Holquist. Trans. Caryl Emerson and Michael Holquist. Austin: University of Texas Press, 1981.

Balibar, Etienne, and Immanuel Wallerstein. *Race, Nation, Class: Ambiguous Identities.* London: Verso, 1991.

Banes, Sally. *Democracy's Body: Judson Dance Theater, 1962–1964.* Ann Arbor: UMI Research Press, 1983.

———. *Greenwich Village, 1963: Avant-Garde Performance and the Effervescent Body.* Durham: Duke University Press, 1993.

———. *Terpsichore in Sneakers.* 2d ed. Middletown, Conn.: Wesleyan University Press, 1987.

Baraka, Amiri. *Dutchman.* New York: William Morrow, 1964.

Barnet, Richard J., and John Cavanagh. *Global Dreams: Imperial Corporations and the New World Order.* New York: Touchstone, 1994.

Barthes, Roland. "From Work to Text." In Josué V. Harari, ed., *Textual Strategies: Perspectives in Post-Structuralist Criticism,* 73–81. Ithaca: Cornell University Press, 1979.

———. *S/Z: An Essay.* New York: Hill and Wang, 1974.

Bartra, Roger. *The Cage of Melancholy: Identity and Metamorphosis in the Mexican Character.* New Brunswick: Rutgers University Press, 1992.

Baumol, William, and William Bowen. *Performing Arts: The Economic Dilemma.* 1966. Reprint, Cambridge: MIT Press, 1968.

Bell, Daniel. *The End of Ideology: On the Exhaustion of Political Ideas in the Fifties.* 1960. Reprint, Cambridge: Harvard University Press, 1988.

Benjamin, Walter. "Theses on the Philosophy of History." In Hannah Arendt, ed., *Illuminations: Essays and Reflections.* New York: Schocken, 1968.

Berlant, Lauren. "Dissemination: Time, Narrative, and the Margins of the Modern Nation." In Bhabha, ed., *Nation and Narration.* London: Routledge, 1990.

———. "National Brands/National Body." In Hortense Spillers, ed., *Comparative American Identities.* New York: Routledge, 1991.

Bhabha, Homi K. *Nation and Narration.* London: Routledge, 1990.

Bhattacharjee, Anannya. "The Public/Private Mirage: Mapping Homes and Undomesticating Violence Work in the South Asian Immigrant Community." In M. Jacqui Alexander and Chandra Talpade Mohanty, eds., *Feminist Genealogies, Colonial Legacies, Democratic Futures.* New York: Routledge, 1997.

Bissell, Bill. "Faith in the Larger Sense." *High Performance* (Fall 1991): 36–39.

Blackburn, Robin, ed. *After the Fall: The Failure of Communism and the Future of Socialism.* London: Verso, 1991.

Blau, Herbert. *The Audience.* Baltimore: Johns Hopkins University Press, 1990.

Blau, Judith. *The Shape of Culture: A Study of Contemporary Cultural Patterns in the United States.* Cambridge: Cambridge University Press, 1989.

Boggs, Carl. *The Socialist Tradition: From Crisis to Decline.* New York: Routledge, 1995.

Bonner, Frances, et al. *Imagining Women: Cultural Representations and Gender.* London: Polity, 1992.

Braudel, Fernand. *On History.* Chicago: University of Chicago Press, 1980.

Brecher, Jeremy, John Brown Childs, and Jill Cutler, eds. *Global Visions: Beyond the New World Order.* Boston: South End Press, 1993.

Brinson, Peter. *Dance as Education: Towards a National Dance Culture.* London: Falmer Press, 1991.

Brown, Michael E. "The Future of Marxism and the Future of Theory." In Chronis Polychroniou, ed., *Socialism, Crisis, Renewal*, 143–56. New York: Praeger, 1993.

———. "History and History's Problem." *Social Text* 16 (Winter 1986/87): 136–61.

———. "Issues in the Historiography of Communism." part 2, "Some Principles of Critical
Analysis." *Socialism and Democracy* 5 (Fall/Winter 1987): 1–37.

———. *The Production of Society: A Marxian Foundation for Social Theory.* Totowa, N.J.: Allen
and Littlefield, 1986.

Brown, Michael E., and Amy Goldin. *Collective Behavior.* Pacific Palisades, Calif.: Goodyear,
1973.

Brown, Michael E., and Randy Martin. "Left Futures." *Socialism and Democracy* no. 18 (1995):
59–90.

———. "Rethinking the Crisis of Socialism." *Socialism and Democracy* no. 14 (1991): 9–56.

Brown, Michael E., Randy Martin, Frank Rosengarten, and George Snedeker, eds. *New Studies
in the Politics and Culture of U.S. Communism.* New York: Monthly Review, 1993.

Browning, Barbara. *Samba.* Bloomington: Indiana University Press, 1995.

Buechler, Steven M. "Beyond Resource Mobilization? Emerging Trends in Social Movement
Theory." *Sociological Quarterly* 34 (May 1993): 217–35.

Buenker, John D., and Lorman A. Ratner. *Multiculturalism in the United States: A Comparative
Guide to Acculturation and Ethnicity.* New York: Greenwood, 1992.

Buhle, Mari Jo, and Paul Buhle, eds. *The Concise History of Woman Suffrage: Selections from the
Classic Work of Stanton, Anthony, Gage, and Harper.* Urbana: University of Illinois Press,
1978.

Burt, Ramsay. *The Male Dancer: Bodies, Spectacle, Sexualities.* London: Routledge, 1995.

Butler, Judith. *Bodies That Matter: On the Discursive Limits of "Sex."* New York: Routledge, 1993.

———. "Endangered/Endangering: Schematic Racism and White Paranoia." In Robert Gooding-Williams, ed., *Reading Rodney King/Reading Urban Uprising.* New York: Routledge,
1993.

Campbell, R. M. "A Test of Faith." *Los Angeles Times,* March 10, 1991.

Case, Sue-Ellen. *The Domain-Matrix: Performing Lesbian at the End of Print Culture.* Bloomington: Indiana University Press, 1996.

Cashmore, Ellis, and Eugene McLaughlin, eds. *Out of Order? Policing Black People.* London:
Routledge, 1991.

Castells, Manuel. *The Informational City.* Cambridge, Mass.: Basil Blackwell, 1989.

Chartier, Roger. *Cultural History: Between Practices and Representations.* Ithaca: Cornell University Press, 1988.

Chatterjee, Partha. *Nationalist Thought and the Colonial World: A Derivative Discourse.* London: Zed, 1986.

Cheney, Gay. *Basic Concepts in Modern Dance: A Creative Approach.* 3d ed. Princeton: Dance
Horizons, 1989.

Clarke, John, Stuart Hall, Tony Jefferson, and Brian Roberts. "Subcultures, Culture, and Class."
In Stuart Hall and Tony Jefferson, eds., *Resistance Through Rituals: Youth Subculture in
Post-War Britain,* 9–74. London: Hutchinson, 1976.

Clement, Catherine. *Opera, or the Undoing of Women.* Minneapolis: University of Minnesota Press, 1988.

Clough, Patricia. *The End(s) of Ethnography: From Realism to Social Criticism.* Newbury Park, Calif.: Sage, 1992.

Cohen, Selma Jeanne. *The Modern Dance: Seven Statements of Belief.* Middletown, Conn.: Wesleyan University Press, 1965.

Cone, James. *Martin and Malcolm and America: A Dream or a Nightmare?* Maryknoll, N.Y.: Orbis Books, 1991.

Copeland, Roger. "A Curmudgeonly View of the American Dance Boom." *Dance Theatre Journal* 4, 1 (1986): 10–13.

Copeland, Roger, and Marshall Cohen, eds. *What Is Dance?: Readings in Theory and Criticism.* Oxford: Oxford University Press, 1983.

Copjec, Joan. "The *Unvermögender* Other: Hysteria and Democracy in America." *New Formations* 14 (Summer 1991): 27–41.

Cowan, Jane. *Dance and the Body Politic in Northern Greece.* Princeton: Princeton University Press, 1990.

Crary, Jonathan, and Sanford Kwinter, eds. *Incorporations.* New York: Zone, 1992.

Croce, Arlene. "Discussing the Undiscussable." *The New Yorker,* December 26, 1994–January 2, 1995, 54–60.

Cubitt, Sean. *Timeshift: On Video Culture.* London: Routledge, 1990.

Daly, Ann. *Done into Dance: Isadora Duncan in America.* Bloomington: Indiana University Press, 1995.

Debord, Guy. *Society of the Spectacle* (1967). Detroit: Black and Red, 1983.

de Certeau, Michel. *The Practice of Everyday Life.* Berkeley: University of California Press, 1984.

Decker, Jeffrey Louis. "The State of Rap: Time and Place in Hip Hop Nationalism." *Social Text* 34 (1993): 53–84.

Deleuze, Gilles. *Nietzsche and Philosophy.* New York: Columbia University Press, 1983.

Deleuze, Gilles, and Felix Guattari. *Anti-Oedipus: Capitalism and Schizophrenia.* Minneapolis: University of Minnesota Press, 1983.

——. *Kafka: Toward a Minor Literature.* Minneapolis: University of Minnesota Press, 1986.

——. *A Thousand Plateaus: Capitalism and Schizophrenia.* Minneapolis: University of Minnesota Press, 1987.

de Man, Paul. *The Resistance to Theory.* Minneapolis: University of Minnesota Press, 1986.

Denby, Edwin. *Dance Writings.* New York: Knopf, 1986.

Denisoff, Serge. *Inside MTV.* New Brunswick, N.J.: Transaction, 1988.

Denning, Michael. "The Academic Left and the Rise of Cultural Studies." *Radical History* (Fall 1992): 20–47.

Dent, Gina, ed. *Black Popular Culture: A Project by Michele Wallace.* Seattle: Bay Press, 1992.

Derrida, Jacques. "Différance." In *Margins of Philosophy.* Trans. Alan Bass. Chicago: University of Chicago Press, 1982.

——. *Spectres of Marx: The State of the Debt, the Work of Mourning, and the New International.* London: Routledge, 1994.

Desmond, Jane C. "Embodying Difference: Issues in Dance and Cultural Studies." *Cultural Critique* 26 (Winter 1993/94): 33–63.

———. *Meaning in Motion.* Durham: Duke University Press, 1997.

Diawara, Manthia, et al. "Popular Culture and Political Correctness." *Social Text* 36 (1993): 1–39.

Dillon, Douglas C. "The Economic Crisis in the Arts." In Gideon Chagy, ed., *Business and the Arts.* New York: Paul Ericksson, 1970.

Donziger, Steven R., ed. *The Real War on Crime: The Report of the National Criminal Justice Commission.* New York: Harper Collins, 1996.

Dubin, Steven C. *Arresting Images: Impolitic Art and Uncivil Actions.* New York: Routledge, 1992.

DuCille, Ann. *Skin Trade.* Cambridge: Harvard University Press, 1996.

Duncan, Isadora. "I See America Dancing." In Sheldon Cheney, ed., *Isadora Duncan: The Art of the Dance.* New York: Theatre Arts Books, 1969.

During, Simon, ed. *The Cultural Studies Reader.* London: Routledge, 1993.

Dyson, Michael Eric. *Between God and Gangsta' Rap: Bearing Witness to Black Culture.* New York: Oxford University Press, 1996.

———. *Reflecting Black.* Minneapolis: University of Minnesota Press, 1993.

Eagleton, Terry. *The Ideology of the Aesthetic.* London: Blackwell, 1990.

Eco, Umberto. *A Theory of Semiotics.* Bloomington: Indiana University Press, 1976.

Edelman, Murray. *The Symbolic Uses of Politics.* Urbana: University of Illinois Press, 1964.

Eder, Klaus. *The New Politics of Class: Social Movements and Cultural Dynamics in Advanced Societies.* London: Sage, 1993.

Elder, Robert E. *The Information Machine: The United States Information Agency and American Foreign Policy.* Syracuse: Syracuse University Press, 1968.

Eure, Joseph D., and James G. Spady, eds. *Nation Conscious Rap.* Brooklyn: PC International Press, 1991.

Eyerman, Ron. *Social Movements: A Cognitive Approach.* University Park: Pennsylvania State University Press, 1991.

Faludi, Susan. *Backlash: The Undeclared War against American Women.* New York: Crown Publishers, 1991.

Feher, Michel, ed. *Fragments for a History of the Human Body.* 3 vols. New York: Zone, 1989.

Ferguson, Russell, Martha Gever, Trinh T. Minh-ha, and Cornel West, eds. *Out There: Marginalization and Contemporary Cultures.* Cambridge: MIT Press, 1990.

Fiske, John. *Power Plays/Power Works.* London: Verso, 1993.

Flores, Juan, and George Yúdice. "Living Borders/Buscando America: Languages of Latino Self-Formation." *Social Text* 24 (1990): 57–84.

Foss, Daniel A., and Ralph Larkin. *Beyond Revolution: A New Theory of Social Movements.* South Hadley, Mass.: Bergin and Garvey, 1986.

Foster, Hal, ed. *The Anti-Aesthetic: Essays on Postmodern Culture.* Port Townsend, Wash.: Bay Press, 1983.

Foster, Susan L. *Choreography and Narrative.* Bloomington: Indiana University Press, 1996.

———. "Dancing Bodies." In Jonathan Crary and Sanford Kwinter, eds., *Incorporations.* New York: Zone, 1992.

————. *Reading Dancing: Bodies and Subjects in Contemporary American Dance.* Berkeley: University of California Press, 1986.

————, ed. *Choreographing History.* Bloomington: Indiana University Press, 1995.

————, ed. *Corporealities: Dancing, Knowledge, Culture, and Power.* London: Routledge, 1995.

Foucault, Michel. *The Archaeology of Knowledge.* Trans. A. M. Sheridan Smith. New York: Pantheon, 1972.

————. *Discipline and Punish: The Birth of the Prison.* Trans. Alan Sheridan. New York: Vintage, 1979.

————. *The History of Sexuality.* Trans. Robert Hurley. 3 vols. New York: Vintage, 1980–86.

————. *Madness and Civilization: A History of Insanity in the Age of Reason.* New York: Vintage, 1973.

————. "Of Other Spaces." *Diacritics* 16 (1986): 22–27.

————. *The Order of Things: An Archaeology of the Human Sciences.* New York: Vintage, 1970.

————. "What Is an Author?" In Josué V. Harari, ed., *Textual Strategies: Perspectives in Post-Structuralist Criticism,* 141–60. Ithaca: Cornell University Press, 1979.

Francher, Gordon, and Gerald Myers, eds. *Philosophical Essays on Dance.* Brooklyn: Dance Horizons, 1981.

Franko, Mark. *Dance as Text: Ideologies of the Baroque Body.* Cambridge: Cambridge University Press, 1993.

————. *Dancing Modernism/Performing Politics.* Bloomington: Indiana University Press, 1995.

Fraser, Nancy. *Unruly Practices: Power, Discourse, and Gender in Contemporary Social Theory.* Minneapolis: University of Minnesota Press, 1988.

Frow, John. *Cultural Studies and Cultural Value.* Oxford: Oxford University Press, 1995.

Fukuyama, Francis. *The End of History and the Last Man.* New York: Free Press, 1992.

Fuss, Diana. *Essentially Speaking: Feminism, Nature, and Difference.* New York: Routledge, 1989.

Gallagher, Catherine, and Thomas Lacquer, eds. *The Making of the Modern Body.* Berkeley: University of California Press, 1987.

Garfinkel, Harold. *Studies in Ethnomethodology.* New York: Prentice-Hall, 1967.

Gates, Henry Louis, Jr. "Beyond the Culture Wars: Identities in Dialogue." *Profession 93* (1993): 6–11.

————. *Loose Canons: Notes on the Culture Wars.* New York: Oxford University Press, 1992.

George, Nelson, Sally Banes, Susan Flinker, and Patty Romanowski. *Fresh: Hip Hop Don't Stop.* New York: Random House, 1985.

Geyer, Michael. "Multiculturalism and the Politics of General Education." *Critical Inquiry* 19, 3 (Spring 1993): 499–543.

Ghirardo, Diane, ed. *Out of Site: A Social Criticism of Architecture.* Seattle: Bay Press, 1991.

Giddens, Anthony. *The Consequences of Modernity.* Stanford: Stanford University Press, 1990.

————. *The Constitution of Society: Outline of a Theory of Structuration.* Berkeley: University of California Press, 1984.

————. *Modernity and Self-Identity.* Stanford: Stanford University Press, 1991.

Gilroy, Paul. *The Black Atlantic: Modernity and Double Consciousness.* Cambridge: Harvard University Press, 1993.

———. *There Ain't No Black in the Union Jack: The Cultural Politics of Race and Nation.* London: Hutchinson, 1987.

Giroux, Henry. *Disturbing Pleasures.* New York: Routledge, 1994.

Goellner, Ellen W., and Jacqueline Shea Murphy, eds. *Bodies of the Text: Dance as Theory/Literature as Dance.* New Brunswick: Rutgers University Press, 1995.

Goffman, Erving. *Stigma: Notes on the Management of Spoiled Identity.* New York: Simon and Schuster, 1963.

Gooding-Williams, Robert, ed. *Reading Rodney King/Reading Urban Uprising.* New York: Routledge, 1993.

Gordon, Avery. "Diversity Management: The Work of Corporate Culture." *Social Text* 44 (Fall 1995): 3–30.

Gordon, David M. *Fat and Mean: The Corporate Squeeze of Working Americans and the Myth of Managerial "Downsizing."* New York: Free Press, 1996.

Graff, Gerald. *Beyond the Culture Wars: How Teaching the Conflicts Can Revitalize American Education.* New York: W. W. Norton, 1992.

———. *Professing Literature.* Chicago: University of Chicago Press, 1987.

Graham, Martha. "Affirmations, 1926–37." In *Martha Graham* (1937). Ed. and with a foreword by Merle Armitage. Brooklyn: Dance Horizons, 1966.

Gramsci, Antonio. *The Prison Notebooks.* Ed. and trans. Joseph Buttigieg. New York: Columbia University Press, 1992.

———. *Selections from the Prison Notebooks of Antonio Gramsci.* Ed. and trans. Quintin Hoare and Geoffrey Nowell Smith. New York: International Publishers, 1971.

Grele, Ronald J., ed. *Envelopes of Sound: The Art of Oral History.* 2d ed. Chicago: Precedent Publishing, 1985.

Griale, Marcel. *Masques Dogon.* Paris: Institut d'ethnologie, 1938.

Grossberg, Lawrence, Cary Nelson, and Paula Triechler, eds. *Cultural Studies.* New York: Routledge, 1992.

Guillory, John. *Cultural Capital: The Problem of Literary Canon Formation.* Chicago: University of Chicago Press, 1993.

Habermas, Jürgen. "Modernity—an Incomplete Project." In Hal Foster, ed., *The Anti-Aesthetic,* 3–15. Seattle: Bay Press, 1983.

———. *The Philosophical Discourse of Modernity.* Cambridge: MIT Press, 1987.

———. *The Theory of Communicative Action.* Vols. 1 and 2. Boston: Beacon, 1984, 1987.

———. *Toward a Rational Society.* Boston: Beacon, 1970.

Hager, Steven. *Hip Hop: The Illustrated History of Break Dancing, Rap Music, and Graffiti.* New York: St. Martin's, 1984.

Hall, Stuart. *Hard Road to Renewal.* London: Verso, 1988.

———. "What Is This 'Black' in Black Popular Culture?" In David Morley and Kuan-Hsing Chen, eds., *Stuart Hall: Critical Dialogues in Cultural Studies,* 464–75. London: Routledge, 1996.

Hall, Stuart, and Martin Jacques, eds. *New Times.* London: Verso, 1990.

Hanna, Judith Lynne. *Dance, Sex, and Gender.* Chicago: University of Chicago Press, 1988.

————. *To Dance Is Human.* Chicago: University of Chicago Press, 1987.

Haraway, Donna J. *Simians, Cyborgs, and Women: The Reinvention of Nature.* New York: Routledge, 1991.

Hardt, Michael, and Antonio Negri. *Labor of Dionysus: Critique of the State Form.* Minneapolis: University of Minnesota, 1994.

Harris, Cheryl I. "Whiteness as Property." In Kimberlé Crenshaw, Neil Gotanda, Gary Peller, and Kendall Thomas, eds., *Critical Race Theory,* 276–91. New York: New Press, 1995.

Harrison, Bennett. *Lean and Mean: The Changing Landscape of Corporate Power in the Age of Flexibility.* New York: Basic, 1994.

Harrison, Charles, and Paul Wood, eds. *Art in Theory, 1900–1990: An Anthology of Changing Ideas.* London: Blackwell, 1992.

Harvey, David. *The Condition of Postmodernity: An Enquiry into the Origins of Cultural Change.* Oxford: Basil Blackwell, 1989.

Hazzard-Gordon, Katrina. *Jookin': The Rise of Social Dance Formations in African American Culture.* Philadelphia: Temple University Press, 1990.

Hebdige, Dick. *Cut n' Mix: Culture, Identity, and Caribbean Music.* London: Methuen, 1987.

Heidegger, Martin. *Being and Time.* Trans. John Macquarrie and Edward Robinson. Oxford: Basil Blackwell, 1962.

Heller, Agnes. *A Theory of History.* London: Routledge and Kegan Paul, 1982.

Hill, Herbert. "Black Workers, Organized Labor, and Title VII of the 1964 Civil Rights Act: Legislative History and Litigation Record." In Herbert Hill and James E. Jones Jr., eds., *Race in America: The Struggle for Equality,* 263–341. Madison: University of Wisconsin Press, 1993.

Hinkle, Roscoe C. *Founding Theory of American Sociology: 1881–1915.* London: Routledge and Kegan Paul, 1980.

Hobsbawm, Eric. *Bandits.* New York: Delacourt, 1969.

————. *Nations and Nationalism since 1780: Programme, Myth, Reality.* Cambridge: Cambridge University Press, 1990.

————. *Primitive Rebels.* New York: W. W. Norton, 1959.

Hodsoll, Frank. "An Interview with Frank Hodsoll." *American Arts,* January 1982.

Hollinger, David. *Postethnic America: Beyond Multiculturalism.* New York: Basic, 1995.

Horosko, Marian. *Martha Graham: The Evolution of Her Dance Theory and Training, 1926–1991.* Chicago: a cappella books, 1991.

Horst, Louis. *Modern Dance Forms.* San Francisco: Impulse, 1961.

Huet, Michel. *The Dance, Art, and Ritual of Africa.* New York: Pantheon, 1978.

Humphrey, Doris. *The Art of Making Dances.* New York: Grove, 1959.

Hunt, Lynn. *New Cultural History.* Berkeley: University of California Press, 1989.

Inglis, Fred. *Cultural Studies.* London: Blackwell, 1993.

————. *Media Theory.* Cambridge, Mass.: Basil Blackwell, 1990.

James, Joy. *Resisting State Violence: Radicalism, Gender, and Race in U.S. Culture.* Minneapolis: University of Minnesota Press, 1996.

Jameson, Fredric. *The Political Unconscious: Narrative as a Socially Symbolic Act.* Ithaca: Cornell University Press, 1981.

———. *Postmodernism, or, The Cultural Logic of Late Capitalism.* Durham: Duke University Press, 1991.

———. *The Prison House of Language.* Princeton: Princeton University Press, 1972.

Jay, Martin. *Downcast Eyes.* London: Verso, 1994.

Jessop, Bob. *State Theory: Putting Capitalist States in Their Place.* University Park: Pennsylvania State University Press, 1990.

Johnson, Richard, Gregor McLennan, Bill Schwarz, and David Sutton, eds., *Making Histories: Studies in History, Writing, and Politics.* Minneapolis: University of Minnesota Press, 1982.

Jones, Simon. *Black Culture White Youth: The Reggae Tradition from JA to UK.* London: Macmillan, 1988.

Jowitt, Deborah. *Time and the Dancing Image.* Berkeley: University of California Press, 1988.

Kelley, Robin D. G. "Straight from Underground." *The Nation* 254, 22 (1992): 793.

King, Martin Luther. *A Testament of Hope: The Essential Writings of Martin Luther King, Jr.* Ed. James Melvin Washington. San Francisco: Harper and Row, 1986.

Koritz, Amy. *Gendering Bodies/Performing Art: Dance and Literature in Early-Twentieth-Century British Culture.* Ann Arbor: University of Michigan Press, 1995.

Krauss, Rosalind. *The Originality of the Avant-Garde.* Cambridge: MIT Press, 1985.

Kruger, Loren. *The National Stage: Theatre and Cultural Legitimation in England, France, and America.* Chicago: University of Chicago Press, 1992.

Kuhn, Thomas. *The Structure of Scientific Revolutions.* Chicago: University of Chicago Press, 1962.

Lacan, Jacques. *The Seminar of Jacques Lacan: Book II, The Ego in Freud's Theory and in the Technique of Psychoanalysis, 1954–1955.* Ed. Jacques-Alain Miller. Trans. Sylvana Tomaselli. New York: W. W. Norton, 1991.

Laclau, Ernesto. *New Reflections on the Revolution of Our Time.* London: Verso, 1990.

Laclau, Ernesto, and Chantal Mouffe. *Hegemony and Socialist Strategy: Towards a Radical Democratic Politics.* London: Verso, 1985.

Landes, Joan B. *Women and the Public Sphere in the Age of the French Revolution.* Ithaca: Cornell University Press, 1988.

Langer, Suzanne. "The Dynamic Image: Some Philosophical Reflections on Dance." In *Problems of Art,* 1–12. New York: Charles Scribner's Sons, 1957.

Larson, Magali Sarfatti. *Behind the Postmodern Facade: Architectural Change in Late Twentieth-Century America.* Berkeley: University of California Press, 1993.

———. *The Rise of Professionalism.* Berkeley: University of California Press, 1977.

Latour, Bruno. "Technology Is Society Made Durable." In John Law, ed., *A Sociology of Monsters: Essays on Power, Technology, and Domination,* 103–31. London: Routledge, 1991.

Le Bon, Gustave. *The Crowd: A Study of the Popular Mind.* New York: Macmillan, n.d.

Lévi-Strauss, Claude. *The Savage Mind.* Chicago: University of Chicago Press, 1966.

Lewis, Lisa. *Gender Politics and MTV.* Philadelphia: Temple University Press, 1990.

Light, Alan. "About Salary or Reality—Rap's Recurrent Conflict." *SAQ* 90, 4 (Fall 1991): 855–70.

Lincoln, Abraham. *The Collected Works of Abraham Lincoln.* Ed. Roy P. Basler. Vol. 8. New Brunswick: Rutgers University Press, 1953.

Lott, Eric. *Love and Theft: Black Face Minstrelsy and the American Working Class.* New York: Oxford University Press, 1993.

Lowe, Donald. *The Body in Late-Capitalist USA.* Durham: Duke University Press, 1996.

Lowry, W. McNeil, and Gertrude S. Hooker. "The Role of the Arts and the Humanities." In Paul J. Braisted, ed., *Cultural Affairs and Foreign Relations,* 45–87. Washington, D.C.: Columbia Books, 1968.

Lubiano, Wahneema. "Like Being Mugged by a Metaphor." In Avery F. Gordon and Christopher Newfield, eds., *Mapping Multiculturalism,* 64–75. Minneapolis: University of Minnesota Press, 1996.

Lukács, Georg. *History and Class Consciousness: Studies in Marxist Dialectics.* Trans. Rodney Livingstone. Cambridge: MIT Press, 1971.

Lynd, Robert S. *Knowledge for What? The Place of Social Science in American Culture.* Princeton: Princeton University Press, 1939.

Magnus, Bernd, and Stephen Cullenberg, eds. *Whither Marxism: Global Crises in International Perspective.* New York: Routledge, 1995.

Mandel, Ernest. *Late Capitalism.* London: Verso, 1975.

———. *The Second Slump.* London: New Left Books, 1977.

Mannheim, Karl. *Ideology and Utopia.* Trans. Louis Wirth and Edward Shils. New York: Harcourt Brace Jovanovich, 1936.

Manning, Susan. *Ecstasy and the Demon: Feminism and Nationalism in the Dances of Mary Wigman.* Berkeley: University of California Press, 1993.

———. "Modernist Dogma and Post-Modern-Rhetoric: A Response to Sally Banes' *Terpsichore in Sneakers.*" *Drama Review* 32, 4 (1988).

Marable, Manning. *Beyond Black and White: Rethinking Race in American Politics and Society.* London: Verso, 1995.

———. *Race, Reform, and Rebellion: The Second Reconstruction in Black America, 1945–1990.* Rev. 2d ed. Jackson: University Press of Mississippi, 1991.

Marcuse, Herbert. *One-Dimensional Man.* Boston: Beacon, 1964.

Marquis, Alice Goldfarb. 1995. *Art Lessons: Learning from the Rise and Fall of Public Arts Funding.* New York: Basic.

Martí, José. 1984. "Nuestra América." In *Tres Documentos.* Havana: Editorial José Martí.

Martin, Carol. 1996. "High Critics/Low Arts." In Gay Morris, ed., *Moving Words: Re-writing Dance.* London: Routledge, 320–33.

Martin, John. *Introduction to the Dance* (1939). Brooklyn: Dance Horizons, 1965.

———. *John Martin's Book of the Dance.* New York: Tudor Publishing, 1963.

Martin, Randy. "Agency and History: The Demands of Dance Ethnography." In Susan L. Foster, ed., *Choreographing History.* Bloomington: Indiana University Press, 1995.

———. "Dance Ethnography and the Limits of Representation." *Social Text* 33 (Winter 1992): 103–23.

———. "Is the Body of Dance Sexed?" *Journal of Dramatic Theory and Criticism* 1 (Fall 1990): 7–24.

———. "Modern Dance and the American Century." In Townsend Ludington, ed., *Modernism in the United States.* Chapel Hill: University of North Carolina Press, 1998.

———. *Performance as Political Act: The Embodied Self.* New York: Bergin and Garvey, 1990.

———. "Resurfacing Socialism: Resisting the Appeals of Tribalism and Localism." *Social Text* 44 (Fall 1995): 97–118.

———. *Socialist Ensembles: Theater and State in Cuba and Nicaragua.* Minneapolis: University of Minnesota Press, 1994.

———. "Who Went to War?" In G. Boulanger and C. Kadushin, eds., *The Vietnam Veteran Redefined: Fact and Fiction,* 13–24. Hillsdale, N.J.: Lawrence Erlbaum Associates, 1986.

Marx, Karl. *Capital: A Critique of Political Economy.* Ed. Friedrich Engels. Trans. Samuel Moore and Edward Aveling. Vol. 1. New York: International Publishers, 1967.

———. *The Eighteenth Brumaire of Louis Bonaparte* (1852). In Karl Marx and Friedrich Engels, *Collected Works,* vol. 11. New York: International Publishers, 1979.

———. *Grundrisse.* Ed. and trans. Martin Niclaus. New York: Vintage, 1973.

McDonagh, Don. *The Complete Guide to Modern Dance.* Garden City, N.Y.: Doubleday, 1976.

McFee, Graham. *Understanding Dance.* London: Routledge, 1992.

McKinlay, John B., ed. *Issues in the Political Economy of Health Care.* New York: Tavistock, 1984.

Mercer, Kobena. " '1968': Periodizing Politics and Identity." In Lawrence Grossberg et al., eds., *Cultural Studies,* 424–49. New York: Routledge, 1992.

———. *Welcome to the Jungle: New Positions in Black Cultural Studies.* London: Routledge, 1994.

Merleau-Ponty, Maurice. *The Phenomenology of Perception.* London: Routledge and Kegan Paul, 1962.

Messer-Davidow, Ellen. "Manufacturing the Attack on Liberalized Higher Education." *Social Text* 36 (Fall 1993): 40–80.

Metzger, Bruce M., and Roland E. Murphy, eds. *The New Oxford Annotated Bible.* New York: Oxford University Press, 1991.

Miller, Daniel. *Material Culture and Mass Consumption.* Cambridge, Mass.: Basil Blackwell, 1987.

Miyoshi, Masao. "A Borderless World? From Colonialism to Transnationalism and the Decline of the Nation-State." *Critical Inquiry* 19, 3 (Summer 1993): 726–51.

Morris, Gay. *Moving Words: Re-writing Dance.* London: Routledge, 1996.

Morrison, Toni, ed. *Race-ing Justice, En-gendering Power: Essays on Anita Hill, Clarence Thomas, and the Construction of Social Reality.* New York: Pantheon, 1992.

Mueller, Carol McClurg. "Building Social Movement Theory." In Aldon Morris and Carol McClurg Mueller, eds., *Frontiers in Social Movement Theory,* 3–25. New Haven: Yale University Press, 1992.

National Endowment for the Arts (NEA). *National Endowment for the Arts Annual Report.* Washington, D.C.: NEA, 1981.

———. *National Endowment for the Arts Annual Report.* Washington, D.C.: NEA, 1986.

———. *National Endowment for the Arts Annual Report.* Washington, D.C.: NEA, 1991.

Ness, Sally Ann. *Body, Movement, and Culture.* Philadelphia: University of Pennsylvania Press, 1992.

Netzer, Dick. *The Subsidized Muse.* Cambridge: Cambridge University Press, 1978.

Newfield, Christopher. "What Was Political Correctness? Race, the Right, and Managerial Democracy in the Humanities." *Critical Inquiry* 19, 2 (Winter 1993): 308–36.

Nietzsche, Friedrich. *The Use and Abuse of History* (1873). Trans. Adrian Craft. Indianapolis: Bobbs-Merrill, 1949.

Novack, Cynthia. *Sharing the Dance: Contact Improvisation and American Culture.* Madison: University of Wisconsin Press, 1990.

Olson, Mancur. *The Logic of Collective Action.* Cambridge: Harvard University Press, 1965.

Omi, Michael, and Howard Winant. *Racial Formation in the United States: From the 1960s to the 1990s.* 2d ed. New York: Routledge, 1994.

Palfy, Barbara, ed., with Claudia Gitelman and Patricia Mayer. *Dance Reconstructed: Modern Dance Art Past, Present, and Future.* New Brunswick: Rutgers University Press, 1993.

Parker, Andrew, Mary Russo, Doris Sommer, and Patricia Yaeger, eds. *Nationalisms and Sexualities.* New York: Routledge, 1992.

Parsons, Talcott. *The Structure of Social Action.* New York: McGraw-Hill, 1937.

Perkins, William Eric, ed. *Droppin' Science: Critical Essays on Rap Music and Hip Hop Culture.* Philadelphia: Temple University Press, 1996.

Phelan, Peggy. *Unmarked: The Politics of Performance.* London: Routledge, 1993.

"Popular Culture and Political Correctness." Ed. Andrew Ross. In *Social Text* 36 (Fall 1993): 1–39.

Poulantzas, Nicos. *Political Power and Social Classes.* London: New Left Books, 1973.

———. *State, Power, Socialism.* London: New Left Books, 1978.

Reed, Adolph L., Jr. 1986. *The Jesse Jackson Phenomenon: The Crisis of Purpose in Afro-American Politics.* New Haven: Yale University Press, 1986.

Retamar, Roberto Fernández. *Caliban and Other Essays.* Minneapolis: University of Minnesota Press, 1989.

Ricoeur, Paul. *Time and Narrative.* 3 vols. Chicago: University of Chicago Press, 1985.

Robbins, Bruce. *Secular Vocations.* London: Verso, 1994.

———, ed. *Intellectuals: Aesthetics, Politics, Academics.* Minneapolis: University of Minnesota Press, 1990.

Roberts, Dorothy. "Motherhood and Crime." *Social Text* 42 (Spring 1995): 99–123.

Rose, Jacqueline. *Sexuality in the Field of Vision.* London: Verso, 1986.

Rose, Tricia. *Black Noise: Rap Music and Black Culture in Contemporary America.* Hanover, N.H.: University Press of New England, 1994.

Rose, Tricia, and Andrew Ross, eds. *Microphone Fiends.* New York: Routledge, 1994.

Ross, Andrew, ed. "Popular Culture and Political Correctness." *Social Text* 36 (Fall 1993): 1–39.

Ross, Dorothy. *The Origins of American Social Science.* Cambridge: Cambridge University Press, 1991.

Rowe, John, and Vivian Schelling. *Memory and Modernity.* London: Verso, 1991.

Rudé, George. *The Crowd in the French Revolution.* Oxford: Oxford University Press, 1959.

Ruyter, Nancy. "Antique Longings: Genevieve Stebbins and American Delsartean Performance." In Susan L. Foster, ed., *Corporealities: Dancing, Knowledge, Culture, and Power.* London: Routledge, 1995.

Sachs, Curt. *World History of the Dance* (1937). New York: Norton, 1965.

Samuel, Raphael, ed. *East End Underworld: Chapters in the Life of Arthur Harding.* London: Routledge and Kegan Paul, 1981.

San Juan, Epifanio, Jr. *Racial Formations/Critical Transformations.* Atlantic Highlands, N.J.: Humanities Press, 1992.

Sarnoff, Allison. "Getting into the Promised Land" and "The Presenter's Challenge." *Dance/ USA,* May/June, 1991, 24–26.

Sassen, Saskia. *Losing Control: Sovereignty in an Age of Globalization.* New York: Columbia University Press, 1996.

Saussure, Ferdinand de. *Course in General Linguistics.* Trans. Wade Baskin. New York: McGraw-Hill, 1966.

Savigliano, Marta. *Tango and the Political Economy of Passion.* Boulder: Westview, 1994.

Scheper-Hughes, Nancy. *Death without Weeping: The Violence of Everyday Life in Brazil.* Berkeley: University of California Press, 1992.

Schlesinger, Arthur M., Jr. *The Disuniting of America.* New York: W. W. Norton, 1992.

Schliefer, Ronald. *Rhetoric and Death: The Language of Modernism and Postmodern Discourse Theory.* Urbana: University of Illinois Press, 1990.

Schwartz, Hillel. "Torque: The New Kinesthetic of the Twentieth Century." In Jonathan Crary and Sanford Kwinter, eds., *Incorporations: Zone 6,* 70–127. New York: Zone, 1992.

Schwarz, Bill. " 'The People' in History: The Communist Party Historians' Group." In R. Johnson et al., eds., *Making Histories.* Minneapolis: University of Minnesota Press, 1982.

Scott, Alan. *Ideology and the New Social Movements.* London: Unwin Hyman, 1990.

Scott, James C. *Weapons of the Weak: Everyday Forms of Peasant Resistance.* New Haven: Yale University Press, 1985.

Scott, Joan Wallach. "The Campaign against Political Correctness: What's Really at Stake." *Radical History* (Fall 1992): 58–79.

Shaw, Arnold. *Black Popular Music in America: From the Spirituals, Minstrels, and Ragtime to Soul, Disco, and Hip-Hop.* New York: Schirmer, 1986.

Shelton, Suzanne. *Divine Dancer: Ruth St. Denis.* Garden City, N.Y.: Doubleday, 1981.

Siegel, Marcia B. *The Shapes of Change: Images of American Dance.* Boston: Houghton Mifflin, 1979.

Siltanen, Janet, and Michele Stanworth, eds. *Women and the Public Sphere: A Critique of Sociology and Politics.* London: Hutchinson, 1984.

Simonson, Rick, and Scott Walker, eds. *Graywolf Annual 5: Multicultural Literacy.* St. Paul, Minn.: Graywolf Press, 1988.

Small, Stephen. *Racialised Barriers: The Black Experience in the United States and England in the 1980s.* London: Routledge, 1994.

Smith, Anthony D. *The Ethnic Origins of Nations.* London: Blackwell, 1986.

Smith, Michael Peter, ed. *Breaking the Chains: Social Movements and Collective Action.* New Brunswick, N.J.: Transaction, 1991.

Smith, Neil. "Contours of a Spatialized Politics: Homeless Vehicles and the Production of Geographical Scale." *Social Text* 33 (Winter 1992): 54–81.

Smith, Paul. *Discerning the Subject.* Minneapolis: University of Minnesota Press, 1988.

Snead, James. "Repetition as a Figure of Black Culture." In Russell Ferguson et al., eds., *Out There: Marginalization and Contemporary Cultures.* Cambridge: MIT Press, 1990.

Soja, Edward. *Postmodern Geographies: The Reassertion of Space in Critical Social Theory.* London: Verso, 1989.

Sommer, Doris. "Irresistible Romance: The Foundational Fictions of Latin America." In Homi K. Bhabha, ed., *Nation and Narration.* London: Routledge, 1990.

Sorell, Walter. *Dance in Its Time: The Emergence of an Art Form.* Garden City, N.Y.: Anchor Press, 1981.

Sparshott, Francis. *A Measured Pace: Toward a Philosophical Understanding of the Arts of Dance.* Toronto: University of Toronto Press, 1995.

Spivak, Gayatri Chakravorty. "Can the Subaltern Speak?" In Cary Nelson and Lawrence Grossberg, eds., *Marxism and the Interpretation of Culture.* Urbana: University of Illinois Press, 1988.

———. "In a Word: Interview." *Outside in the Teaching Machine,* 1–23. New York: Routledge, 1993.

———. *In Other Worlds.* London: Routledge, 1988.

———. *The Post-Colonial Critic.* Ed. Sarah Harasym. New York: Routledge, 1990.

Starr, Paul. *The Social Transformation of Medicine: The Rise of a Sovereign Profession and the Making of a Vast Industry.* New York: Basic, 1982.

Stewart, Gary. *Breakout: Profiles in African Rhythm.* Chicago: University of Chicago Press, 1992.

Stodelle, Ernestine. *The Dance Technique of Doris Humphrey and Its Creative Potential.* Princeton: Princeton Book, 1978.

Stowe, Harriet Beecher. *Uncle Tom's Cabin* (1852). Introduction by Ann Douglas. New York: Viking, 1981.

Stuckey, Sterling. *Slave Culture: Nationalist Theory and the Foundations of Black America.* New York: Oxford University Press, 1987.

Suleiman, Susan Rubin, ed. *The Female Body in Western Culture.* Cambridge: Harvard University Press, 1986.

Sussman, Leila. "Anatomy of the Dance Company Boom, 1958–1980." *Dance Research Journal* 16, 2 (1984): 23–38.

Sztompka, Piotr. *The Sociology of Social Change.* Oxford: Basil Blackwell, 1993.

Tagg, John. *The Burden of Representation.* Amherst: University of Massachusetts Press, 1988.

Takaki, Ronald. "A Tale of Two Decades: Race and Class in the 1880s and 1980s." In Herbert Hill and James E. Jones Jr., eds., *Race in America: The Struggle for Equality,* 402–16. Madison: University of Wisconsin Press, 1993.

Tarrow, Sidney. *Power in Movement: Social Movements, Collective Action, and Politics.* Cambridge: Cambridge University Press, 1994.

Taussig, Michael. *Mimesis and Alterity: A Particular History of the Senses.* New York: Routledge, 1993.

Taylor, Charles. *Multiculturalism and "The Politics of Recognition": An Essay.* With commentary by Amy Gutmann, Steven C. Rockefellar, Michael Walzer, and Susan Wolf. Princeton: Princeton University Press, 1992.

Thomas, Helen. "An-other Voice: Young Women Dancing and Talking." In Helen Thomas, ed., *Dance, Gender, and Culture*, 69–93. New York: St. Martin's, 1993.

———. *Dance, Modernity, and Culture: Explorations in the Sociology of Dance.* London: Routledge, 1995.

———, ed. *Dance, Gender, and Culture.* New York: St. Martin's, 1993.

Thompson, Edward Palmer. *The Making of the English Working Class.* New York: Knopf, 1963.

———. *The Poverty of Theory.* London: New Left Books, 1978.

Thompson, Paul. *The Voice of the Past: Oral History.* Oxford: Oxford University Press, 1978.

Thomson, Charles A., and Walter H. C. Laves. *Cultural Relations and U.S. Foreign Policy.* Bloomington: Indiana University Press, 1963.

Tomko, Linda. "Fete Accompli: Gender, 'Folk-Dance,' and Progressive Era Political Ideals in the United States." In Susan L. Foster, ed., *Corporealities: Dancing, Knowledge, Culture, and Power.* London: Routledge, 1995.

Toop, David. *Rap Attack 2.* London: Serpent's Tale, 1991.

———. *The Voice and the Eye: An Analysis of Social Movements.* Trans. Alan Duff. Cambridge: Cambridge University Press, 1981.

Touraine, Alain. *Return of the Actor: Social Theory in Postindustrial Society.* Trans. Myrna Godzich. Minneapolis: University of Minnesota Press, 1988.

Trouillot, Michel-Rolph. "Anthropology and the Savage Slot: The Poetics and Politics of Otherness." In Richard G. Fox, ed., *Recapturing Anthropology: Working in the Present*, 17–44. Santa Fe: School of American Research Press, 1991.

Turner, Graeme. *British Cultural Studies.* Boston: Unwin-Hyman, 1990.

Van Dyke, Jan. *Modern Dance in a Postmodern World: An Analysis of Federal Arts Funding and Its Impact on the Field of Modern Dance.* Reston, Va.: National Dance Association, 1992.

Vattimo, Gianni. *The Transparent Society.* Cambridge: Polity, 1992.

Wallace, Maya. "In Search of the Promised Land." *Dance*, October 1991, 56–59.

Weber, Max. "Politics as Vocation." In H. H. Gerth and C. Wright Mills, trans. and eds., *From Max Weber: Essays in Sociology*, 77–128. New York: Oxford University Press, 1958.

West, Cornel. *Prophesy Deliverance! An Afro-American Revolutionary Christianity.* Philadelphia: Westminster Press, 1982.

———. *Prophetic Fragments.* Trenton: World Africa Press, 1988.

West, Cornel, and John Rajchman. *Post-Analytic Philosophy.* New York: Columbia University Press, 1985.

Williams, Patricia. *The Alchemy of Race and Rights.* Cambridge: Harvard University Press, 1991.

Williams, Raymond. *Marxism and Literature.* Oxford: Oxford University Press, 1977.

———. *The Politics of Modernism: Against the New Conformists.* London: Verso, 1989.

Willis, Paul. *Learning to Labor: How Working Class Kids Get Working Class Jobs.* New York: Columbia University Press, 1981.

Wilson, Robert, and Wimal Dissanayake, eds. *Global/Local: Cultural Production and the Transnational Imaginary.* Durham: Duke University Press, 1996.

Wood, Joe, ed. *Malcolm X: In Our Own Image.* New York: St. Martin's, 1992.

Yúdice, George. *We Are Not the World.* Durham: Duke University Press, forthcoming.

Zald, Mayer N., and John D. McCarthy. *The Dynamics of Social Movements: Resource Mobilization, Social Control, and Tactics.* New York: Little, Brown, 1979.

Ziff, Bruce, and Pratima V. Rao. *Borrowed Power: Essays on Cultural Appropriation.* New Brunswick: Rutgers University Press, 1997.

Zimmer, Elizabeth. "Moving Truths." *Elle,* November 1990.

——. "Ten Hours at Uncle Tom's Cabin." *Dance/USA,* May/June 1991, 24–26.

Žižek, Slavoj. *Tarrying with the Negative: Kant, Hegel, and the Critique of Ideology.* Durham: Duke University Press, 1993.

Zoete, Beryl de, and Walter Spies. *Dance and Drama in Bali.* London: Faber and Faber, 1952.

Index

Rudé, George, 41

Sachs, Curt, 56
Saussure, Ferdinand de, 37, 161, 215
Schelling, Vivian, 119
Schwartz, Hillel, 172
Schwarz, Bill, 42
Segal, Lewis, 82–83
Semiotics, 36
Shawn, Ted, 169
Simpson, O. J., 98
Smith, Andre, 70
Smith, Neil, 137
Smith, Sid, 82
Sojourner Truth, 67
Soviet Union, 97
Speech act, 37
State Department (U.S.): Division of Cultural Relations, 91; United States Information Agency (USIA), 91
St. Denis, Ruth, 169
Stowe, Harriet Beecher, 17, 63, 66–67, 75, 78
Structure of feeling, 107, 147
Stuckey, Sterling, 127

Taglioni, Filippo (*Revolt in the Harem*), 169
Taussig, Michael, 162–163
Taylor, Paul, 90

Technique, 20, 155, 166, 171
Tharp, Twyla, 202
Thompson, Edward Palmer, 41–42
Tönnies, Ferdinand Julius, 116
Touraine, Alain, 44
2 Live Crew, 124

Underreading, 55, 60
Utopia of the real, 63, 95, 103

Vattimo, Gianni, 122
Video, 35–36, 126, 131–132
Voting Rights Act, 98

Weak link, 21, 111, 139, 149, 182
Weber, Max, 118
West, Cornel, 72
White, Hayden, 202
Whiteness, 148
Wicked, 19, 110, 130–139
Williams, Janine, 80
Williams, Patricia, 195
Williams, Raymond, 13, 147, 210
Wilson, Robert, 88
Wood, Joe, 121
Woods, Andrea, 68

Zero degree, 36

Randy Martin is Chair and Professor of Sociology in the
Department of Social Science and Management at Pratt
Institute. He is the author of *Socialist Ensembles: Theater and
State in Cuba and Nicaragua* and *Performance as Political Act:
The Embodied Self* and editor of *Chalk Lines: The Politics of Work
in the Managed University* (also published by Duke University
Press).

Library of Congress Cataloging-in-Publication Data
Martin, Randy.
Critical moves : dance studies in theory and politics
Randy Martin.
Includes bibliographical references (p.) and index.
ISBN 0-8223-2203-X (alk. paper).
ISBN 0-8223-2219-6 (pbk. : alk. paper)
1. Dance — Sociological aspects.   2. Dance — Political aspects.
3. Dance — Philosophy.   4. Multiculturalism.   I. Title.
GV1588.6.M37   1998   792.8 — dc21   97-49360 CIP